Applied Anthropology

DATE DUE

MY07 '99			

Applied Anthropology

An Introduction

John van Willigen

REVISED EDITION

BERGIN & GARVEY
Westport, Connecticut • London

Library of Congress Cataloging-in-Publication Data

van Willigen, John.
   Applied anthropology : an introduction / John van Willigen.—
Rev. ed.
      p.   cm.
   Includes bibliographical references and index.
   ISBN 0–89789–298–4. — ISBN 0–89789–303–4 (pbk.)
   1. Applied anthropology.   I. Title.
GN397.5.V36   1993
307.1′4—dc20   92–31722

British Library Cataloguing in Publication Data is available.

Library of Congress Catalog Card Number: 92–31722
ISBN: 0–89789–298–4
     0–89789–303–4 (pbk.)

First published in 1993

Bergin & Garvey, 88 Post Road West, Westport, CT 06881
An imprint of Greenwood Publishing Group, Inc.

Printed in the United States of America

The paper used in this book complies with the Permanent Paper
Standard issued by the National Information Standards
Organization (Z39.48–1984).

10 9 8 7 6 5 4 3 2 1

Contents

PART IV   BEING A PROFESSIONAL

Preface

SOLVING PROBLEMS ANTHROPOLOGICALLY

Ever since anthropology has existed as a research discipline it has had a practical, problem-solving aspect, although this has attracted more attention in recent years. Historically this aspect of anthropology has been called applied anthropology. As the number of anthropologists who apply their knowledge and skills to activities other than basic research and teaching has increased, so has the number of different terms for practical activities. Besides applied anthropology, many other terms are used for the different forms of practice, including: practicing anthropology, development anthropology, action anthropology, research and development anthropology, and advocacy anthropology. In addition to these, an increasing number of anthropologists engaged in practical employment call themselves practicing anthropologists; they may not choose to call what they do applied anthropology. All of these terms carry meanings appropriate to specific circumstances, which are considered in this book. We will use applied anthropology as a general label for the entire array of situations and approaches for putting anthropology to use. In doing this we must recognize that some will disagree with this usage.

The text is based on a number of my experiences dealing with the applications of anthropology. The first was special training in applied anthropology at the University of Arizona, including an internship served with the tribal government of the Gila River Indian Reservation doing manpower research and other activities. The second consisted of experiences as a development administrator for the Tohono O'odham Tribe of Arizona. This provided first-hand experience in community development as an intervention process. The third experience is nineteen years of teaching applied anthropology at the University of Kentucky. The fourth experience is the creation and ongoing management of the Applied Anthropology Documentation Project, an archive for applied anthropology technical literature. This has brought me in contact with the written products of applied and practicing anthropologists.

The fifth area of experience consists of a number of activities done in conjunction with the Society for Applied Anthropology and the National Association for the Practice of Anthropology. In conjunction with the Society for Applied Anthropology I have served as chair of the Ethics Committee during the period when the current ethics statement was developed, and I served as the editor of the first two editions of the *Guide to Training Programs in the Applications of Anthropology* (1987). I am working with both the Society for Applied Anthropology and the National Association for the Practice of Anthropology in their efforts at developing standards for training in applied anthropology.

The view of applied anthropology expressed here has both research and intervention aspects. It provides anthropologists with a number of effective action strategies that can be used to assist communities in reaching their goals within the context of self-determination. Applied and practicing anthropologists can draw upon experiences from the past as effective guides for work in both intervention and research; thus, knowledge of history is very useful. Activities done by anthropologists in both the past and present provide choices for problem solving. The foundation of most of the techniques presented here is the ideology of self-determination by communities and individuals. The research techniques presented also have at their base the idea of systematically identifying local viewpoints and needs as these relate to development efforts or program functioning.

SHARING A TRADITION OF PRACTICE

While this book is intended to teach the reader how to put anthropology to use, reading it is not the best way to learn this skill. The way to learn it is to do it, especially, when possible, under the supervision of a qualified applied anthropologist. Basically, it is too much an art to convey efficiently through books, term papers, and other more traditional assignments; one needs direct experience. So why read this book? The answer is simple enough: many applied anthropologists work in isolation, operating in agencies or firms that hire few other anthropologists. They spend time tracking over the same ground and solving many of the same problems in ways that may seem to them unique. This book attempts to describe applied anthropology in its breadth and to build a shared tradition of practice, as much as to teach some techniques of application. It is useful to grasp the breadth of activity found in anthropological practice because it helps us see the power of the ideas produced within the discipline. That discovery will enhance our own ability to be effective users of anthropological knowledge. Further, the knowledge presented in this book will help link the experiences associated with contemporary practices to those of the past.

The basic point is a simple one: there are many kinds of anthropological practice, and knowledge of these different ways of practice is useful for the applied or practicing anthropologist. Not all useful practices are represented in this book.

ORIENTATION OF THE TEXT

Before we go on to consider the content of the book, it is useful to say something about its orientation. While this text presents approaches that are useful in many different settings and political traditions, it will be immediately clear that the tradition of application drawn upon and presented is that of anthropologists from the United States of America. There are, however, other national traditions that also present useful experiences for us to consider. For example, contemporary Canadian applied anthropology is undergoing very rapid development (Price 1987), and application has been at the core of Mexican anthropology since the 1917 revolution. Certainly, one could consider other regional traditions as well.

The value orientation of the applied anthropology described in this text is consistent with the political culture within which it developed, that is, it is pragmatic and democratic. It is pragmatic in that it stresses practices that work to achieve people's goals. It is democratic in that all the approaches, whether they are for research or intervention, have at their core the commitment to discover and communicate the community's perspective. A function of the democratic orientation is a consistent regard for the interests of the local community. You will see these attributes manifested continually throughout the text. You may find it useful to regard these features as a kind of bias.

Depending on the circumstances, the approaches can be both radical and conservative. In some cases, these different kinds of applied anthropology can be used to slow and redirect change that political authorities are advocating. In other cases, the practices discussed here can be used to transform communities into more powerful organizations, giving control where none existed previously. It is important for you, the reader, to realize these features are at the core of all the approaches to using anthropology that are discussed here. Applied anthropology is not about getting people to change against their will, it is about helping people express their will. Yet the framework for action that we discuss here is practical; it has to do with the job market, and it has to do with politics, power, and will.

Although most of the technique chapters have to do with change-producing strategies, this book is also about cultural persistence. You will notice that even in the more explicit change-producing approaches there is a strenuous commitment to identifying the community perspective in the development process. None of the approaches involve unilateral imposition of development goals from outside the community. The basic task is to foster acceleration of the adaptation process. Sometimes expressed simply as "getting more" for the community, the process involves creating a better adaptation for the people of the community. Adaptation questions are ultimately survival questions. Therefore, we should recognize that community-defined development aided by the applied anthropologist is basically a culture-conserving activity.

IS IT ANTHROPOLOGY?

This book does not ask the question, "Is this anthropology?" The question itself is viewed as basically destructive from both intellectual and action perspectives in that it generally limits competition and protects vested intellectual interests. In the case of applied anthropology the question is particularly problematic. Further, if we look at the effect of applied anthropological work on the rest of the field through time we can see that applied work often has functioned as the cutting edge of the discipline. Consequently, applied anthropologists have always been the targets of the "but is it. . . . " refrain. As we permanently set aside the "but is it anthropology?" question, we should be reminded of more relevant questions: "What is the problem?," "What are the solutions to it?," and most important, "What are the skills and knowledge necessary to implement the solution?"

CONTENT OF THE BOOK

The book is divided into four parts. The first part, "Introduction and Overview," includes chapters intended to provide background for better understanding the core of the text, as presented in Parts II and III. The fourth part of the book deals with some issues of the professional's role.

The first chapter, entitled "The Domain of Application," will consider both the relationship between theoretical and applied anthropology and the content of contemporary anthropologists' work situations. An explicit definition of applied anthropology is presented to give the reader a more systematic and comprehensive understanding of what applied anthropologists do. The relationship between application and theory is seen as poorly understood within the discipline. Two aspects of the relationship between theory and application are stressed. First, good knowledge of theory is a necessity for the applied anthropologist because it guides research and increases the scope of applicability of the information obtained. Second, theory that is useful to the applied anthropologist will concern variables that can be acted upon. The chapter maps out a strategy for self-instruction concerning potential employment situations.

The second chapter, entitled "The Development of Applied Anthropology," provides a synthesis of the history of applied anthropology from the standpoint of developments in the United States. This synthesis is based on work done in conjunction with the Applied Anthropology Documentation Project at the University of Kentucky. Among the points made in this chapter: the theoretical and applied aspects of anthropology have developed simultaneously, and, to a large extent, activities in the academic realm have often been motivated or at least rationalized by the information needs of governments, research funding organizations, and other policy research consumers.

The "Introduction and Overview" section of this book concludes with a chapter on ethics, organized around fundamental principles for ethical professional behavior. These principles are derived from the "Statement of Ethical and Professional Responsibilities" of the Society for Applied Anthropology. The research component of this chapter discusses the core of ethical research practice: informed consent, voluntary participation by informants, and the issue of risk. The discussion of ethics is expanded to include consideration of the conflicts that may exist between the different groups with which anthropologists work.

Although most research or action situations can be carried out without facing overly difficult dilemmas, even very simple situations can turn into a labyrinth of apparently insoluble conflicts. While it is best to be prepared for these problems, they cannot all be anticipated because real learning requires experience. Situations of irreconcilable conflict are easy to read about, and can even be discussed around seminar tables with some benefit, but being faced with harmed communities, betrayed colleagues, and unfulfilled contracts is quite another thing. All these complexities aside, it is important to understand that standards of ethical practice need not be viewed solely as constraints, but more importantly as good guides for effective professional action. Indeed, ethical behavior is more often than not the most effective action.

The second part of this book, "Interventions in Anthropology," contains chapters descriptive of six intervention techniques that have been developed within anthropology or with substantial participation by anthropologists. These modes of intervention are presented using, where appropriate, the prototypical case as the starting point in the discussion.

In the fifth chapter, research and development anthropology is exemplified by the Vicos Project, which was directed at establishing an independent community of former serfs in highland Peru. The sixth chapter discusses community development as it was applied to bring about improved aspects of life in a number of communities on the Tohono O'odham Indian Reservation in southern Arizona. The seventh chapter is about a kind of advocacy anthropology. Advocacy anthropology is depicted using a Chicago Community Mental Health Project in which anthropologists, working with activists in the Chicago Latino community, used their research skills to increase the political power of the Latino community and to improve available health, education, and recreational facilities in an area of Chicago's South Side. In the eighth chapter, cultural brokerage is illustrated by a case study based on Miami's Community Mental Health Project, which used anthropological knowledge and skills to develop and maintain a linkage between five different ethnic communities in Miami and a large county hospital.

The ninth chapter, new to this edition, is on social marketing. In the described project the goal was the promotion of breastfeeding among low-income women in the southeastern United States.

Action anthropology, research and development anthropology, and community development are similar in approach, purpose, and result. Each varies somewhat, and it can be argued that each represents a somewhat different array of techniques to achieve certain goals. All of these approaches can be used to achieve development of different kinds at the community level. To varying extents these approaches all stress what has been called developmental change—change that improves a community's long-term adaptability. One can often observe two parallel strands of development in projects that use these approaches. The first is more public and results in physical transformations and improved services, and serves as a medium for the second. The second thread is more obscure and results in strengthened community organization and improved decision making. It is more focused on educational change, and results in the creation of social structures rather than physical structures. The three approaches vary enough to provide a set of alternatives for dealing with different development problems in different kinds of communities.

Advocacy anthropology and cultural brokerage seem better suited to complex urban environments. Advocacy anthropology is used here as a general term for situations in which the anthropologist is directly working on behalf of community groups. This often entails working in opposition to more powerful political forces. The approach that is used to illustrate advocacy anthropology was developed by Stephen Schensul. This type is quite different from the three approaches described above. Here, the anthropologist acts more as a research auxiliary to community leadership than as a direct change agent, as is the case in action anthropology, research and development anthropology, and community development. Certainly, this is not to say that the anthropologist is not involved in the action— in fact, the advocacy process requires very close affiliation between the anthropologist and the community. The anthropologist's role reflects the development of increased political sophistication of ethnic minorities in American cities as much as a shift in the way anthropologists work. This is simply an appropriate adjustment to changes in ethnic communities.

Cultural brokerage, too, seems appropriate to contemporary urban ethnic politics. In this approach, developed by anthropologist Hazel H. Weidman, the anthropologist serves as a link between a community service-providing institution, such as a hospital, and an ethnic community that receives services from the institution. In contrast with the other approaches, the primary goal of cultural brokerage is not change per se, but increased efficiency through effective culture contact. That is, cultural brokerage aims at improving services for ethnic groups through enhanced communication, as well as changing the service provider and the ethnic community.

Social marketing makes use of techniques derived from commercial marketing to promote new behaviorals that are socially useful, such as safer sex, smoking reduction, and changes in diet. These efforts benefit from the anthropologist's research skills and community knowledge.

The third part of this book is entitled "Policy Research in Anthropology." The tenth chapter provides an overview of anthropology as a policy science by discussing various application domains. This chapter contains an expanded version of the discussion on policy that appears in Chapter 1. A special section on using policy research data is also included. Anthropologists are on both the producing and using ends of policy research these days. In fact, one anticipates that more and more anthropologists will take on the role of policy maker as they gain experience in the agencies and firms that employ them.

The next two chapters, "Social Impact Assessment" and "Evaluation," provide practical instruction in the two most important policy research areas. The chapter on social impact assessment (SIA) describes a generalized approach for doing this type of analysis. It is important to note here that SIA is usually done in response to a set of agency guidelines. Social impact assessment is most often done in response to specific federal laws, such as the National Environmental Policy Act of 1969, and consequently is limited to domestic situations in the United States. This chapter contains an extended illustrative case, an SIA done for a dam and reservoir project to be built on the Rio Grande in New Mexico. Other projects are mentioned in order to describe some of the variety of such research efforts.

The twelfth chapter deals with evaluation research. For certain kinds of evaluation tasks traditionally trained anthropologists are quite well equipped. This chapter focuses on those tasks that best fit the traditional array of research skills. Basically, we can say that anthropologists are usually best prepared to evaluate smaller scale programs or local components of larger national programs. One might also say that ethnography works best in evaluation strategies that respect qualitative data or are interested in the community perspective. The potential of anthropologists goes much beyond the qualitative evaluation of smaller programs. Because of this, the chapter describes a variety of evaluation modes, including a number of case presentations.

The last chapter of this section of the book deals with technology development research. In this type of research the anthropologist's goal is to increase the cultural appropriateness of new technology as it is developed. The case used to illustrate this kind of research is from the Farming Systems Research literature. The illustrative case is a research effort done in the Sudan as part of the International Sorghum and Millet Project.

The intervention component (Part II) and the policy research component (Part III) are the core of this text. These intervention and research approaches represent most of the major types of practice found in contemporary American anthropology. There are many other activities, most of them specific to particular new occupations for anthropologists, which are an important part of the total picture. Many of these activities are commented upon throughout the text. Increasingly, these diverse areas of practice will come to dominate applied anthropology.

Below is an outline of the major approaches presented in this text. Cultural resource assessment and social soundness analysis are briefly treated in Chapter 10, "Anthropology as a Policy Science."

Major Types of Anthropological Practice

I. Intervention Anthropology
  A. Action Anthropology
  B. Research and Development Anthropology
  C. Community Development
  D. Advocacy Anthropology
  E. Cultural Brokerage
  F. Social Marketing
II. Policy Research
  A. Social Impact Assessment
  B. Evaluation Research
  C. Technology Development Research
  D. Cultural Resource Assessment

The fourth and concluding section of this book includes one chapter, entitled "Making a Living." This last chapter focuses on skills that are important in anthropological practice. Above all, anthropologists need to be able to produce useful knowledge for their clients. Important communication skill areas that are discussed include report writing and proposal writing. Many anthropologists find that these skills are extremely important in their jobs. Some would say they were hired because of these skills, not for their ability to do cultural analysis or ethnography. Proposal writing holds an especially enticing lure, since it often allows one to create one's own employment, either in self-organized consulting firms, or for various other organizations, including universities, agencies, and firms. A variety of organizational skills are treated in this chapter. In addition, this chapter also looks at the role of the consultant. Topics discussed include: why people use consultants, different styles for being a consultant, and marketing your skills as a consultant.

The chapter gives practical advice on employment. The core of the chapter is about the job search and its component parts. It includes the selection of appropriate education and training experiences, selecting appropriate courses, how to build marketable credentials, investigating the domain of application, writing resumes, and carrying out job interviews. Survival skills after employment are also discussed. These include networking and collaboration, and skill maintenance.

ABOUT THE REVISED EDITION

In preparing the revised edition, I reviewed the text line by line and eliminated any statements that the intervening six years had made obsolete, and I added updates on particular issues. I entirely replaced or added new sections, including sections on the use of policy research and on needs assessment. Chapter 2, on the history of applied anthropology, received special attention, which resulted in new bibliographic references. Chapter 9, on social marketing, is entirely new, and is representative of a new approach to application. Finally, I updated the lists of further reading that follow each chapter.

Acknowledgments

Many people have assisted in the preparation of this book. These people include Tom Arcury, George Castile, Erve Chambers, Kathleen DeWalt, Tony DiBella, Shirley Fiske, George Foster, Tim Frankenberger, Art Gallaher, Sue-ellen Jacobs, Gil Kushner, John Peterson, Jay Schensul, Steve Schensul, Norm Schwartz, Rich Stoffle, Allen Turner, M. G. Trend, Tom Weaver, and Bob Wulff. I especially appreciate the assistance provided by Carol A. Bryant and Doraine F. C. Bailey in developing the chapter on social marketing. I wish to thank Hazel Weidman for materials on culture brokerage and Billie R. DeWalt for information on farming systems research. I thank Barbara Rylko-Bauer for allowing me to use materials from our essay, "A Framework for Conducting Utilization-Focused Policy Research in Anthropology," to be published in *Speaking the Language of Power: Communication, Collaboration and Advocacy*, ed. David Fetterman.

Part I

Introduction and Overview

1

The Domain of Application

The number of anthropologists employed to solve practical problems has increased dramatically in the last decade. Rather than working in the traditional academic roles of teaching and research in a college or university, large numbers of anthropologists work for many other kinds of organizations such as government agencies, non-government agencies, and firms in a wide range of content areas. While many work for government agencies, opportunities have also developed in not-for-profit private service agencies as well as profit-making firms, including those owned and operated by anthropologists. Still others free-lance through temporary contracts. These persons may describe themselves as practicing anthropologists or applied anthropologists. At their workplace they take many roles, including: policy researcher, evaluator, impact assessor, needs assessor, planner, research analyst, advocate, trainer, culture broker, expert witness, public participation specialist, administrator/manager, change agent, and therapist. These roles are briefly described below.

PRACTITIONER ROLES IN ANTHROPOLOGY

Policy researcher. Policy makers require information upon which to base policy decisions. This somewhat generalized role involves providing research results to them. It may involve traditional ethnographic research or a variety of specialized research techniques. This role may be the most common and can be activated at various stages in the research process, from research design to data collection. The research function is common to many applied positions, and therefore, all potential applied anthropologists need to have preparation as policy researchers. In a recent survey, 37 percent of members of the National Association for the Practice of Anthropology (NAPA) reported involvement as researchers (Fiske 1991:vi).

Evaluator. Evaluator is a specialized policy research role that involves the use of research skills to determine if a project, program, or policy is working effectively or has had a successful outcome. The basic task is to determine objectively the worth or value of something. Some kinds of evaluation are called program monitoring. This role is common; in the NAPA survey 31 percent reported using evaluation skills (Fiske 1991:vi).

Impact Assessor. Impact assessor is also a specialized policy research role that involves the prediction of the effects of a project, program, or policy. An impact assessor usually attempts to determine the effects of planned government projects on the nearby human communities. The information produced is usually intended to influence the design of a project, thus an impact assessor often considers various design alternatives. Particular attention is paid to the unintended consequences of projects such as reservoir, highway, and airport system construction. The term social impact assessment is often used to describe this kind of activity. This role is common; 24 percent of the NAPA membership reported expertise in social impact assessment (Fiske 1991:vi).

Needs Assessor. Needs assessor is a specialized policy research role that involves the collection of data on public program needs in anticipation of social, health, economic, and education program design. The needs assessor contributes to the process of program design and justification. This role is relatively common and is closely related to evaluation.

Planner. As planners, anthropologists participate in the design of future programs, projects, and policies. This may involve data collection and research analysis in support of decision makers. This role is not common.

Research analyst. The research analyst role consists of interpretation of research results for decision makers of various kinds. The analyst may serve as an auxiliary to planners, policy makers, and program managers. This is a common role.

Advocate. Advocate is a label for a complex role that involves acting in support of community groups and individuals. It almost always involves direct political action consistent with the community's self-defined goals. Advocacy may be part of other roles, but in itself is not common.

Trainer. Trainers develop and use training materials referenced to a number of different client groups and content areas. Often this involves preparation of technicians for cross-cultural experiences. This is a role with a long history in applied anthropology.

Culture Broker. Culture brokers serve as links between programs and ethnic communities. The role appears especially useful in reference to health care delivery and the provision of social services. Many other roles have culture brokerage functions attached to them. In a few cases, it is the primary role. Brokerage is always a two-way communication role.

Expert Witness. The expert witness role is usually activated on a part-time basis, mostly by those academically employed. It involves the presentation of research data through legal documents, that is, briefs and direct testimony on behalf of the parties to a legal case or as a friend of the court. This role is not common.

Public Participation Specialist. The public participation specialist's role is newly developed in response to the need for public input in planning. It closely resembles the culture broker role, although it tends to occur on a case-by-case basis rather than continuously as with culture brokerage. The role may involve organizing public education, using the media, and conducting public meetings. The amount of anthropological involvement in this role is increasing.

Administrator/Manager. Some anthropologists have direct administrative responsibility for the programs within which they work. These roles are usually not entry-level, but develop out of employment in the other roles mentioned here. The number of anthropologists working as administrators and managers has increased in the last decade as practicing anthropologists proceed with their careers. In some agencies anthropologists have become very influential because they are in charge.

Change Agent. Change agents work to stimulate change. This is a generalized function and is part of a variety of other tasks. In some cases the change agent role is carried out as part of a specific strategy of change, such as action anthropology or research and development anthropology. This role is not common.

Therapist. The therapist role is quite rare. It involves the use of anthropology along with knowledge of various "talk" therapies to treat individuals with various problems. In some cases these people refer to themselves as "clinical anthropologists." Clinical anthropologists are more often involved in brokerage roles than in the therapist role. This type of application of anthropology is not dealt with in this text to any extent.

To summarize this introduction to practitioner roles: the most frequent role is that of researcher. The various social action roles have great utility and potential, but are not often used. While we might associate teaching with academic employment, teaching is important in practitioner work settings. There is a general tendency for the number of roles to increase.

Typical applied anthropology jobs consist of many roles. Sometimes the job title reflects the role, and other times not. "Anthropologist" is not commonly used as a job title. This is because most of the jobs applied anthropologists do are also available to other kinds of social scientists. Some typical applied and practicing anthropologist's job titles, as shown in the *NAPA Directory of Practicing Anthropologists* (1991), are: administrator, advisor, analyst, anthropologist, archaeologist, caseworker, chief, consultant, coordinator, curator, director, ethnographer, extension anthropologist, manager, partner, president, research associate, social scientist, socioeconomist, specialist, supervisor, and therapist. It is difficult to tell from the job title what is entailed in a particular job, of course.

CONTENT AREAS FOR APPLIED WORK

In addition to working in many different roles, applied anthropologists work in a variety of different content areas. This can be seen in the contents of *Anthropology in Use: A Source Book on Anthropological Practice* (van Willigen

Figure 1.1
Content Areas Found in Anthropology in Use (1991)

Agriculture

Alcohol and Drug Use   Human Rights, Racism, and Genocide

Community Action   Industry and Business

Criminal Justice and Law Enforcement   Land Use and Land Claims

Cultural Resources Management   Language and Action

Design and Architecture   Media and Broadcasting

Development Policies and Practices   Military

Disaster Research   Missions

Economic Development   Nutrition

Education and Schools   Policy Making

Employment and Labor   Population and Demography

Energy Extraction   Recreation

Environment   Religious Expression

Evaluation   Resettlement

Fisheries Research   Social Impact Assessment

Forestry and Forests   Training Programs

Geriatric Services   Urban Development

Government and Administration   Water Resources Development

Health and Medicine   Wildlife Management

Housing   Women in Development

1991). This volume contains descriptions of cases in which anthropology was used to solve a practical problem, and is based upon materials in the Applied Anthropology Documentation Project collection at the University of Kentucky. This is a collection of technical reports and other documents prepared by practitioners. The content areas are listed in Figure 1.1. The most frequently cited topics are agricultural development, health and medicine, and education. Most frequently cited in the survey of NAPA members are "public health and health services, agricultural development, natural resources, and education" (Fiske 1991:vi). Because of the nature of the collection process of the Applied Anthropology Documentation Project, the listing emphasizes content areas where the research role dominates. Nevertheless, it serves as a useful indicator of areas of work.

APPLIED ANTHROPOLOGY: WHAT IS IT?

Clearly, anthropologists apply their knowledge in a wide variety of ways in many situations. Further, the extent to which their backgrounds as anthropologists can be expressed directly in their work varies a great deal. Their work is often defined by the problem and not by the discipline. In addition, new terms for the role and the work have emerged. All this makes defining the content of the field quite difficult.

We can start our discussion of a definition by simply saying that applied anthropology is anthropology put to use. Given the changes that are occurring in applied anthropology these days, it is tempting to leave the definitional question at that, and go on to the next question. Simply asserting that use defines the field has significant advantages. The generalized and fuzzy quality of that definition is appropriate to the changing job market. Yet in spite of the utility of flexible definitions it is useful for us to think about what we do somewhat more precisely.

The conception of applied anthropology used in this book is quite general. It is viewed as encompassing the tremendous variety of activities anthropologists do now, and have done in the past, when engaged in solving practical problems. The view taken here is that the various kinds of anthropological problem-solving activities are types of applied anthropology. This book is about the different kinds of applied anthropology. While this may seem like a simple idea, some people contrast action anthropology with applied anthropology, cultural brokerage with applied anthropology, and public-interest anthropology with applied anthropology.

More important, practicing anthropologists often conceive of themselves as being something different from applied anthropologists. This view, more common in the late 1980s, is that applied anthropology is something that is done by academic anthropologists when doing consulting work relating to practical problems. The term practicing anthropologist may be more frequently applied to persons who are employed by firms and agencies on a full-time basis. While this distinction holds up imperfectly in use, there are some very important differences in the working conditions of these two kinds of people that lead to differences in knowledge, attitudes, and reference group. Yet the view taken here is that these all represent kinds of applied anthropology.

At a general level, one can think of anthropology as having two aspects, one of which is concerned with the solution of theoretical problems, and another which is concerned with the solution of practical problems. The first we will call theoretical anthropology, or sometimes basic anthropology, and the second, applied anthropology or practicing anthropology. Both terms encompass a lot of diversity. Actually, the terms theoretical and basic are problematic. Much theoretical anthropology is not very theoretical, really. We just use the term to describe its implied purpose. Basic is also a misleading term because it suggests that it comes before, or first, and serves as a basis for more practical work. As will be shown later, practical work often serves as the basis of important theoretical developments. In spite of these semantic problems, the applied versus theoretical contrast is a useful distinction.

While there are no previous definitions that dominate the published literature on the definitional issue, one widely disseminated statement was written by George Foster for his textbook, *Applied Anthropology* (1969). He defined the field in the following way: ''Applied anthropology is the phrase commonly used by anthropologists to describe their professional activities in programs that have as primary goals changes in human behavior believed to ameliorate contemporary social, economic, and technological problems, rather than the development of social and cultural theory'' (1969:54). In many ways this definition remains quite serviceable. Foster identifies the major theme in applied anthropology as ''problem solution. The definition is limited in a number of ways. His use of the phrase ''in programs'' seems to imply that applied anthropologists do not work directly for communities. Advocacy anthropology and collaborative anthropology are kinds of applied anthropology that do just that (Stull and Schensul 1987). The definition also seems to emphasize change as the goal, while there are some examples of anthropology being used to assure stability (van Willigen 1981b).

The definition used in this text is based on review of large numbers of different types of anthropological practice. Considering those activities that are typically labeled applied anthropology, let us define the field in the following way: applied anthropology is a complex of related, research-based, instrumental methods that produce change or stability in specific cultural systems through provision of data, initiation of direct action, and/or the formation of policy. This process can take many forms, varying in terms of problem, role of the anthropologist, motivating values, and extent of action involvement.

The definition used here states that applied anthropology has a broad range of products. These are information, policy, and action. In the past and in the present, the most typical product of applied anthropologists seems to be information; information that can be used to construct policy or motivate action. Action and policy are less frequently the products of the process. Parts II and III of this book deal with different types of products: action products, policy products, and information products. The situation within which these products are produced is very complex. For our purposes here we can call this situation the *domain of application*.

DOMAIN OF APPLICATION

By domain of application we mean the knowledge and technique that are relevant to a particular work setting. The domain of application includes the methodology that maps the relationships between information, policy, and action, and the context of application, which includes the knowledge relevant to a particular problem area and work setting.

Application methodology consists of the intellectual operations by which applied anthropologists produce their products and have their effects. This view is consistent with the conception of research methodology presented by Pelto and Pelto (1978). It is simply an extension of that scheme to include action and policy.

Information. Information is seen as the foundation of the other two products, and can exist in a number of forms. The information we deal with can range from raw data to general theory. Mostly, applied anthropologists deal with information between these two poles. Through these methods of research we are able to move from observation, through various levels of abstraction, to more general theoretical statements. While the goal of applied work is not the production of theory, the patterns of research logic are similar to those used in theoretical pursuits.

Policy. The second product of applied anthropologists is policy. Policies are guides for consistent action. Policy can be developed in reference to a wide variety of situations. Cases of anthropologists actually developing policy are relatively rare, however. For the most part an anthropologist's involvement in the policy formulation process is as a researcher providing information to policy makers, or as an analyst who evaluates research data for policy makers. The experiences of anthropologists in this process will be discussed in more concrete terms in Chapter 2, "The Development of Applied Anthropology," and Chapter 10, "Anthropology as a Policy Science."

Action. The third product is action. Here are included the various interventions carried out by anthropologists. Part II of this text deals with the various action or intervention strategies that are used by anthropologists. These include: action anthropology, advocacy anthropology, community development, cultural brokerage, research and development anthropology, and social marketing. Each one of these strategies consists of a set of related ideas about role, procedures, and values that can be used to guide action.

The three products of applied anthropology are related in the following way: information is obtained through research, information is used to formulate policy, and policy guides action. Of course, nothing is ever that neatly rational; everything is subject to the struggles of politics. The relationship also operates in the opposite direction. The needs of action and policy often result in information being collected through research. Typically, in fact, there is a cycling back and forth through research, policy making, and action. The process of social impact assessment described in Chapter 10 is a good example.

Social impact assessment is done to help predict the effects of an action taken in the future, such as building a dam and reservoir. The research is often determined by which alternative plan would have the least social cost. This information would be fed back to the decision makers and used to determine which course of action would be the best considering many factors, including the political, economic, and social. The chapters on action anthropology and research and development describe the continual interplay between information and action. In thinking about this process it is possible to be either too cynical or too naive. Think pragmatically—the process is workable.

In addition to the relationship between information, policy, and action, we can also think about these categories at different levels of abstraction. Information, policy, and action can be thought of in terms of a progression from the simple and concrete to the complex and abstract. Anthropologists as social scientists are most familiar with this kind of relationship in terms of the linkage between observed data and general theory. The same kind of relationship exists in the realms of policy and action. The most important point is that the three realms have somewhat similar logical structures.

The general structure of the relationships across the information, policy, and action categories, and between the simple and complex levels, is shown in Figure 1.2. This figure is derived from the conception of the Domain of Methodology described by Pelto and Pelto (1978). Their model depicts aspects of the scientific research process, while the model presented here attempts to show the articulation between information, policy, and action as well as the general structure of the logic of the process.

The diagram depicts elements of a large and complex process within which the practitioner works. The work that individuals do only rarely encompasses the whole process. A typical function for an applied anthropologist would be to collect information, which would be turned over to a policy maker. The policy would be used to guide action carried out by yet another person. The process is, of course, not unique to anthropology. Collaboration with nonanthropologists would be typical at various points in the process. This often requires what might be called conceptual translation. The information that is communicated may be derived from special purpose research, secondary sources, or the general expertise of the anthropologist. The point is that not everything requires or allows the execution of a research process to solve a specific problem. In some cases, what is required is the transmission of just a few informally derived facts or interpretations. Thus there is great variation in the degree of formality. In my own work in development administration, I was struck by how rapidly one could act under certain circumstances. Information flow can vary from a crucial fact based on one's expertise communicated in a meeting, to the presentation of an elaborate research report based on a formal design to a policy maker. Information may also flow to the public to influence debate.

Most training that we receive as anthropologists relates to either research methodology or informational content. We receive very little training about the process of application as such, depicted here as the flow across the elements of information, policy, and action. Various aspects of this process are dealt with at various points in this text. The model of the application process and the definition presented above stresses the importance of research in the whole process. The foundation of all of this is objective knowledge obtained using the canons of scientific research as a guide and standard. While this may involve special research efforts, it can also be derived from the literature or our accumulated expertise. As Sol Tax asserted, an applied anthropology that is not based on research is simply a kind of propaganda (Tax 1958, in Gearing, Netting, and Peattie 1960:415).

The research base of the application process goes much beyond that which can be legitimately called anthropology. The informational basis of applied

Figure 1.2
Methodology of Application

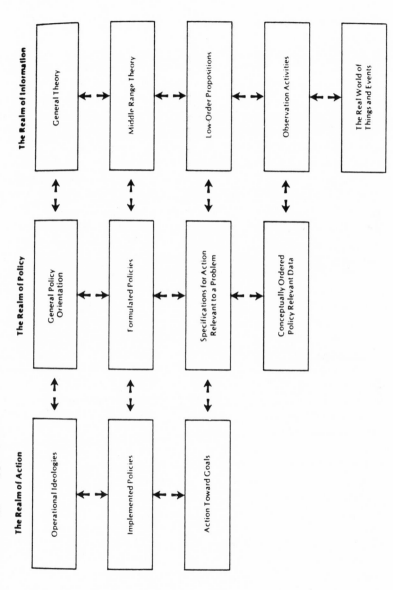

The Realm of Action

Operational Ideologies

Implemented Policies

Action Toward Goals

The Realm of Policy

General Policy Orientation

Formulated Policies

Specifications for Action Relevant to a Problem

Conceptually Ordered Policy Relevant Data

The Realm of Information

General Theory

Middle Range Theory

Low-Order Propositions

Observation Activities

The Real World of Things and Events

anthropology is defined by the problem, not the discipline. If we limited ourselves to knowledge exclusively from anthropology, we could not adequately deal with the problems at hand. This is not to say that anthropology is an uninformed discipline, it simply says something about reality. Further, the information that we tend to apply has certain characteristics that allow it to be efficiently applied. Good applied anthropologists have the skill to relate information to practical problems.

The discussion of anthropology as a policy science will deal with the process of knowledge utilization. There are at least three major issues or questions that are the basis of successful knowledge utilization practice. First, knowledge should be provided in reference to areas where the client can act. Telling someone about a problem on which they can not act is a waste of time. The applied anthropologist needs to be able to identify where action is possible. Second, knowledge has to be provided on time. Oftentimes action can only be effective within a specific time window. Research design has to allow for timely completion. If your goal is application, time becomes a crucial factor. Third, knowledge has to be communicated in a way that facilitates action. The basic conclusions of the process are best expressed as a recommendation for action with a justification.

In addition to the methods of application, such as effectively providing information, or skillfully converting information to effective action, the practicing anthropologist needs to know a great deal about the work context. Most important is knowledge about the particular policy area being dealt with. Each setting in which anthropologists work requires certain kinds of knowledge and experience for effective practice. It is to these practice areas that we bring our knowledge and techniques as anthropologists. In most areas of practice the anthropologist must learn a great deal from outside of anthropology in order to function in a professional manner. As mentioned above, we refer to the work context and its related knowledge as the context of application. This simple idea, along with the idea of methodology of application, helps focus our attention on information that is essential for being an applied anthropologist. In addition to these areas of special knowledge, we also need to understand those aspects of anthropological method and knowledge that are necessary for the work with which we are engaged.

KNOWING THE DOMAIN OF APPLICATION

The basis for effective practice is knowledge of the substantive aspects of a particular context of application. The first kind of knowledge that you should master is derived from the works of other social scientists relevant to a work context. Some content areas, such as health care delivery, are associated with immense bodies of literature. Other areas, such as fisheries management, are relatively limited. In addition to knowing the collateral social science literature referenced to a particular context of application, it is necessary to learn something of the technical basis of a particular field. If you are interested in agricultural development, knowledge of agronomy, soils, and marketing may be useful, if only to allow you to talk with your development colleagues. While not many of us can master both the collateral social science literature and a technical field in addition to our knowledge of anthropology, it is important to add continually to our knowledge of these areas.

The anthropologist's understanding of the domain of application may also be enhanced by knowledge of the legal basis for a particular area of application. In the United States, for example, many contemporary opportunities for work in various context areas are made possible and shaped by federal statute and regulation. The whole social impact assessment enterprise came about through a series of laws (most notably the National Environmental Policy Act of 1969), regulations, and agency guidelines. Often, the law mandates our work. The regulations and guidelines substantially tell us how to do it. These issues are discussed in Chapter 2, "The Development of Applied Anthropology," and Chapter 11, "Social Impact Assessment." The legislative and regulatory basis for the different areas of application are rather difficult to keep up with.

The next aspect of the domain of application for us to consider is its social organization. Here we can stress three components: the agencies and firms that hire anthropologists to do this type of work, the professional organizations established for people doing this work, and the social networks of the people employed in a particular context. It is important to identify the firms and agencies that hire people to deal with this type of work. It is especially useful to come to understand something about their hiring practices, job classifications, employment evaluation criteria, and even their previous experiences with anthropologists. Knowledge of professional organizations is useful because these organizations often afford a point of access into the social organization of a particular content area before employment. Such organizations may have newsletters and other publications that serve as information sources.

As a student, it is difficult to tap into social networks in the area of application. As you seek employment, you will begin to build your own network. It is important in this regard to begin to collect names of anthropologists who work in a domain. This will minimally give you an indication of where and whether anthropologists are working in a specific area. It may also serve as a basis for networking. Some local associations of anthropologists, such as the Washington Association of Professional Anthropologists, provide situations at their meetings that facilitate networking. Networking provides one with a source about work opportunities, agency plans, and information that may lead to the establishment of more network links. You will find those who have gone before are very willing to share certain kinds of information about opportunities. Their willingness to share is based on their continued use of the same sources of information into which you are trying to tap.

Students need to systematically collect information about potential work contexts. I often suggest to my students that they prepare a "pathfinder" to a particular content area in order to guide their learning. A pathfinder is a guide to learning resources and information, and can be thought of as a road map for self-instruction. The pathfinder idea was developed at the library of the Massachusetts Institute of Technology as a means of sharing information.

You should start your pathfinder with a "scope note" that defines the area of application. In your scope note you may find it useful to include reference to content, service population, and role. Some examples are: water resources development, with reference to social impact assessment and public input to planning reservoir construction; community development program administration among American Indian reservation communities; nutritional assessment techniques as used in determining the impact of economic development; and evaluation of curriculum innovations in education in the framework of the classroom.

A good pathfinder should be thought of as only a starting point. For the purposes of an applied anthropologist, a pathfinder should include information sources of the following types: guides to literature, review articles, indexing services, abstract services, major journals, newsletters, as well as computerized data bases. All of these should refer to anthropology, the collateral social science fields, and substantive technical fields. In addition, reference should be made in the pathfinder to relevant professional organizations, agencies and firms that do work in this area, and any special research facilities. A listing of anthropologists working in the content area is useful, as is a listing of the relevant statutes and regulations that are important to applied anthropologists working in the area.

SUMMARY

Applied anthropologists need to know the domain of application. This includes knowledge of the methods of application and the work context. Knowledge of method includes the practices associated with producing and communicating useful information in a policy or action setting. It can also involve various skills associated with being a development administrator or a change agent. Knowledge of the work context should include: knowledge of the literature of collateral social science fields; knowledge of the substantive technical field; knowledge of statute, regulation, and policy issued from government sources; knowledge of firms and agencies that work in a content area; knowledge of professional organizations in the content area; and knowledge about which anthropologists are doing what in the content area.

It is sometimes difficult to learn the context and method of application to any great extent through course work in anthropology departments. Students with a serious commitment to becoming practitioners should expect, in addition to their anthropological course work, course work in other departments, self-study, and practical experiences through internships and practica. While there are a number of training programs in applied anthropology, even these programs have to rely on a number of extradepartment resources (van Willigen 1987, Society for Applied Anthropology 1989), making it clear that anthropologists must expect that less of their training will fit traditional conceptions of what anthropology is. They must expect to be continually learning through their own efforts.

Start your self-instructional efforts right now. The first step is to consider your goals and interests, along with an assessment of opportunities. A starting point might be to review the content areas listed in the early part of this chapter. The possibilities go beyond this list, but it is an informed starting point. In addition to the content area, the knowledge and techniques needed vary with role (researchers, trainer, evaluator, planner, analyst, etc.), organizational type (public/ private, profit/not-for-profit, etc.), and service population (ethnicity, age, sex, etc.).

Define a content area for yourself that you can use as a focus for your own development and career planning. Be realistic, but really reflect on your goals. This reflection process is very important, and you will find that it sets the scene for the employment process. Try to project yourself into the future. This process of planning should start now and continue through all of your training, job hunting, and employment. As you do this, your conception of your own future will become refined and more specified. This process can serve as a reference point for your development. As this process unfolds, you can increase your focus and mastery, and take better advantage of learning opportunities in your area of focus.

FURTHER READING

Chambers, Erve. 1989. *Applied Anthropology: A Practical Guide*. Prospect Heights, Ill.: Waveland Press.

Presents a very useful discussion of work specializations in applied anthropology. Also useful for discussion of policy and policy research.

Society for Applied Anthropology. 1978. *Practicing Anthropology: A Career-Oriented Publication of the Society for Applied Anthropology* (College Park, Md.: Society for Applied Anthropology.

Provides information on current practice in applied anthropology. Most articles are written by practitioners, many focusing on their personal experiences.

2

The Development of Applied
Anthropology

This chapter interprets the history of the development of applied anthropology as it is currently practiced in the United States, with some reference to developments in other countries. The sequence of development is divided into five periods, which are defined on the basis of interpretations of the different kinds of practice done by applied anthropologists. In addition, the chapter also comments upon changes that are occurring in contemporary applied anthropology. This chapter is based upon the review of materials in the Applied Anthropology Documentation Project, as well as such published sources as Eddy and Partridge (1978b), Goldschmidt (1979), Spicer (1977), Mead (1977), and van Willigen (1991).

Awareness of history does much to reduce the antipathy that exists between theoretical and applied anthropologists. Historic awareness teaches a number of important points, perhaps most important among them, that the theoretical realm is historically based on application. While this is increasingly recognized, many continue to view theoretical anthropology, inappropriately, as the genitor. The fundamental reason for this is that applied anthropology tends not to be published in traditional formats and therefore exists primarily as "fugitive literature" (Clark and van Willigen 1981). Thus, while we are continually made aware of the historic development of theoretical anthropology through the literature, the historic development of applied anthropology and its relationship to the formation of the discipline is muted by the lack of documentation. This problem is especially acute in the earliest phases of the history of the field. While some of the experiences from the past are no longer applicable in new contexts, many current activities would benefit from knowledge of the past. To paraphrase a comment made by Karl Heider in a discussion of the history of the ethnographic film, those who don't understand the history of applied anthropology will be lucky enough to repeat it (Heider 1976). George Foster expresses clearly the importance of understanding history: "Current forms and place of applied anthropology within the broad discipline can be fully appreciated only with knowledge of the several stages of its development'' (1969:181). This chapter attempts to define the "several stages."

From my perspective, there are five stages: the predisciplinary stage, the applied ethnology stage, the federal service stage, the role-extension, value-explicit stage, and the policy research stage. The scheme as presented is additive. That is, general patterns of practice that emerged in earlier periods are continued in subsequent stages. The discussion of each stage includes the identification of the rationalization for the dating of the stage, a discussion of the primary patterns of practice with some examples, and a discussion of those external factors that seem to be relevant for the formation of the key patterns of practice. In reading this chapter it is important to keep in mind that the discipline is also changing. Especially significant among these changes is the radical change in the scale of the discipline.

THE PREDISCIPLINARY STAGE (Pre–1860)

If we consider early historic sources that deal with cultural interrelationships, we find recognition of the usefulness of cross-cultural data to solve problems identified in an administrative or policy context. This is most common in contexts of expansive political and economic systems. In the case of early recorders of cross-cultural description, such as Herodotus (circa 485-325 B.C.), or Lafitau (1671-1746), their basic motivation was to provide information for some practical purpose. Virtually all proto-anthropology of the predisciplinary stage was representative of a kind of applied work. Most frequently, as in the case of Herodotus, the research was done to gather data about potential enemies or colonial subjects. In the case of Lafitau, the purpose was to inform plans for trade and marketing expansion. Later, it is possible to find examples of proto-anthropology being used to provide research data to support certain philosophical or theological positions. Although Thomas Aquinas (1225-74) wrote about kinship and incest rules, he was attempting to support current church marriage laws (Honigmann 1976:2).

There are very early cases where cross-culturally informed administrators used their knowledge to facilitate better ''culture contact.'' During the Middle Ages, Pope Gregory urged his missionaries to the Irish to link Catholic saints' days to pagan Irish ceremonies and to convert animal sacrifices to forms more appropriate for newly converted Catholics (Honigmann 1976:45). Later, the most typical activities of the period included individuals appointed to carry out basic cultural research to assist in the administration of an area. A very early example of this is Francis Buchanan's appointment in 1807 by the East India Company to study life and culture in Bengal (Sachchidananda 1972). With increasing cross-cultural contact in the colonial period, more and more concern over the welfare of native populations developed. This can be observed in the establishment of such organizations as the Aborigines Protection Society, founded in London in 1838;

(Keith 1917; Reining 1962). The society was concerned with both research and social service for native populations.

In the predisciplinary stage it is possible to point to a number of examples of social reformers, ministers, and administrators who were able to make use of cultural knowledge in order to carry out the tasks at hand. This includes such documented cases as the work of Hinrich Rink, who served as an administrator for the Danish Government of Greenland. Rink, trained as a natural historian, contributed to the early development of self-determination among Greenland natives in the 1860s (Nellemann 1969).

There are a number of North American examples of early usages. Perhaps the earliest documented is the ethnological work of the Jesuit priest, Father Joseph Lafitau. Posted to New France as a missionary, Lafitau set about to document life in the Northeast. This resulted in the publication of *Customs of the American Indians Compared with the Customs of Primitive Times* (1724). While this is framed as a theoretical work, he did engage in various practical studies. One such inquiry was his quest for ginseng, a medicinal herb in the woodlands bordering the St. Lawrence. Introduced from Asia to Europe by a fellow Jesuit, ginseng became much sought after in European markets. Lafitau attempted to find the plant in North America. To do this he sought the help of Mohawk herbalists, whom he interviewed about native plant knowledge and other topics. This inquiry seemed to lead him to more general research, which contributed to his compendium on customs. He did find ginseng and became well known for this (Lafitau 1724; Fenton and Moore 1974).

An interesting example from the United States is the work of Henry R. Schoolcraft, one of the founders of the American Ethnological Society. Schoolcraft was retained by the United States Congress to compile *Information Respecting the History, Condition and Prospects of the Indian Tribes of the United States* (Schoolcraft 1852-1857). This imposing six-volume set is nothing if not a policy research report. It was prepared with the explicit purpose of providing reliable information upon which to base United States Indian policy. Schoolcraft started his career as an American Indian specialist as an administrator. His professional identity as an ethnologist emerged with the development of the discipline; his career paralleled changes that occurred within applied anthropology. The missionary work of William Duncan among various Northwest Indian groups serves as an example of the impact of a cross-culturally informed change agent. Working in the 1860s, Duncan made significant efforts in the area of social reform (Barnett 1942).

In this period there were some examples of the development of ethnologically informed training programs for colonial officers. Great Britain started such programs in 1806, and the Netherlands offered such programs by 1819. There is no evidence for such developments in the United States.

To summarize, contemporary anthropologists have rather little to learn about the methodology of application from the predisciplinary stage. Documentation is poor, and therefore it is difficult to develop a sense of the nature of the approaches used. The one important lesson to be learned is that anthropology in its prototypical stage had an important applied component. This contradicts the idea that applied anthropology somehow grew out of general anthropology. Later it becomes clear that the foundation of general anthropology is application and practice. The most objective view would suggest that the proto-anthropologists, for the most part, did their general interest work on the basis of what were applied research assignments. This stage ends with the emergence of anthropology as a distinct discipline. Here we use 1860 as a starting point, following Voget's view of the history of the discipline (1975:115).

THE APPLIED ETHNOLOGY STAGE (1860-1930)

With the emergence of anthropology as a distinct discipline, the basic style of applied work typical of the next seventy years is manifested. Typically, the applied anthropologists of this stage worked as training or research specialists in support of government or private foundation-supported administrative programs. For the most part, these efforts supported the establishment of direct administrative control over native populations in internal and external colonial settings. Later in the stage, applied anthropologists carried out the same pattern of activity in the context of development programs. It is important to emphasize that the anthropologist's role tended to be limited to providing data for policy making and problem solving. Very rarely were anthropologists involved as administrators or change agents. There were a number of administrators that became anthropologists, however.

The ethnology phase is very long, and is marked by significant changes in anthropology itself. This stage covers the transition from the dominance of classical evolution theory to the structural-functionalism and historical anthropology of the 1920s. The other significant process that occurred between the beginning and end of this period was the institutionalization of the discipline. That is, the basic infrastructure of a scientific discipline was formed. Professional associations were organized, degree programs were established, academic departments were formed as a body of knowledge grew and accumulated.

A fundamentally important fact that is not acknowledged in the literature on the history of anthropology is that applied anthropology served as the foundation for the development of much disciplinary infrastructure. This can be seen in four contexts. The earliest learned societies in anthropology developed out of associations that were primarily concerned with application and social reform (Reining 1962, Keith 1917). The first organizations that hired anthropologists in the United States were policy research organizations (Powell 1881, Hinsley 1976). The first academic department of anthropology at Oxford University was established on the basis of a justification to train colonial administrators, that is as a kind of applied anthropology training program (Fortes 1953). The first use of the term applied anthropology occurred in a description of the program at Oxford

(Read 1906). The first professional code of ethics in anthropology was developed by an applied anthropology organization (Mead, Chapple, and Brown 1949).

While the effects of application on the discipline were significant, the basic approaches to using anthropological knowledge remained the same throughout the period. For the most part, anthropologists carried out their research activities using an explicitly "value-free" approach. In fact, anthropologists writing in support of limiting anthropology to the style characteristic of this era often argued that their utility would be dramatically impaired if they did not approach their research from a "value-free" perspective. This was also done in conjunction with issues relating to role extension. Anthropologists argued that the anthropologist *qua* anthropologist cannot legitimately engage in roles other than the core consultant's role. This view was argued repeatedly and effectively until rather late in this particular period in the development of applied anthropology. The essence of this position is simply that when the anthropologist extends her role beyond that of researcher-consultant-instructor she is no longer an anthropologist, she is acting as some other kind of specialist. Others held that involvement beyond the core role required that the value-free position often stressed had to be relinquished.

An early manifestation of anthropology in the United States took the form of the Bureau of American Ethnology (BAE). The BAE is known to us today as a basic research institute. It was, in fact, created as a policy research arm of the federal government. The bureau's first Annual Report notes that it was founded to "produce results that would be of practical value in the administration of Indian affairs" (Powell 1881). The label used to describe this stage, "applied ethnology," was coined by James Mooney for a discussion of the BAE's commitment to policy research in the 1902 Annual Report (Hinsley 1976). Mooney's claims for political relevance were not hollow: his classic account of the Ghost Dance Religion is described by Anthony Wallace as an early policy study done in anthropology (Mooney 1896; Wallace 1976).

The creation of the BAE antedates the organization of the first academic anthropology department in the United States, at Clark University, by a number of years. The bureau served as a model for the social research foundation of some American colonial administration experiences. A similar organization was established by the American government, in the Philippines, in 1906, which was directed by Albert E. Jenks (Kennard and MacGregor 1953). According to Hinsley, the Bureau of American Ethnology's involvement in policy studies lasted only until Charles C. Royce's study of Indian land cessions was published in 1899 (Hinsley 1979).

There are examples of privately sponsored research from this period. One such example is the work of the Women's Anthropological Society of Washington. This organization supported research into the apparently deplorable housing conditions of Washington, D.C. As an outcome of this research an organization was established to improve the quality of housing to the poor. This research was done in 1896 (Schensul and Schensul 1978).

Franz Boas, although not usually thought of as an applied anthropologist, completed some important policy research. Most noteworthy is his research sponsored by the United States Immigration Commission. He documented morphological changes in the substantial United States immigrant population. The research contradicted a number of racist ideas concerning the impact of immigration on the American population. Boas was, of course, a committed anti-racist. This research was published in 1910. Also related to the issue of United States immigration was the work of Albert Jenks at the University of Minnesota. He established an Americanization training course for immigrants in conjunction with the existing anthropology curriculum (Jenks 1921).

As early as 1864, ethnological studies were included in the colonial service training program of the Netherlands (Held 1953; Kennedy 1944). Such training was developed for the Union of South Africa in 1905 (Forde 1953), Anglo-Egyptian Sudan in 1908 (Myres 1928), Belgian territories in 1920 (Nicaise 1960), and Australian-mandated New Guinea in 1925. This type of training was not emphasized in the United States. As colonial administrative experience increased there seemed to be more interest in ethnological training.

The British also made early and intensive use of anthropologists as government staff or contract research consultants. Anthropologists or anthropologically trained administrators provided research products ranging from short-term trouble-shooting to long-term basic research. Such individuals were hired by the foreign office, colonial office, and India office, as well as the military.

During the applied ethnology period there was significant growth and development in applied anthropology. This growth occurred in certain sectors, but was, with few exceptions, limited to research or instructional activities. These developments occurred most dramatically in the United States, Great Britain, Mexico, and the Netherlands. Most typically the activities consisted of the following: first, a number of anthropologists were involved in instruction of government personnel for administrative positions in cross-cultural settings. Second, there are a number of examples of short-term troubleshooting research in which the anthropologist provided cultural data to an administration to solve a problem that had developed precipitously; in some locales, the anthropologist-on-staff seemed to be retained for this purpose. Third, anthropologists were also hired to carry out research in various problem areas at the request of administrators. These activities included national and regional ethnographic surveys, single-culture focused ethnographies, and topic-specialized single-culture ethnographies.

During this era, applied activities made a significant and often overlooked contribution to the anthropological literature. The typical output of anthropologists during this period were research reports. If we consider the output of anthropologists hired to do problem-oriented research for the government or other sponsoring agencies, it becomes apparent that much of the distinguished ethnographic literature produced in the first half of the twentieth century was a product of applied efforts. This is particularly apparent in African and Pacific ethnography done by British social anthropologists, and North and South American ethnography done by anthropologists from the United States and Mexico.

In summary, during the applied ethnology stage the policy research and administrative training needs of governments were an important stimulus both for early applied work and for the establishment of much organizational infrastructure for the basic discipline. Most applied anthropologists functioned in roles confined to research and teaching. The effects of applied anthropology on the basic discipline consisted largely of stimulating research in new areas and topics. And importantly, the potential for application was used as a justification for the establishment of many of the important academic programs.

THE FEDERAL SERVICE STAGE (1930-1945)

With the coming of the Great Depression and the New Deal, the number of anthropologists employed in application grew dramatically in the United States. This related to an apparent increased need for information on the part of government, as well as a need to provide jobs for anthropologists. It is important to note that the annual production of anthropologists was still quite small. At the same time the academic job market was very limited until World War II. The intensification of anthropological employment in applied work reached a climax with the war. This period is named for the dominant kind of employment.

During the period of federal service, anthropologists came to work in an increasingly large number of problem areas and political contexts. Further, it is apparent that the work of anthropologists improved in quality and appropriateness. In terms of problem orientation the research seemed initially to focus on general ethnography. Later, the research typical of applied anthropologists came to include education, nutrition, culture contact, migration, land tenure, and various other topics. This pattern is particularly characteristic of the development in British colonial territories, but can be applied to describe the development of applied anthropology in the United States as well. Foster suggests at least one difference between the subdiscipline as it was practiced by its British and American practitioners: "the interest of Britain's applied anthropologists in the social aspects of technological development has been relatively modest as compared to that of the Americans" (1969:194).

In the United States a number of applied research organizations were created during this period. One of the first of these groups was the Applied Anthropology Unit established in the Office of Indian Affairs. The purpose of the unit was to review the prospects of certain American Indian tribes to develop self-governance organizations in response to the Indian Reorganization Act of 1934. Research topics included settlement patterns, education policy, and prospects for economic development (Collier 1936; Mekeel 1944; Rodnick 1936; Thompson 1956). The researchers produced a number of reports that had very little impact on the policy-making process. The Applied Anthropology Unit was created by John

Collier, who had been appointed Commissioner of Indian Affairs by Franklin D. Roosevelt in 1932. Collier's advocacy of the utility of anthropology is widely viewed as crucial to the rapid expansion of federal employment of anthropologists.

At approximately the same time, the Bureau of Indian Affairs (BIA) received the services of a group of anthropologists employed by the U.S. Department of Agriculture. This program, referred to as the Technical Cooperation Bureau of Indian Affairs, carried out projects relating to economic and resource development on various Indian reservations (Kennard and MacGregor 1953). This group worked in conjunction with various physical scientists, such as geologists, hydrologists, agronomists, and soil conservationists, and produced various studies on the sociocultural aspects of environmental problems. Similar use of anthropologists occurred in the large-scale research project carried out by the U.S. Department of Agriculture in the Rio Grande Basin of the United States (Provinse 1942; Kimball and Provinse 1942). Analysis was directed at Native American, Mexican-American, and Anglo-American residents of the Southwest. Research focused on the cultural factors that had influenced land use.

Involvement of anthropologists in the study of policy questions among rural American communities increased from this point well into the war years. This took a variety of forms. For example, some anthropologists participated in the U.S. Department of Agriculture's Rural Life Studies, which produced a series of six community studies that focused on community potential for change. Perhaps most interesting among the policy research done by anthropologists in rural America was that of Walter Goldschmidt, who was involved in a number of studies for the U.S. Department of Agriculture, Bureau of Agricultural Economics. These included a study of war mobilization in a rural California county and a study of the political economy of agribusiness in the San Joaquin valley of California. The second study produced a classic account of economic exploitation and led to Goldschmidt's vilification by vested interests in California's agribusiness (1947).

During the mid-1930s early use of anthropology in the context of nursing occurred with the work of Esther Lucille Brown. In addition, pioneering work in educational policy studies were carried out in American Indian education in the form of the Pine Ridge and Sherman-California vocational education surveys.

In 1941, the Indian Personality and Administration Research Project was established. For the most part this was a policy-focused basic research project, which resulted in a number of useful studies of American Indian reservation life, including Papago (Joseph, Spicer, and Chesky 1949), Hopi (Thompson and Joseph 1944), Navajo (Kluckhohn and Leighton 1946; Leighton and Leighton 1944), Sioux (MacGregor 1946), and Zuni (Leighton and Adair 1946). One aspect of this project made use of action research methodology, which exemplifies the primary change associated with this stage. Action research was developed outside of anthropology, largely by psychologist Kurt Lewin. Laura Thompson applied this technique to stimulate change in Hopi administration. Thompson's description of the technique is cited below:

Action research is normally distinguished by the following characteristics: (1) it stems from an urgent practical problem, a felt need on the part of a group, and is generally solicited voluntarily by the potential users of the findings; (2) it involves both scientists and the user-volunteers as participants in a cooperative effort—namely, the solving of the practical problem; and (3) the scientists involved normally function both as scientist-technicians and as integrative or "democratic" leaders in Kurt Lewin's sense of the term. That is, they endeavor to stimulate, draw out, and foster the talents and leadership qualities of the members of the participant group and to minimize their own roles except as catalysts of group potentialities. In their role as integrative leaders, the staff scientists train and supervise the work of the volunteer user-participant. (Thompson 1950:34)

Also indicative of the expansion into new research areas during this period was the work of the anthropologists associated with the Committee on Human Relations in Industry at the University of Chicago. Included among the anthropologists associated with the committee were W. Lloyd Warner and Burleigh B. Gardner. This period saw major advancements in what came to be called the scientific study of management. The most significant project was the classic Western Electric, Hawthorn Works study of the relationships between working conditions and productivity. This area of work developed very rapidly for a period of time.

The National Research Council established at least two research committees that were to have significant impacts on policy research done by anthropologists in this period. These included the Committee on Food Habits, which included Margaret Mead, Ruth Benedict, and Rhoda Metraux, among others. This group was to obtain scientific information on nutritional levels of the American population. Also established was the Committee for National Morale, consisting of Gregory Bateson, Elliot Chapple, and Margaret Mead, among others. This committee was to determine how anthropology and psychology could be applied to the improvement of national morale during the war.

This stage in the development of applied anthropology started in the national crisis caused by the Great Depression and concluded in the crisis of war. The intensification of involvement in application caused by World War II is astounding. Mead (1977) estimates that over 95 percent of American anthropologists were involved with work in support of the war effort during the 1940s. By way of contrast, the war in Vietnam had very much the opposite effect on anthropologists. In 1941, the American Anthropological Association passed a resolution placing the "specialized skill and knowledge of its members, at the disposal of the country for the successful prosecution of the war" (American Anthropological Association 1942:42). This effort seemed to increase the self-awareness of applied anthropologists, as well as their concentration in Washington and other places.

Perhaps the most well-known war effort involvements by American anthropologists are the activities on behalf of the War Relocation Authority. The War Relocation Authority was responsible for managing the internment camps established early in the war to incarcerate Japanese-Americans. The use of social scientists grew out of the experiences of the one camp that was under the administrative responsibility of the Bureau of Indian Affairs. At that time the BIA was directed by John Collier. In response to the problems that developed at the other camps, social science programs were developed at all War Relocation Authority facilities (Arensberg 1942; Kimball 1946; Leighton et al. 1943; Spicer 1946a, 1946b). The anthropologists who served in the camps served as liaisons between inmates and camp administration, and as researchers. This involvement by anthropologists is frequently characterized as unethical, being viewed by some as supportive of an illegal and inhumane government program. If one reads their writings or discusses this involvement with them it is clear that they viewed themselves as ameliorators of a potentially much worse situation. One should read Rosemary Wax's chilling account of her experiences as a community analyst in a camp to get some feeling for the problem (Wax 1971).

In addition to the War Relocation Authority, anthropologists were involved in a variety of other programs. The Far Eastern Civil Affairs Training School was established to prepare administrators for areas that were being recaptured from the Japanese by the Allies. This operation, established at the University of Chicago, was headed by anthropologist Fred Eggan (Embree 1949). The Foreign Morale Analysis Division was created within the Office of War Information. Using various data sources, this organization reported intelligence on the Japanese and other adversaries to the Departments of War, State, and Navy. Some of the information was collected from internment camp inmates. Benedict's *The Chrysanthemum and the Sword* (1946) was a by-product of this operation.

During the war the Smithsonian Institution initiated a number of activities that had significant applied research components. The Institute of Social Anthropology of the Smithsonian, established in 1943, engaged in both basic and applied research projects. The applied activities included very early use of anthropological research to plan and evaluate health programs. The applied aspect of the Institute of Social Anthropology's research program developed under the leadership of George M. Foster. Contemporary applied medical anthropology was, to a large extent, shaped by the program of the Institute of Social Anthropology.

Also of interest are the various war-related compilation and publication programs. These include the Civil Affairs Handbooks published by the Chief of Naval Operations on Japanese-held Pacific territories, and the Handbook of South American Indians published as part of a program to promote relations with Latin America. In addition to the efforts mentioned here, there were activities related to the immediate postwar period. These included research into the effects of the nuclear attack on Japanese cities (Leighton 1949), and studies of occupation problems (Bennett 1951; Gladwin 1950; Embree 1946; Hall 1949; Rodnick 1948).

It is quite clear that applied anthropology grew dramatically during this period and that the major cause was employment opportunities with the federal government relating to the depression and war. One of the products of this expansion was the organization of the Society for Applied Anthropology. Spicer refers to this as "one of the most important events in the development of anthropology in the twentieth century" (1976:335). Now over fifty years old, the society has gone through considerable change and development through the years. In its early phases the society seemed most concerned with bringing together social scientists and administrators, reporting cases where anthropological knowledge had been usefully applied, and advocating the idea that there existed an applicable body of anthropological theory (Spicer 1976:336). An important component of the program of the Society for Applied Anthropology was the publication of the journal *Applied Anthropology*, which was subsequently named *Human Organization*.

The Society for Applied Anthropology developed around local interest groups in Washington, D.C. and Cambridge, Massachusetts, and then subsequently expanded to a national membership. The changes in the Society for Applied Anthropology will be discussed in conjunction with the next two periods in the history of American applied anthropology. In the early days of the society's existence most activities of the organization were directed at creating a professional identity for applied anthropologists.

This period saw major changes in applied anthropology. These included dramatic intensification of involvement of anthropologists in application and the development of a more definite professional identity through the creation of the Society for Applied Anthropology and its publications. For the most part, applied anthropology roles were still limited to policy researcher and trainer, the roles that dominated both the applied ethnology and predisciplinary stages. There are some examples of pioneering assumption of change-producing, action-involved roles, which are a striking feature of the next phase, the value-explicit, role-extension phase.

THE ROLE EXTENSION, VALUE-EXPLICIT STAGE (1945-1970)

The historic course of the development of applied anthropology up to 1945 is characterized by relatively little change in the applied anthropologist's operational strategy. From the initial professionalization of the discipline, around the middle of the nineteenth century, there was little deviation from the core applied anthropology role, which might best be labeled "instructor-researcher-consultant." The history of the field up to 1945 is characterized by continued elaboration of this theme.

The basic pattern of the applied ethnology stage became elaborated as it became more widely accepted by both anthropological producers and administrative consumers. It is inappropriate to suggest that the acceptance of applied anthropology was complete or even extensive. It became more and more useful, more and more important, but one senses a certain reluctance to participate in applied roles. A cadre of applied anthropologists did not develop as such, but a group of anthropologists did exist who oscillated between academic and applied appointments. Further, much employment was in service to colonial regimes (Asad 1973). This may have related to the historic tendency to switch back to academic careers.

In any case, the radical critique of applied anthropology derived a great deal of its impact from an analysis of the anthropologists who served in these capacities (for example, Horowitz 1967; Gough 1968; Berreman 1969; Hymes 1974; Moore 1971). We are faced with an evaluation dilemma, however, for even an unsympathetic review of these efforts reveals that most anthropologists were struggling to increase the fairness and humaneness of various domestic and international colonial systems. To be sure, the anthropological perspective was more ameliorative than revolutionary, and given the power relations extant, it would seem fair to assume that the most positive impact of anthropology on colonialism could be achieved within the system. As history became reconstructed in the post-colonial period, these anthropologists took the brunt of various aggressive criticisms.

The shift in applied anthropology practice that occurred in this stage can be best understood in terms of three basic changes. First, the range of legitimate roles for applied anthropologists expanded beyond the researcher-instructor-consultant core. With role extension came increases in the intensity of participation, that is, the number of aspects of a particular applied problem with which the anthropologist dealt. Anthropologists became more directly involved in implementation and intervention. Instead of merely providing information and an occasional recommendation, anthropologists began to take responsibility for problem solution. Anthropologists were no longer merely monitors and predictors of change but came actually to work as agents of change. In addition, other new roles were explored.

The second major shift occurred in terms of the extent to which anthropologists confronted their own values, directly and explicitly. The "value-free" or, more accurately, the value-implicit approach, came to be more openly questioned. Some anthropologists came to recognize the value-explicit approach as legitimate, after substantial debate. This means that certain anthropologists came to feel that social scientists cannot separate their work from real-world values, and that to do so creates a dangerous illusion of true objectivity. The value-explicit stance implied a willingness on the part of anthropologists openly to define goals and values for clients and client communities. This, of course, led to intense debates concerning ethics for cultural anthropologists of all types. It also led anthropologists to increased political exposure.

The third shift came as a corollary to role extension and value-explicitness. That is, applied anthropology was increasingly action-involved. This means, as suggested above, that the users of the new patterns came to be directly engaged in change-producing behavior. Their contacts with the *dramatis personae* of the real world were transformed. No longer was their activity limited to the basic researcher-instructor-consultant role, but was extended to include a much wider array of action-involved roles. This change did not result in a single new approach, but a multiplicity of new approaches for applying anthropological knowledge. In addition to the retained and still important activities characteristic of the earlier stages, at least five new value-explicit, role-extended, and action-involved approaches to applications began to emerge during this period. These approaches are: action anthropology, research and development anthropology, community development, community advocacy anthropology, and culture brokerage. Cultural brokerage actually appeared early in the next period, as specified in the historic scheme reported here.

Action Anthropology. Perhaps the first action-involved, value-explicit approach to be developed within anthropology was action anthropology, which grew out of a University of Chicago field school organized by Sol Tax among the Mesquakie residents near Tama, Iowa. The action orientation was not part of the original intent, but emerged because of the sentiments of the participating students. The Fox Project, as it was called, consisted of a dual program of action and research that addressed a complex of ideas associated with self-determination and some more generalized research goals.

Some of the key concepts of the approach are community self-determination and the idea of what might best be called interactive planning. This last idea is rooted in the work of John Dewey and is manifested in a tendency to stress an ambiguous distinction between means and ends, and to reduce the linearity of social planning. The primary proposition is that means and ends are interdependent, and are determined through an oscillating interaction between problems inherent in a situation and various development alternatives. Additionally, goal specification tends to be very general and open-ended. The Fox Project was initiated in 1948 (Gearing, Netting, and Peattie 1960). The action anthropology approach was used in a wide variety of settings.

Research and Development Anthropology. The research and development approach was first attempted in the well-known Vicos Project. Like action anthropology, the research and development process has both scientific and development goals. Defined technically, research and development anthropology is a means of bringing about increases in the net amount and breadth of distribution of certain basic human values through research-based participant intervention in a community. The writings of Allan Holmberg, the primary initiator, are good sources for understanding the transition toward a value-explicit anthropology. Holmberg and his associates assumed that value-free social science was unobtainable, and that the research inevitably influenced the community. He argued that this tendency was better dealt with if it was made explicit and used for the betterment of the society, as well as for scientific advancement.

The goal of research and development anthropology is the wider sharing of the content of basic value categories. The value categories conceptualized in research and development anthropology are power, respect, enlightenment, wealth, skill, well-being, affection, and rectitude. The conceptualization benefited from the contribution of the political scientist, Harold Lasswell. The specific content of the approach involved identifying baseline data relevant to the specific value categories, and then devising an action response that was calculated to increase the amount and breadth of distribution of the valued content. The Vicos Project took place in highland Peru, and was initiated in 1952 (Dobyns, Doughty, and Lasswell 1971). The approach has been used in a variety of other settings.

Community Development. The community development approach was developed outside of anthropology in the context of British colonial administration, and the social work and agricultural extension disciplines in the United States. It is listed here because a number of anthropologists used and contributed to the approach. A widely used definition of the approach is contained in manuals produced by the International Cooperation Administration (a predecessor of the Agency for International Development):

Community Development is a process of social action in which the people of a community organize themselves for planning and action; define their common and individual needs and problems; make group and individual plans to meet their needs and problems; execute the plans with a maximum of reliance upon community resources; supplement these resources when necessary with services and materials from government and nongovernmental agencies outside the community (1955:1)

Projects using this approach often speak of concepts like felt needs, self-help, and self-determination.

The most visible contributions of anthropologists to this approach are various textbooks, which include *Cooperation in Change* (Goodenough 1963), and *Community Development: An Interpretation* (Brokensha and Hodge 1969). In addition to this, anthropologists have made use of the approach directly (van Willigen 1971, 1973, 1977; Willard 1977).

Community Advocacy Anthropology. Action research, action anthropology, and research and development anthropology represent the first generation of value-explicit applied anthropology approaches. In addition to these approaches, various advocacy anthropology approaches developed in the early 1970s. These were supplemented by an approach called cultural brokerage around the same period. Generally, the advocacy approaches are characterized by a closer administrative relationship between the community and the anthropologist. In some cases, the anthropologist is actually hired by the local community. While this is not strictly true of the case example we are using for this type of anthropology, the relationship between the community and the anthropologists was quite close. It was developed by Stephen Schensul for use in a Latino barrio of Chicago. In this case, the anthropologist worked primarily as a research technician in support of indigenous community leadership. Goals of the sponsoring organization were addressed to a limited extent. The anthropologist also provided technical assistance in training for research and proposal writing.

While the community advocacy role is diverse, it is somewhat more focused upon research done in support of community-defined goals. The anthropologist, although involved in the action, does not serve as a direct change agent, but as an auxiliary to community leaders. The anthropologist does not work through intervening agencies, but instead has a direct relationship with the community. The relationship is collaborative, drawing upon the anthropologist's research skills and the organizational skills of the community's leadership. Typically, the anthropologist's activities include evaluation of community-based programs, whether they are sponsored or managed by people from within or outside the community; needs assessments in anticipation of proposal writing and program design; proposal writing and a wide variety of generalized inputs of a less formal nature. The Chicago project was initiated in 1968 (Schensul 1973).

Cultural Brokerage. Cultural brokerage is an approach to using anthropological knowledge developed by Hazel H. Weidman (Weidman 1973). It is based on a conception of role defined originally by Eric Wolf to account for persons who serve as links between two cultural systems (1956). While Wolf conceptualized the role in the context of the naturally occurring roles that exist between peasant communities and the national system, Weidman applied the term to structures created to make health care delivery more appropriate to an ethnically diverse clientele.

Stimulated by research findings of the Miami Health Ecology Project, Weidman created a position for culture brokers in the Community Health Program of the Department of Psychiatry of the University of Miami. These individuals were social scientists who were familiar with the various ethnic groups found in the "catchment area" of a large county hospital. Within this area, it was possible to find Cubans, Puerto Ricans, blacks, Haitians, and Bahamians, as well as whites. While the cultural brokerage role is quite diverse, its primary goal is the establishment of links between the politically dominant structures of the community and the less powerful, in a way that restructures the relationship in terms of equality.

The commitment to egalitarian intercultural relations in cultural brokerage is manifested in other elements in its conceptual structure. The most important of these conceptual elements are coculture and culture mediation. Coculture is the label used for the components of a culturally pluralistic system. It is a conceptual substitute for subculture.

The development of intervention techniques within anthropology is the most striking characteristic of this particular stage of the development of applied anthropology. Parallel with this new development is the continuation of the basic pattern of research for various administrative authorities that was characteristic of the applied ethnology stage. Much of this research received its stimulus in the early years of the role-extension, value-explicit stage from the forces put in place by World War II. These forces were substantial.

While intervention strategies were developed and used within anthropology, the most important factors that shaped applied anthropology were simple economic ones. During this phase there was a tremendous expansion of the academic job market. According to Spicer, "It became a world of academic positions far in excess of persons trained to fill them" (1976:337). This caused a "retreat into the academic world" of substantial proportions. While economic factors associated with the expansiveness of the academic job market were important, the tendency not to take federal employment was enhanced by objections many anthropologists had toward the war the government was waging in Vietnam.

A variety of research projects motivated by basic policy questions led anthropologists to study a variety of new research areas, including native land rights (Goldschmidt and Haas 1946), government policy toward native political organization (Gluckman 1943, 1955), ethnohistory (Stewart 1961), health care (Leighton and Leighton 1944), land tenure (Allen, Gluckman, Peters, and Trapnell 1948), urban life (Beaglehole and Beaglehole 1946), migrant labor (Schapera 1947), relocation (Kiste 1974; Mason 1950, 1958), water resources development (Cushman and MacGregor 1949, Padfield and Smith 1968), health care delivery (Kimball 1952, Kimball and Pearsall 1954), disasters (Spillius 1957), health development (Foster 1953), racial discrimination (Southern Regional Council 1961), and others.

New roles activated by anthropologists include: expert witness (Lurie 1955; MacGregor 1955; Kluger 1976; Stewart 1961; Dobyns 1978), evaluator (Aiyappan 1948; Sasaki 1960; Sasaki and Adair 1952; Foster 1953; Honigmann 1953; Dupree 1956a, 1956b, 1958, Lantis and Hadaway 1957; Ingersoll 1968, 1969; Halpern 1972; Mathur 1977; Elwin 1977; Messing 1965, 1964; Pearsall and Kern 1967; Cain 1968; Sorenson and Berg 1967; Jacobsen 1973), planner (Peattie 1968, 1969a, 1969b; Peterson 1970, 1972, 1978), as well as roles associated with various clinical functions (Landy 1961; Aberle 1950).

Anthropologists invested more effort in the documentation of sound practices for themselves and others. A number of manuals and texts published in this period were intended to provide guidance to development administrators, public health officials, and change agents. These included *Human Problems in Technological Change* (Spicer 1952), *Cultural Patterns and Technological Change* (Mead 1955), *Health, Culture and Community: Case Studies of Public Reactions to Health Programs* (Paul 1955), *Traditional Cultures and the Impact of Technological Change* (Foster 1962), *Cooperation in Change: An Anthropological Approach to Community Development* (Goodenough 1963), and *Applied Anthropology* (Foster 1969).

An important event during this period was the development of an ethics statement by the Society for Applied Anthropology. The statement, written in 1949, was the first within the discipline. This effort has continued to the present day. Interestingly, the statement was developed in reaction to a specific basic research project rather than problems associated with application. The American Anthropological Association did not consider development of an ethics statement for about twenty years.

In summary, the role extension stage saw anthropologists designing and implementing strategies for social change. Alongside this development anthropologists increased the array of new research-based roles. Although the social change strategies developed within anthropology during this stage appear to remain useful, their application has been infrequent in the latest stage of the development of applied anthropology. The development of strategies for social change within the discipline seems to be most common in the United States and Mexico. Perhaps the most important change that shaped applied anthropology during this period was the tremendous expansion of the academic job market.

THE POLICY RESEARCH STAGE (1970 TO THE PRESENT)

The policy research stage is characterized by the emergence of what Angrosino calls the "new applied anthropology" (1976). Expressed simply, this means an increased emphasis on policy research of various kinds done outside of academic employment. The typical pattern of the value-explicit, role-extension period, where the applied anthropologist would take temporary assignments of an applied nature while working as an academic, has been replaced by more employment by consulting firms or as a direct-hire staff member of the agency. This kind of employment results in a dramatic increase in new kinds of research.

This stage appears to be more clearly a return to the pattern of the federal service period than an outgrowth of the role-extension period. It is different in a fundamental way, however. During the federal service period applied anthropologists returned to academia once the employment pressure was off. It appears unlikely that the large numbers of anthropologists entering the job market as practicing anthropologists now will take academic jobs in the future. They will not return because there will not be jobs for them, their salary expectations can not be met, and they just do not want to. It is for this reason that this period is unique.

Applied anthropology of this stage is more clearly a product of external factors. There are two primary external factors: the dramatically shrinking academic job market (D'Andrade, Hammel, Adkins, and McDaniel 1975; Cartter 1974; Balderston and Radner 1971), and (at least in the United States) the creation of a wide array of policy research functions mandated by federal regulation and statute.

The effect of the shrinking academic job market is substantial and increasing. An early estimate predicted that two-thirds of new Ph.D.s produced in anthropology would find employment outside of academia (D'Andrade, Hammel, Adkins, and McDaniel 1975). Recent research on employment summarized by Elizabeth Briody shows that the percentage of each annual cohort of Ph.D.s that enters employment outside academia is increasing (Briody 1988:77). An American Anthropological Association survey indicated that in the 1989-90 cohort of Ph.D.s 59 percent were employed outside of academic departments, although most anthropologists still work in academic positions (American Anthropological Association 1991:1).

Coupled with this big push factor are the pulling effects of legistalively mandated policy research opportunities. To some unspecified degree, the so-called surplus of Ph.D.s is absorbed by other opportunities created by the expansion in policy research. Some of the legislation relevant to this problem is the National Environmental Policy Act of 1969, the Foreign Assistance Act as amended in 1973, and the Community Development Act of 1974. In addition to employment directly related to these policy research needs, a very large array of new types of employment was accepted by anthropologists. Some of this employment involved research, much of it involved assuming other roles. The effects of these pull factors varied considerably. Levels of funding have varied substantially through the years with changing economic conditions, changing political styles, and periodic disillusionment with the utility of policy research.

A confounding factor in employment choice is the political attitude of anthropologists formed by their experiences in the era of the Vietnamese War. For some, employment in United States government agencies with overseas programs was unacceptable for ideological reasons, no matter how hard the push or attractive the pull. This, so it seems, has changed significantly as the job situation has worsened and agency programs have changed.

The changes in anthropology associated with the increase in nonacademic employment are substantial. These can be addressed in terms of three general categories: academic program content, publication and information dissemination, and social organization, as well as some general changes in style.

Academic program content. The most obvious effect has been the creation of academic programs that are specifically focused upon preparation for nonacademic careers (Kushner 1978:23; Trotter 1988; Hyland and Kirkpatrick 1989). Increasingly, these programs are coming to be focused upon more specific policy areas rather than having a general orientation toward applied anthropology (van Willigen 1988). These programs tend to make wider use of internships and practica in their instructional strategy (Hyland et al. 1988; Wolfe, Chambers, and Smith 1981). The number of programs that have application as a focus have increased dramatically (van Willigen 1985; Hyland and Kirkpatrick 1989). It is conceivable that in the future a professional society will develop standards for certification and accreditation.

Publication and information dissemination. The most noteworthy change in publication and information dissemination has been the creation of the publication *Practicing Anthropology*. *Practicing Anthropology* publishes articles that report the experiences of anthropologists in various kinds of nonacademic employment. Currently its readership is over two thousand. In addition, the Applied Anthropology Documentation Project at the University of Kentucky has resulted in the establishment of a collection of the written products of applied anthropologists (Clark and van Willigen 1981; van Willigen 1981a, 1991). A similar collection of Canadian applied anthropological work, sponsored by the Society for Applied Anthropology in Canada has been organized at McMaster University in Hamilton, Ontario, by Wayne Warry.

The increased interest in application has influenced the publication policies of the major journals. *Human Organization* shows some tendency to return to the publication of application case study materials that dominated its pages in the first decade of publication. *American Anthropologist* publishes book reviews of technical reports that are applied in nature, and a limited number of articles based on practice. The National Association for the Practice of Anthropology publishes a bulletin series that features materials on application.

Social Organization. The most significant change caused by increases in non-academic employment have been the creation of a large number of local practitioner organizations (LPOs). The first of these was the Society of Professional Anthropologists (SOPA), established in Tucson, Arizona in 1974 (Bennett 1988; Bainton 1975). Although now disbanded, SOPA served as a model for others. Among the organizations currently operating are those in Washington, D.C., Los Angeles, Tampa, Tallahassee, Ann Arbor, and Memphis. In addition the High Plains Society for Applied Anthropology serves a regional consituency in the high plains. These groups are quite variable in size and current levels of activity. The Washington Association of Professional Anthropologists (WAPA) and the High Plains Society for Applied Anthropology (HPSFAA) are clearly the most active. WAPA publishes a newsletter and directory and regularly holds workshops at national association meetings on topics like "Seeking Federal Employment." HPSFAA has a lively annual meeting and a regular publication. Most importantly, the LPOs serve as a mechanism for effective networking in the profession.

At the national level there has been considerable organizational development that has benefited American applied anthropologists. Most important is the National Association for the Practice of Anthropology, organized as a unit of the American Anthropological Association to replace the Society for Applied Anthropology. SfAA and NAPA are currently engaged in various cooperative activities. Canadian anthropologists benefit from the activities of the Society for Applied Anthropology in Canada, organized in 1981 (Price 1987).

Both the American Anthropological Association and the Society for Applied Anthropology have used academically employed and nonacademically employed slates for their elections for some time. Other adaptations have included changing the mix of the national meeting programs so as to increase activities relevant for nonacademically employed anthropologists, and to decrease the part of the program designed for scholarly purposes. Innovations in this area include workshops for gaining skills in various policy research areas, such as social impact assessment and program evaluation. NAPA has provided considerable creative leadership in this regard.

The American Anthropological Association has issued a number of publications that address practical or applied issues. These include publications on the structure of training programs, produced with the Society for Applied Anthropology (Leacock, Gonzalez, and Kushner 1974), the development of training programs (Trotter 1988), approaches to practice (Goldschmidt 1979), practicing anthropologists (Chatelain and Cimino 1981), and employment (Bernard and Sibley 1975). Also published were a series of training manuals in applied anthropology on various topics including development anthropology (Partridge 1984), medical anthropology (Hill 1984), policy ethnography (van Willigen and DeWalt 1985), and nutritional anthropology (Quandt and Ritenbaugh 1986).

Another potentially significant development has been the modification of ethics statements by the national organizations. The Society for Applied Anthropology approved a new version of their ethics statement in 1983. The committee was charged with adjusting the existing statement to the conditions faced by practicing anthropologists. With this in mind, the committee developed a statement that recognized the "legitimate proprietary" interests of clients in terms of the dissemination of research data, the need for truthful reporting of qualifications, and the need for continuing education to maintain skills, as well as other issues (Committee on Ethics, Society for Applied Anthropology 1983). NAPA also recently issued an ethics statement.

As in the two previous stages, the anthropologists working in application are exploring new areas of research. The growth of new areas of inquiry is dramatic. Some examples of the new developments are research into forestry (Collins and Painter 1986; Murray 1987), drug rehabilitation (Weppner 1973; Marshall 1979), human waste disposal (Elmendorf and Buckles 1978), welfare program reform (Trend 1978), broadcast media (Eiselein and Marshall 1976), social services in boomtowns (Uhlman 1977a, 1977b), educational evaluation (Wax and Breunig 1973; Fitzsimmons 1975; Burns 1975; Clinton 1975), commodity marketing (Lample and Herbert 1988), housing needs and effects (Wulff 1972; Weaver and Downing 1975; Kerri 1977), commodity-focused agricultural research (Werge 1977), wildlife management (Brownrigg 1986), radioactive waste storage siting (Stoffle, Evans, and Jensen 1987), energy extraction (Softestad 1990), rural industrial development (Grinstead 1976), office management (Weaver et al. 1971), employment training (Wolfe and Dean 1974; Naylor 1976), market development (Zilverberg and Courtney 1984), corrections (Alexander and Chapman 1982), building and landscape design (Esber 1987; Low and Simon 1984), fisheries (Stoffle, Jensen, and Rasch 1981; Johnson and Griffith 1985; McCay and Creed 1990), recreational planning (Wulff 1976; Scott et al. 1982), and the effects of power generation (Callaway, Levy, and Henderson 1976). There are, of course, others.

At a somewhat more general level, one can cite development in the areas of social impact assessment and program evaluation. Anthropologists have been involved in some of the pioneering efforts that attempted to predict, for the benefit of planners, some of the social costs and benefits of various kinds of development projects. In domestic settings, we find anthropologists engaged in team research that has developed social impact assessment manuals and standards (Maruyama 1973; Vlachos 1975). Anthropologists have been involved in direct assessment of project effects (Nugent et al. 1978; Jacobs, Schleicher, and Ontiveros 1974; Millsap 1978; Jacobs 1977; Parker and King 1987; Preister 1987;

Stoffle, Evans, and Jensen 1987; McGuire and Worden 1984; Van Tassell and Michaelson 1977; Dixon 1978), and field testing of social impact assessment methodologies (Clinton 1978).

Although the legislative mandate was substantially different, anthropologists have also been engaged in social impact assessment work in the context of international development. These efforts include the development of manuals for impact assessment methodology (Harza Engineering Company 1980), baseline studies to inform development planning (Werge 1977; Maloney, Aziz, and Sarker 1980; Brown 1980; Scaglion 1981; Green 1982; Reeves and Frankenberger 1981; DeWalt and DeWalt 1982), development of regional development plans (Brokensha, Horowitz, and Scudder 1977), needs assessments (Mason 1979; Practical Concepts, Inc. 1980), social soundness analysis (U.S. Agency for International Development 1975; Cochrane 1979; McPherson 1978), project evaluations (Blustain 1982; Brown 1980; Pillsbury 1986; Williams 1980, 1981), and analysis of program planning documents (Ingersoll, Sullivan, and Lenkerd 1981; Hoben 1980; Britan 1980; Collins and Painter 1986). In addition, there has been basic research into various aspects of development such as decentralization in development (Ralston, Anderson, and Colson 1981), indigenous voluntary associations (Miller 1980), and women in development (Elmendorf and Isely 1981).

The involvement of anthropologists in the evaluation of various domestic social action programs is quite common. Evaluation studies occur in a wide variety of areas, including American Indian education (Fuchs and Havighurst 1970), housing development (Kerri 1977), American Indian tribal governance (Weaver et al. 1971), employment training programs (Wolfe and Dean 1974), rural education (Everhart 1975), welfare reform (Trend 1978), alternative energy source development (Roberts 1978), innovative education programs (Wilson 1977; Fetterman 1987), alcohol abuse curtailment projects (Marshall 1979), and minority employment (Buehler 1981).

The dramatic increase in policy research efforts of various types is not associated with an increase in the use of social intervention techniques, which this chapter describes as characteristic of the pattern of application in the previous stage. There are examples of the use of action anthropology (Schlesier 1974; Stull 1979), research and development anthropology (Turner 1974; Wulff 1977), and various advocacy research approaches. The approaches based on cultural brokerage models developed by Hazel H. Weidman earlier in this stage are still in use. There are two factors that seem to have caused the reduction of this type of application: the radical critique of much of applied anthropology, and the increasing political sophistication of many of the traditional client groups of anthropologists.

A factor that will influence the future of anthropology is the changing circumstances of employment. First, the academic to nonacademic mix has changed. The nonacademic realm is quite variable within itself. The conditions of employment affect both motivation and opportunity to publish, tendency to participate in anthropological learned societies, extent of interdisciplinary orientation, and the training of future anthropologists. Working in a governmental organization is different than working in the private sector. There are significant differences between profit and nonprofit organizations in the private sector. The biggest differences may occur where the anthropologist owns the firm. Academic employment is also changing in many of the same ways. There seems to be a stronger commitment to consulting and, of course, many nonacademically employed anthropologists have to compete with the academics. Some academics take on research commitments in the policy area so as to provide students with marketable work experiences.

SUMMARY

What is called applied anthropology has grown dramatically since the inception of anthropology as a discipline. In its growth, applied anthropology has manifested an array of tendencies. First, the applied and theoretical aspects of the discipline developed in parallel, application potentials being used as a rationale for the development of academic programs and theoretical research programs. The effect of applied anthropology on theoretical anthropology was often masked because of the nature of publication in applied anthropology and its relative lack of prestige. Second, a major effect of applied anthropology on theoretical anthropology has been the stimulus of interest in new research topics and populations. This effect too has been masked. Third, the development of applied anthropology is best thought of in terms of an additive expansion of research context, topics, and techniques. While there have been intervention techniques developed within anthropology, today these are infrequently applied. Fourth, applied anthropology should be thought of as primarily a product of important external forces rather than a consistent pattern of internally generated change. Mostly, the external forces have been manifested in employment and funded research opportunities brought about by the needs of colonial governance, war, and foreign policy. More recently, a major external factor has been the nature of the academic job market, and to a limited extent an increase in policy research opportunities mandated by federal law.

The nature of the academic job market has resulted in the creation of a large cadre of anthropologists employed outside of academic contexts. The changes wrought by this significant demographic shift are being felt in the discipline now. It is anticipated that other more significant changes will occur in the discipline as the number of nonacademically employed increases to majority, and beyond. Those employed in nonacademic settings will continue to occupy roles that relate in some way to policy research rather than intervention.

FURTHER READING

Eddy, Elizabeth M., and William L. Partridge, eds. 1987. *Applied Anthropology in America*. New York: Columbia University Press.

Contains a number of chapters useful for understanding the history of applied anthropology.

van Willigen, John. 1991. *Anthropology in Use: A Source Book on Anthropological Practice*. Boulder, Colo.: Westview Press.

Contains brief descriptions of over five hundred cases of the use of anthropology to solve practical problems. It is an excellent source for research paper topics.

3

Ethics

As one prepares to assume an occupational role as an applied anthropologist, one becomes increasingly concerned with standards of performance and behavior in that role. This connotes a concern for the quality of the services produced as a result of one's action, as well as concern for how and under what circumstances one produces these services. Such standards of performance and behavior are the substance of ethics. The essential core of the ethics of applied anthropology is the nature of the potential and manifested impact on the people involved.

In his important discussion of ethical issues, Joseph G. Jorgensen distinguishes between the anthropologist and various other "information seekers" whom persons confront. As he notes, "our situation is unlike that of the priest, the lawyer, or the physician, whose help is *requested by the client* and whose right to privileged communication is deemed necessary (by law, in the United States) if he is to serve his clients. In contrast, as anthropologists we *ask for the help* of our subjects and we *offer* confidentiality as an *inducement* to informants for their cooperation" (Jorgensen 1971:327).

In light of this, then, the applied anthropologist by implication would have a status distinct from the research anthropologist in terms of various ethical considerations. First, because we may have change as a goal as well as scientific understanding, we must be especially concerned about the impact of our efforts on the populations with whom we work. Second, because we may be working for an agency that is from outside or is marginal to the community, we may be forced to deal with an especially complex set of ethical concerns. Applied anthropologists typically face more complex ethical situations than other anthropologists.

Though the term *ethics* connotes an absolute standard of behavior, applied anthropologists, like other human scientists both pure and applied, must, to be realistic, deal with the concept relativistically. That is to say, ethical standards are difficult enough to specify, let alone apply consistently. In each of the applied anthropologist's constituencies we find different kinds of ethical requirements. That is, different ethical issues are raised in the case of the applied anthropologist's relations with research subjects, project sponsors, or fellow anthropologists. The somewhat different requirements of these relationships are sometimes in conflict.

ETHICAL ISSUES

This is a complex period in the history of anthropology. The discipline has achieved a very high level of theoretical and methodological complexity. New areas of inquiry emerge with surprising frequency. Further change is brought about by the growth of applied activities. All this change creates new challenges and an increased concern for ethical issues. The debate has continued through the years, reaching a peak during the war in Vietnam. The tensions of that period were exacerbated by a series of ill-conceived and unethical research projects.

The debate is not limited to the recent past, but has substantial time depth. As early as 1919, Franz Boas raised concerns in a letter to the *Nation* in which he accused four anthropologists of serving as spies under the guise of their researcher role. Boas wrote: ''A person, who uses science as a cover for political spying, who demeans himself to pose before a foreign government as an investigator and asks for assistance in his alleged researches in order to carry on, under this cloak, his political machinations, prostitutes science in an unpardonable way and forfeits the right to be classed as a scientist'' (Boas 1919, in Weaver 1973:51).

From the time of Boas to the present, the debate continues with only a trace of its intensity revealed in published articles, letters to the editor, resolutions passed at national meetings, American Anthropological Association ethics committee reports, and the ethics codes published by the American Anthropological Association and the Society for Applied Anthropology.

The primary issue in the ethical debate is the potential negative effect that the activities of the anthropologist may have on a community or a specific person. There are many important issues, but this is the core of anthropology's ethical concerns. This is something that an anthropologist should understand. We are inextricably linked to the communities we work with, and therefore, our actions can be continually ramified, and may have serious unanticipated effects.

Cora Du Bois relates an incident that exemplifies this potential in a frightening way. Du Bois had carried out her well-known study, *The People of Alor*, in an area of what is now Indonesia, which came to be occupied by the Japanese during World War II. It was reported to Du Bois after the war that persons she had studied had innocently mentioned that they wished the Americans would win the war, because they were good people. The Alorese in question had never heard of America prior to Du Bois's field work. She reports that the Japanese heard that certain Alorese were stating that America would win the conflict. The Japanese military government rounded up the persons in question and publicly beheaded them as an example to the populace. As Du Bois notes, "There is no end to the intricate chain of responsibility and guilt that the pursuit of even the most arcane social research involves. 'No man is an island' " (Du Bois 1944, in Weaver 1973:32). However unusual this horrifying case is, it dramatically emphasizes the potential for unexpected harm our science has. Let us here engage in a discussion of some of the issues identified in the literature on anthropological research ethics.

PRIVACY

The fieldwork process is based largely on overcoming the boundaries that exist between the personality of the researcher and that of the informant. We call this breakdown of protective boundaries "rapport building." Through the building of rapport, we erode the informants' tendency to protect their private personalities. It is possible, even probable, that with the development of rapport, informants provide information that could be damaging to them, if not properly protected.

Why do people give us information? Many do so because they value the goals of science. However, in many cases the goals of science are irrelevant or unknown to them and they may be responding for a whole range of other reasons. These might include their own standards of hospitality, their perceptions of the anthropologist's power, and their own need for recognition and attention. The importance of this last aspect is very clearly indicated in Joseph Casagrande's *In the Company of Man* (1960). This volume contains descriptions of important informants written by anthropologists. These sketches are quite revealing because of the rather heavy reliance these anthropologists place on the isolated and often disaffected members of a community. The Casagrande volume depicts anthropologists' informants as very young, very old, very marginal, and very powerful, but rarely very "typical." This raises methodological issues as well as ethical ones.

In any case, we must be wary of any tendency to use whatever power and prestige the anthropologist might have to produce positive responses in informants. Clearly, it is possible to use our relative power to obtain data. One might even argue that "rapport-building skills" are in fact the most insidious deception.

We often give our research subjects assurances about anonymity, yet our capacity to protect the information is not absolute, although one might argue that it is reasonably assured. We do not have the legal right to claim that our information is privileged. Anthropologists' legal status is not unlike that of journalists, whose data and data sources can be subpoenaed. Yet the ethical standards of the discipline, and more recently the legal requirements of federally funded research, seem to suggest that absolute control is possible. These conditions cause us to work as if we had absolute control over access to our data. In applied research settings, control of the use of data may be in the hands of the sponsor rather than the researcher.

We value our research and its products. It is possible to build substantial justification for the continuation of such research efforts. The question is, however, what costs must individual research subjects bear in order for the research to go on? The respondent's costs include loss of opportunity, loss of control of data, as well as any physical risks.

CONSENT

Perhaps the paramount issue in the ethical debate is the issue of consent. Our discipline should expect that its practitioners carry out their activities with the permission of research subjects. That is to say, the anthropologist must ask the question, "May I do this?" Further, the informant must know the circumstances in which the question is asked. It is only with adequate knowledge that the subject can give permission in a way that is ethically meaningful. Sufficient knowledge is a relative concept to be sure, but nevertheless, would include an understanding of the purposes of the research activity; the identity of the funding agency and its goals; the final disposition of the data; and the potential impact the data would have on the individual. Further, the informant must understand that his or her participation is voluntary. Such are the components of what is referred to as "informed consent."

Informed consent is the foundation of ethical research. Much impetus for formalizing ethical issues, such as informed consent, has come from the medical research area. This impetus is derived from the real and immediate risk of much medical research that uses human subjects. Further, many of the most abusive human-subject research projects have been carried out by medical researchers. The abuses of medical research and other disciplines have led to increasing public concern. Associated with this concern is an increased government involvement in the ethical dimension of large-scale federally funded research projects. Most individual research projects that are considered for federal funding must be evaluated in terms of key ethical issues such as informed consent.

In spite of this concern, there is still a significant amount of ambiguity concerning these issues. Let us present here a widely applied definition of informed consent. This definition of informed consent was provided by the Board of Regents of the State of New York in 1966. It provides clear guidelines for medical investigators, though it could also be used for anthropologists.

No consent is valid unless it is made by a person with legal and mental capacity to make it, and is based on a disclosure of all material facts. Any facts which might influence the giving and with-holding of consent is material. A patient has the right to know he is being asked to volunteer and to refuse to participate in an experiment for any reason, intelligent or otherwise, well-informed or prejudiced. A physician has no right to withhold from a prospective volunteer any fact which he knows may influence the decision. It is the volunteer's decision to make, and the physician may not take it away from him by the manner in which he asks the question or explains or fails to explain the circumstances. (Langer 1966:664)

Though informed consent is rather easy to specify as a requirement, it is sometimes very difficult to achieve. Part of our task in establishing the conditions of informed consent is to convey the implications of our research when we may not fully understand these implications. The type of research populations we, as anthropologists, deal with tend not to be in the position to recognize adequately the implications of our research. As Jorgensen notes,

Because our research is usually conducted among illiterate or semiliterate [people] who have scant knowledge of the uses to which data can be put, we are doubly obligated to spell out our intentions and not to exploit their naivete. The extent to which we must explain our intentions will vary with the problems we address and the knowledge possessed by the host population. Our host populations, in particular, will vary greatly in their understandings of the implications of the ways in which research conducted among them could damage their own interests. I am not suggesting that it will be easy to apprise them of everything they ought to know, nor to make them immediately understand all they ought to know. The anthropologist himself is often naive about the implications of his own research. (Jorgensen 1971:328)

The fact that anthropologists tend to use inductive research designs also causes a certain amount of difficulty in legitimately achieving the goal of informed consent. Anthropologists create strictly deductive research designs infrequently. With such designs, the ultimate range and breadth of a research project can be more easily determined. In the field, topics grow and change.

A question is raised by these changes: how and under what circumstances does consent have to be obtained again? Does consent to carry out one aspect of the research imply that consent is given for other aspects of the study? Oftentimes, the researcher begins his or her project with uncontroversial topics, and then slowly changes focus to the more controversial ones, for the very reason that if the latter topics had been broached during the initial stages of the research project, the anthropologist would have been run off. This represents a difficult problem. There are those that suggest that "consent should be requested for the research ends that are anticipated" (Jorgensen, 1971:328). This may be difficult in certain social contexts. The goal of informed consent implies that the research activities are carried out without deceit and misrepresentation. Jorgensen writes:

I accept the premise that anthropologists, by the very nature of their dedication to free and open inquiry and the pursuit of truth, cannot condone deceit in research. If the anthropologist seeks truth, exposes falsehood, feels an ethical obligation to others of his profession not to compromise them or make their own legitimate research suspect, and feels he has a right and a duty to honor the obligations he has made to his informants in requesting their help in giving him information about which they are protective, he cannot assume a masquerade at all. (1971:329)

UTILITY

As suggested above, anthropologists' research means that certain costs will accrue to the research subject and thereby to the subject community. In most cases it would seem that the loss of time to the informant is inconsequential. Most humans have sufficient leisure to allow some interaction with a social scientist. Further, it seems in most cases the research efforts of anthropologists will tend not to harm informants if the data is properly protected. Yet there are cases where the work of the anthropologist has caused harm.

The most important idea here is that information can be used to control people, that is, knowledge is power. That phrase has become meaningless because we rarely take time to examine the mechanism by which knowledge is used to control people. Just how anthropological data plays into the hands of an exploitative, multinational corporation, an oppressive, totalitarian organization, or a secret intelligence agency is not clear. It is difficult to find out, given that it is not even clear how more "righteous" organizations make use of such data. The implications of the potential for harm, however, are so serious that we must develop our position in terms of the *potential* for harm rather than the real probabilities. When we do this, we are confronted with a number of serious problems.

In most cases in pure anthropological research, the costs of research accrue to the researched, whereas most of the benefits accrue to the researcher. At least it seems improbable that given the normal research process in anthropology, research subjects will receive any significant benefit from the enterprise. These communities are rarely equipped to use such data; the topics selected by the researcher are often irrelevant to the information needs of the community, and the researcher rarely provides information to the community.

This kind of research might be construed as the ultimate kind of anthropological self-indulgence, if it were not so common. The Dutch applied anthropologist Gerrit Huizer refers to this self-indulgent anthropology as hobbyism (1975:64). He notes:

It seems as if the most immediate purpose of the research is the satisfaction of a rather arbitrary curiosity (or urge for knowledge) of the social researcher. The satisfaction of this urge according to the rules of the game of scientific effort and the passing on of the knowledge gained to others determines the career and promotion of the research worker. (1975:64)

The remedy for this problem is the active and conscientious consideration of the interests of the research population in the research design process. Huizer notes, however:

That the research could possibly serve the interests of the people investigated or even remedy their distress, hardly occurs to most social scientists. Such a thing might occur by chance, but generally the interference with the realities under investigation is seen as disturbing or dangerous for the scientific quality of the research. (1975:65)

Huizer advocates a close identification between anthropologist and research subjects so that the interests of the subject population may be protected.

The best treatment for this problem is the direct negotiation of the content and goals of the research design between researcher and community. The negotiation may result in modifications of the research procedure so that objectionable procedures may be removed. But, more importantly, the project can be modified to help meet the information needs of the subject community. It may simply be required that the research design remain unchanged but that reporting requirements be changed so as to improve the community's access to the research results. Other alternatives might mean "piggybacking" community research needs on the researchers' topic, selecting a community-defined topic as the primary focus of the project, or providing another kind of service in lieu of research.

The point is that the utility of a project to the community is a relevant ethical dimension that can be addressed. In applied research these issues may be simplified in the sense that the research design and goals are determined by, or through, negotiation with the client community. The question remains, however, who is the client community and who are its representatives? Oftentimes applied anthropologists must work on research problems for clients who, although they serve a community, are not truly representative of the community. Ethical issues must be dealt with most carefully in this situation. The anthropologists must consider the impact of their behavior when they are acting as agents of service organizations, development agencies, or political action groups. In cases where the client group is part of the community, the extent of representativeness must also be considered. It is not always clear to what extent subgroups, such as the "leadership" elite, are representative of the total community.

COMMUNICATION

There is a great deal of tension in anthropology concerning the ethics of publication. This multidimensional problem is particularly relevant to the ethical concerns of the applied anthropologist. As applied anthropologists, we are faced with complying with diverse standards of information dissemination. As scientists, we are obliged to communicate results so that others may share in our contribution to knowledge. The research process is thought to end only with effective communication of research results. The assumption is that there is "an immortal open record of research results where all scientists are able to present their results for the benefit and scrutiny of their scientific peers" (Price 1964:655).

Though it seems that applied anthropologists tend not to emphasize the publication of their applied results, like most scientists they are motivated to get things on the record for a wide variety of rather intense motivations. These motivations include the lure of immortality in print, the publish-or-perish tenure struggle for those who are employed in academic jobs, and the need for non-academically employed anthropologists to establish some academic credentials so as to maintain the possibility for academic employment, if they so choose. Publication by practicing anthropologists can serve to increase personal influence in the domain of application.

The potential applied anthropology author faces a number of problems. First, few journals are actually geared up to publish materials that have applied relevance. Applied research results sometimes have limited appeal for the general social science audience. Oftentimes the components of an applied project that see the light of publication are not the parts that were significant in accomplishing the goals of the project. What often gets published are those components that have an academic cast to them. There is not even a consistent tendency to document or archive materials produced in the course of applied anthropologists' activities. These deficiences of information exchange seem to limit the cumulative improvement of applied anthropology.

This is by no means the most crucial issue applied anthropologists face in the realm of publication and the communication of information. The primary issue is the extent to which the applied anthropologist can make information public. Our employers often have some control over the disposition of the research results. As Price notes, the problem also occurs in the realm of physical science:

Historically, there has been a very interesting contrast between the literature ethics of basic science and those of technology. In basic science, the motivation is always for the most complete publication that will ensure the payoff, of recognition of the contribution of the individual scientist and his reward by eponymic fame, Nobel prizes or similar honors or at least by appreciation. In technological research and development, with profit or military ascendancy substituted so largely for honor, the effort is toward publication only as an epiphenomenon, not as an end product. (Price 1964:655)

All researchers are enjoined ethically to control the release of collected data. For example, it is absolutely necessary to maintain the anonymity of our research subjects. No matter what our relationship is with a client, we must maintain the privacy of the informant. Our job is not to collect data about individuals for other individuals. But even if we are capable of maintaining the anonymity of informants, serious ethical problems remain. The most difficult kinds of ethical problems are caused by research in which the anthropologist, in a clandestine manner, researches a community on behalf of another group or agency. The researcher may mask his researcher role, his real questions, or any working relationships that he might have with a third party.

SOME RECENT PROBLEM CASES

Although there have been sad occurrences of unethical behavior by anthropologists throughout the history of the discipline, the most questionable activities have occurred in the recent period. The two most frequently cited are the so-called Project Camelot initiated in Latin America, and the various sponsored research activities carried out in Northern Thailand.

Project Camelot. Project Camelot was initiated in 1964 under the sponsorship of the Special Operations Research Office (SORO) of the United States Army (Horowitz 1967:4). It was the largest grant for social science research up until that time. A citation from the prospectus of the project mailed to a number of well-known scientists provides an excellent summary of the project's intent.

Project Camelot is a study whose objective is to determine the feasibility of developing a general systems model which would make it possible to predict and influence politically significant aspects of social change in the developing nations of the world. Somewhat more specifically, its objectives are: first, to devise procedures for assessing the potential for internal war within national societies; second, to identify with increased degrees of confidence, those actions which a government might take to relieve conditions which are assessed as giving rise to a potential for internal war; and finally, to assess the feasibility of prescribing the characteristics of a system for obtaining and using the essential information needed for doing the above two things (Horowitz 1967:4-5)

The project was ultimately to encompass studies in a large number of countries in Asia, Latin America, Africa, and Europe. Initially, the activities were to start in Chile.

The response to Camelot was substantial in the involved disciplines, the countries of study, and in the American political arena. In spite of the stir it caused in anthropology, there was only one anthropologist involved, and he served as a short-term consultant. The project died a quick death and resulted in substantial interpretive literature (Horowitz 1967; Sjoberg 1967). It is difficult to identify the most important criticism in this literature, and there is some criticism of its objectivity (Beals 1969).

Many persons objected to the use of social science to maintain the social order in countries where there are such clearly identifiable oppressed classes. Although couched in social science jargon, the project was perceived as having a conservative bias. For example, "The use of hygienic language disguises the anti-revolutionary assumptions under a cloud of powder puff declarations" (Sjoberg 1967:48). The most strenuous objections concerned participating in research that had such strong political implications. The basic question became, should social scientists be involved in research that would facilitate interference in the affairs of other nations?

Belshaw notes: "Within the American Anthropological Association, the reaction was immediate and sharp. Resolutions were passed condemning 'clandestine' research and research dealing with 'counterinsurgency' " (Belshaw 1976:261). More important, the reaction included a major study of the problem of ethics, which formed the basis for Ralph L. Beals's study entitled *Politics of Social Research* (1969). These efforts led to the creation of the American Anthropological Association's Committee on Ethics, which reviews cases of alleged unethical behavior brought before it.

Thailand Project. A project that had more severe implications in anthropology was the so-called Thailand Project. The exposure of this project caused a great controversy among anthropologists worldwide.

Northern Thailand is occupied by various hill tribes. These people have little political or economic leverage in the national affairs of Thailand. They have been depicted as the minority suppressed by the politically dominant lowland majority. These groups were relatively isolated, although connected to the outside world through the opium trade. Opium poppies were the major cash crop. Pressure from the international community of nations on the Thai government to control the opium traffic increased.

Government officials came to realize that policy makers had little information with which to develop a plan for dealing with the northern people (Belshaw 1976:264). The significance of the region increased dramatically as the Vietnam War expanded. These factors encouraged a prodigious increase in the amount of research carried out. In the early 1960s, Western social scientists "flooded" the area (Jones 1971:347), and the Hill Tribes Research Centre was established (Belshaw 1976:265). The relationship that existed between the hill people and the flat landers was unequal. The low landers "tend to look down on the hill people, call them by derogatory names, etc." (Jones 1971:347). These high groups were viewed as good candidates for subversive activities and had not demonstrated loyalty to the Thai government.

Jones raises the most basic question:

Did the anthropologists who rushed into the area to do basic descriptive studies consider these political facts? It is safe to say that most of us did not. Was it an accident that the strategic and political concerns about the hill areas and the questionable loyalty of the hill people to Thailand coincided with the growing anthropological concern about the lack of knowledge of the area? Was it also an accident that, about that same time, a considerable amount of money became available for basic research on this "little known area?" The situation which developed led to a decade of concentrated research on hill people to the almost total neglect of valley culture and society. (1971:348)

As the apparent strategic significance of the region increased, the amount of research fund sources increased. Scholars could make use of funds from agencies of the American government such as the Advanced Research Projects Agency (ARPA) of the Department of Defense. Research carried out on the basis of "cleaner" money, for the most part, ended up in the hands of ARPA anyway.

ARPA's goals were clearly directed at counterinsurgency (Jones 1971:348). They were interested in maintaining the status quo, and saw the utility of basic descriptive cultural data. To these ends they supported the data collection process.

ARPA wanted basic information on culture and society in Thailand, and was willing to pay to have the research done. Since most of us who have conducted basic research in Thailand have in fact contributed to that end, we might as well have taken ARPA's money. The question of ethics and responsibility may have little to do with the source of funding and much more with the social and political context within which the data are produced. (Jones 1971:348)

The presence of anthropologists in Thailand was brought under attack in 1970 by the Student Mobilization Committee to End the War in Vietnam for doing what they referred to as "counterinsurgency research." This too resulted in a major crisis in the discipline, which seems to have intensified interest in various ethical concerns. It is clear that the conflicts generated during the Vietnam era concerning ethics contributed a great deal to the understanding of our responsibilities. The process that these discussions developed was very painful and disturbing. In retrospect, many respected scholars were unfairly accused, yet the increase in understanding may have been worth it.

GUIDES TO ETHICAL PROFESSIONAL PRACTICE

For our purposes the most useful statements on ethical practice for application are the statements of the Society for Applied Anthropology and the National Association for the Practice of Anthropology. These statements were written with reference to the work circumstances of the applied or practicing anthropologist.

The statement of the Society for Applied Anthropology is quoted below. This statement is intended as a guide. Approved in 1983, the statement applies to the membership of the society, although it can serve as a guide to others (Committee on Ethics, Society for Applied Anthropology 1983).

Statement on Professional and Ethical Responsibilities, Society for Applied Anthropology. This statement is a guide to professional behavior for the members of the Society for Applied Anthropology. As members or fellows of the Society we shall act in ways that are consistent with the responsibilities stated below irrespective of the specific circumstances of our employment.

This statement is the fourth version of the society's ethics statement. It was modified in response to concern about the increase in the number of anthropologists employed in applied roles outside of universities. This statement is not associated with a system of certification or licensing. Because of this, the society's Ethics Committee is not equipped with sanctions against unethical behavior.

The first paragraph states the basic components of ethical research practice—voluntary participation, informed consent, and confidentiality. This is supplemented with a reference to risk:

1.) To the people we study we owe disclosure of our research goals, methods, and sponsorship. The participation of people in our research activities shall only be on a voluntary and informed basis. We shall provide a means throughout our research activities and in subsequent publications to maintain the confidentiality of those we study. The people we study must be made aware of the likely limits of confidentiality and must not be promised a greater degree of confidentiality than can be realistically expected under current legal circumstances in our respective nations. We shall, within the limits of our knowledge, disclose any significant risk to those we study that may result from our activities.

One point must be emphasized: disclosure of sponsorship is especially important in research that has a practical effect. Individuals who are asked to give consent must be made aware of sponsorship so that they can better calculate their own interest in reference to the goals of the sponsoring organization.

The paragraph contains reference to the fact that in the United States the promise of confidentiality from a researcher will not protect against a legal subpoena. Researchers are not legally protected as are physicians. We are more like journalists in this regard. Risk is primarily viewed in terms of the physical or psychological risk associated with a research procedure as applied on an individual basis. The risks that are generated by social science research tend to be psychological, political, and economic. These risks should be disclosed.

The statement's second paragraph is clearly keyed to social survival:

2.) To the communities ultimately affected by our actions we owe respect for their dignity, integrity, and worth. We recognize that human survival is contingent upon the continued existence of a diversity of human communities, and guide our professional activities accordingly. We will avoid taking or recommending action on behalf of a sponsor which is harmful to the interests of a community.

The view taken here is that cultural diversity is adaptive and the destruction of it reduces the species' potential to survive. Thus, the scheme is not based upon a relativistic conception of what is right or fair, but on a fundamental view of what behaviors relate to and support survival of the species. The last reference to community interests is particularly important to the action-taking anthropologist. The statement means that in a basic sense, even though employed by an organization, a basic overriding responsibility toward communities exists.

The third paragraph addresses the area that produces the most difficulty in ethics—relationships with colleagues:

3.) To our social science colleagues we have the responsibility to not engage in actions that impede their reasonable professional activities. Among other things this means that, while respecting the needs, responsibilities, and legitimate proprietary interests of our sponsors we should not impede the flow of information about research outcomes and professional practice techniques. We shall accurately report the contributions of colleagues to our work. We shall not condone falsification or distortion by others. We should not prejudice communities or agencies against a colleague for reasons of personal gain.

While the entire research community benefits from the free flow of information, sponsoring organizations may have legitimate needs that may result in restrictions on the flow of information. We should not engage in unfair competition with a colleague.

People who train applied anthropologists have the obligation to remain up-to-date in their skills:

4.) To our students, interns, or trainees we owe nondiscriminatory access to our training services. We shall provide training which is informed, accurate, and relevant to the needs of the larger society. We recognize the need for continuing education so as to maintain our skill and knowledge at a high level. Our training should inform students as to their ethical responsibilities. Student contributions to our professional activities, including both research and publication, should be adequately recognized.

Further, persons offering training in applied anthropology need to consider continually the needs of society in terms of the training that they offer.

The fifth paragraph points to one of the important uses of ethics statements, the protection of the employee from requests for unethical practice:

5.) To our employers and other sponsors we owe accurate reporting of our qualifications and competent, efficient, and timely performance of the work we undertake for them. We shall establish a clear understanding with each employer or other sponsor as to the nature of our professional responsibilities. We shall report our research and other activities accurately. We have the obligation to attempt to prevent distortion or suppression of research results or policy recommendations by concerned agencies.

The best protection is up-front discussion of the constraints. This may serve as a means for supporting the applied anthropologist in cases where the agency that employs him or her is suppressing or distorting research results.

The ethics statement concludes:

6.) To society as a whole we owe the benefit of our special knowledge and skills in interpreting sociocultural systems. We should communicate our understanding of human life to the society at large.

Restated in simple terms, we need to communicate to the public anthropological knowledge that will be useful to them and provide positive influences on their lives.

SUMMARY

The ethical concerns of applied anthropologists are complicated by the fact that their work is intended to have a practical effect. Ethics for action are closely related to ethics for research, because our action and policy products are rooted in research. The foundation of ethical research practice can be conveyed in a few words: confidentiality, voluntary consent, and risk disclosure. Action and policy must, for ethical reasons, be initiated in reference to community interests as well as the interests of sponsoring agencies. At this point applied anthropologists must be self-policing from the standpoint of ethics, because the discipline does not have a mechanism for certification of individuals or accreditation of training programs.

Ethics need not be considered as a constraint, but as a guide to effective practice. That is, through ethical practice more effective action and policies can be developed. Why is this so? The primary reason is that relationships between researchers and those researched are made more regular and predictable. Further, the long-term potential of these relationships is enhanced. Thus, we all have a stake in ethical practice. It is important that each applied anthropologist share in the responsibility.

FURTHER READING

Beals, Ralph L. 1969. *Politics of Social Research: An Inquiry into the Ethics and Responsibilities of Social Scientists*. Chicago: Aldine Publishing.

This thorough and objective discussion of ethical issues, especially as they relate to government contract research, was based on Beals's work for the American Anthropological Association.

Rynkiewich, Michael A., and James P. Spradley. 1976. *Ethics and Anthropology: Dilemmas in Fieldwork*. New York: John Wiley and Sons.

Collection of real cases that would be useful for class discussion.

Part II

Interventions in Anthropology

4

Action Anthropology

Action anthropology is significant in the history of applied anthropology because it was the first of the value-explicit approaches. Comparison with the other approaches reveals a consistent concern with culture and with strategies that would have effects on it. Action anthropologists attempt both to understand communities and to influence the rate and direction of change within these communities.

Action anthropology is a value-explicit activity focused on two general goals of essentially equal priority. These are the goals of science and the goals of a specific, culturally defined community. Working in conjunction with community members, the action anthropologist works to discover community problems and to identify potential solutions, with continual feedback between its scientific and community subprocesses. The duality of the process can be seen in the two key base values in action anthropology, which are community self-determination and scientific truth.

DEVELOPMENT OF THE APPROACH

Although Sol Tax is credited with the development of action anthropology, the approach was developed by a group of student-anthropologists largely from the University of Chicago under "the non-directive direction" of Tax (Gearing, Netting, and Peattie 1960:1) The group changed through time as students went on to other activities and as new students replaced them.

The approach was developed in the Fox Project, which was initiated to give University of Chicago anthropology students an opportunity to gain field experience. Tax, having done his research with the Fox people in the mid-1930s, attempted to develop an opportunity for his students among a group of Fox Indians who lived near Tama, Iowa. The original group of students who arrived in Fox country in mid-summer of 1948 intended to engage in traditional social anthropology research.

Very quickly the goals of the research group changed to include development. It has been suggested that the field team turned toward development because of three factors. The first was the changes in the Fox community itself since Tax had engaged in field work some fifteen years earlier. Second, Tax had made a commitment to a Bureau of Indian Affairs official, John Provinse, also an anthropologist, to provide Provinse with whatever information might be useful to the Bureau of Indian Affairs. The third influencing factor was that the project was not committed to any specific research problem. According to program participants, "that relative absence of structure permitted the field party to focus their interests wherever they wanted but, at least as importantly, it created a greater freedom for the Fox, in conversations with the field party, to guide the subject matter as they would" (Gearing, Netting, and Peattie 1960:26). This served as a germ for the role relationship characteristic of action anthropology.

The transition from vague scientific goals to the complex goals of action anthropology was not without difficulty. The field party had doubts about the legitimacy of the emerging approach. Tax himself had to reverse his earlier position on applied anthropology, which called for a separation of the role of scientist and the role of the practitioner. As he notes in an article published only three years before the initiation of the Fox Project:

A scientific observer or reasoner, merely as such, is not an advisor for practice. His part is only to show that certain consequences follow from certain causes, and that to obtain certain ends, certain means are the most effectual. Whether the ends themselves are such as ought to be pursued, and if so, in what cases and to what great length, it is no part of his business as a cultivator of science to decide, and science alone will never qualify him for the decision. (Tax 1945, in Gearing, Netting, and Peattie 1960:16).

It should be made clear that Tax was not saying that the scientist should not become directly involved in the affairs of life, it is just that in doing so he was no longer acting in the role of scientist. As will be seen, the Fox Project and its resultant formulation, action anthropology, represented a major transformation in his conception of the scientist's role. He even went so far as to suggest that anthropology can have only one goal, namely, that of advancing knowledge. Anything else, however valuable, was not science.

In spite of inconsistency with Tax's earlier position, the commitment to a program of intervention emerged quickly. Though rooted in the humane values of the student field staff, the tendency to get involved was encouraged by Tax, who was quick to argue that an action research approach might not only be practically useful, but in fact might represent superior science. A few months after the beginnings of the project it became quite clear that the field party was going to become involved in development as well as research. From this decision action anthropology emerged as an alternative model for applied anthropology.

KEY CONCEPTS

Self-determination is a key concept in action anthropology, which is expressed as a principle of action and a goal. The action anthropologist works to achieve self-determining communities. This goal consistently determines or influences the behavior of the action anthropologist in the field. Self-determination implies the opportunity to be right or wrong. As Tax has put it, the *freedom to make mistakes*. That is, a truly self-determining community has the responsibility for both success and failure. As Gearing notes, "Any other freedom is false. And any less freedom will destroy a human community" (1960c:414).

The action anthropologist works to achieve self-determination. In logical terms that is something of a paradox; that is, one attempts to generate self-determination by influencing the behavior of the group. Tax admits to the paradox, yet is within reason when he suggests that the concept is practically workable.

Tax expresses the complex meanings associated with self-determination:

All we want in our action programs is to provide, if we can, genuine alternatives from which the people involved can freely choose—and to be ourselves as little restrictive as is humanly possible. It follows, however, that we must try to remove restrictions imposed by others on the alternatives open to Indians and on their freedom to choose among them. We avoid imposing our values upon the Indians, but we do not mean to leave a vacuum for other outsiders to fill. Our program is positive, not negative; it is a program of action, not inaction; but it is also a program of probing, listening, learning, giving in. (Tax 1958, in Gearing, Netting, and Peattie 1960:416)

Action anthropologists have a special relationship with power—that is, they must avoid assuming power. Action anthropology is not based on authority, but on persuasion and education. The process can therefore only go as "far as the community would voluntarily follow" (Gearing 1960d:216). Even when the action anthropologist is not linked to a power-providing agency and has personally disavowed power and authority, he or she must actively resist the accumulation of power. If the anthropologist is placed in an administrative role defined as power-holding, the approach becomes virtually impossible to use. In other words, the view of the client or target community as a passive entity to be manipulated is rejected.

As the action anthropologist avoids the accumulation and use of power, he or she also attempts to foster its growth and accumulation in the community. This implies the creation of social organization and the fostering of community leadership. Among the Fox, this represented a serious challenge. Power was diffusely distributed in the Fox community. Further, power was often used to express factionalism rather than purposive action toward the achievement of community goals.

Action anthropology rejects a linear view of planning. The approach used might be best termed interactive planning, because of the tendency to stress ambiguous means and ends distinctions and the continual consideration of the interaction of goals and action.

Interactive planning is characterized by a number of attributes. The primary proposition is that means and ends are interdependent. Ends are appropriate to means, and means are appropriate to ends. Action can be initiated in terms of means or ends. Ends and means are determined through an interactive process that is motivated by both the problem inherent in a situation and the apparent opportunities. The problem is defined as "everything that is wrong or missing about the situation. Problems and possibilities also interact. As Diesing notes,

> The area of the problem to be investigated is continually being limited by reference to what changes are possible, and vice versa. Supposedly wrong things that cannot be changed are excluded from the problem, since they cannot be made right, and a study of them would be a waste of time. Likewise, possible changes which are not changes of something that is wrong are also excluded, since they are irrelevant to the problem. Instead, only those problems are investigated which could conceivably have some effect on a part of the problem. (Diesing 1960:185)

It is obvious that the key function of the anthropologist is to discover what is the problem and what are the possibilities for change. The problem represents a complex of problems complicated, by the limitations of the community and the external interventionist. Further, the capacity to solve problems is thought to increase through time. With these increases, the complexity of the problem-solutions engaged also increases. These increases may be attributed to decreasing community divisiveness and increasing community integration. According to Peattie, the goals of the action anthropologist "tend to be open-ended objectives like growths in understanding, clarification of values and the like" (Peattie 1960b:301). The desired end-states are really expressions of a value stance, or as Peattie refers to them, "modes of valuing," used to analyze the continuous process. This approach generates severe difficulties in terms of evaluation, though in a sense evaluation is inevitable. It tends to be nonempirical and intuitive.

BASE VALUES

It is in the realm of values that the essence of action anthropology can be discovered. The value system that characterizes action anthropology is in part relativistic and situational. That is, the realities of the situation affect value judgments up to certain limits. The relevant values of a situation are those that are indigenous to it. This means that the action anthropologist must discover the value orientation of the community within which she works. She does not derive the plan from her own values. These values are important guides to action. In addition to the relativistic core, there are values that are regarded as universal and are accepted absolutely by action anthropologists. The absolute component of the action anthropology value system consists of two elements.

The first value is truth. The primacy of truth is rooted in the continued identification of the action anthropologist as an anthropologist. It is from this value that action anthropology is legitimized as anthropology. This value is expressed strongly.

We are anthropologists in the tradition of science and scholarship. Nothing would embarrass us more than to see that we have been blinded to verifiable fact by any other values or emotions. We believe that truth and knowledge are more constructive in the long run than falsehood and superstition. We want to remain anthropologists and not become propagandists; we would rather be right according to canons of evidence than win a practical point. But also we feel impelled to trumpet our truth against whatever falsehoods we find, whether they are deliberate or psychological or mythological. This would be a duty to science and truth, even if the fate of communities of men were not involved. (Tax 1958, in Gearing, Netting, and Peattie 1960:415)

The second prime value is freedom—freedom for individuals, and communities, to be self-determining. The action anthropologist does not, therefore, advocate specific value choices. The process does involve the presentation of alternatives of choice to the community. This also implies working to free the client community from restrictions placed on their freedom by forces external to the community.

These values are consistent with the two general goals of action anthropology. These goals, expressed simply, are "to help people and to learn something in the process." These goals are explicitly described as equal in importance by Tax (Tax 1960a, in Gearing, Netting, and Peattie 1960:379). Tax attempts to show that these two goals are not in conflict. In fact, they are mutually supportive. Through truth more beneficial change can be caused, and through action more can be learned. Action anthropologists argue that the emotional intensity associated with action-involvement can increase the perceptivity of the field observer. Participation in the action increases the extent to which the anthropologist comes to understand the nature of the situation that he or she is investigating. The critical events in the action process teach because they determine activities in the future.

Being an action anthropologist forces one to be a maker of value judgments. This can be stressful and burdensome. Tax and the other action anthropologists sought to limit this stress in three ways. Allusions to the first two limiting factors have already been made. The most basic is the assumption of a value-explicit position, which allows the anthropologist to escape the potential hypocrisy of the value-implicit approaches, and "places" values where they can be more closely watched. The second limiting factor is the recognition of paramount values. The self-determination value, for example, forces most value judgments into the hands of the community. The third stress-reducing mechanism used in action anthropology is the "principle of parsimony," which suggests that the action anthropologist need not resolve value-questions that do not concern him or her. Tax illustrates the principle:

In the beginning of our Fox program, having decided to interfere for some good purpose, we were beset with value problems. Some of us were for and some of us were against the assimilation of the Indians; what a marvelously happy moment it was when we realized that this was not a judgement or decision we needed to make. It was a decision for the people concerned, not for us. Bluntly, it was none of our business. (Tax 1958, in Gearing, Netting, and Peattie 1960:416)

This means that many value-questions are never resolved because it is not necessary or appropriate for the action anthropologists to resolve them. Many value-problems are illusory.

ACTION ANTHROPOLOGY PROCESS

The process is goal-oriented, gradual, self-directed, and self-limiting based on education and persuasion. Action anthropologists proceed step by step, basing the rate of intervention on the community's capacity to assimilate change. The process can be thought of as a complex of concrete actions that are interrelated through feedback and are consistent with community values.

The process starts with the determination of the facts relevant to action and means-ends determination. This component of action anthropology includes the determination of relevant ethnographic facts about the community in its cultural setting and the value-stances of the participating anthropologists. The process necessitates the mutual participation of both the anthropologists and the community members in the determination of goals. Based on this, action is carried out to achieve the defined goals.

Action anthropologists express goals as open-ended objectives rather than quotas. Growth in understanding or clarification of values may be stated as an objective. As Peattie notes, "They are not properly speaking 'ends' at all, for they can never be said to have been reached. They are more properly modes of valuing—modes of valuing all stages in a continuous and infinite process" (Peattie 1960b:301).

The action anthropologist does not initiate projects but instead points out alternatives. The alternative selection process is a key concrete activity. It requires that the social and physical environment be known, and thereby draws upon community research activities. Let us consider the process by which action alternatives are designed.

The process requires that the nature of the problems inherent in the situation are very clearly identified. This is complex and difficult. As Diesing notes, "Almost any serious social problem turns, upon investigation, into an endlessly ramified network of conflicts and maladjustments. It has no beginning and no end" (Diesing 1960:186). It is from this complex situation that the anthropologist must select a problem to engage. Focus has to be maintained so as to avoid dissipating one's efforts.

Problems should be selected only if they are significant and can be solved.

The action anthropologist must determine the possibilities for change in the specific problem areas as these relate to her personal inclinations and capabilities. With this in mind, it may be useful to consider what changes have been successfully made in the past.

Diesing poses two rules for problem selection:

One rule is: determine the relative possibilities of change of each problem area, and select the areas of greatest possible change as the areas within which the solutions can start. The reason for this rule is evident, since the easier the changes are, the greater is the likelihood that the changes will actually occur and persist. (Diesing 1960:190)

This suggests that the problems engaged initially should be small, so that sufficient resources can be directed toward them.

The second rule is that one should begin the solution in areas from which an expansion of the solution is possible. Ideally, one should try to discover a starting point from which a solution can expand to cover the major problem areas in the whole community and beyond. This rule is the natural complement to the first rule, since a solution to a circumscribed problem is insignificant unless it leads to solutions of broader problems. (Diesing 1960:191)

The selected problem areas may be characterized by high levels of stress and conflict. This conflict may preclude effective action by the focusing of community energies on contentiousness. Because of this, a prime responsibility of the action anthropologist may be the quelling of community factionalism and contentiousness. It is presumed that success in dealing with a single problem area that is limited in scope may result in increased capacity to deal with problems. This is an important kind of growth in action anthropology. It really represents an expression of the hope that significant transformations will emerge from modest if not trivial beginnings.

CASE STUDY: THE FOX PROJECT

The project involved the development of a special kind of relationship between a changing community of Fox Indians and a changing group of anthropologists.

The Fox community is located on a thirty-three-hundred-acre reservation in central Iowa, about two miles west of Tama. The five hundred Fox farm their river valley lands, but earn the bulk of their living by being employed as skilled and unskilled workers in the nearby towns of Tama, Montour, and Waterloo.

The persistence of the Fox through time represents a remarkable story. They were originally from Wisconsin, and have only resided in Iowa for about 120 years. The period of Fox history following the appearance of the French in Wisconsin was marked by tenacious resistance to change. They were described as the most independent of the Wisconsin tribes and were the last to submit to the influences of the French. They were determined to maintain their cultural system in the old way, unmodified by the influences of white men.

Their skill and tenacity, however, only delayed their inevitable displacement from their Wisconsin lands. The conflict was temporarily quelled by moving to Kansas. Finally in 1854, the Fox purchased eighty acres of white farm lands, an act rare in American Indian history. They continued to invest money in expanding their land base whenever they had the opportunity. By the early 1950s they had accumulated over three thousand acres.

The land itself is an important component of Fox society in that it provides a permanent framework for social interaction, and physical evidence for the contrast between the Fox and the surrounding white population. It "expresses visually the invisible barriers between Fox society and the white society" (Peattie 1960a:41). The Iowa farmer dominates the land with the geometric precision of rationalized agriculture. On the encapsulated Fox land the precise regularities of large soybean and corn fields of the Iowans gives way to the organic irregularities of the Fox woodlots, gardens, and fields.

The land's importance is more than economic. This is expressed by Peattie:

The Fox were never wholly agricultural people, and used to live in settled villages only during the summer, dispersing to hunt during the winter months. During the historical period, we know that under white pressure they moved about over a wide territory. Even today, only a few Fox families are supported primarily by agriculture, and much of the tribal land stands idle. Why, then, the feeling for the land? The land, to the Fox, is the symbol, not of life and livelihood as to the peasant, but of refuge from oppression. It is a place of safety. (Peattie 1960a: 43).

The three thousand acres of Iowa river bottoms is a self-made shelter for the Fox. It is from this enclave that the Fox encounter the white world, working at local factories and construction sites, and shopping at stores as far away as Des Moines, Marshalltown, Waterloo, and Cedar Rapids (Gearing 1970:10).

The Fox lands are also a framework for Fox social organization. The community is sufficiently small so that everyone knows everyone else. The community exists as a system of familiar actors. Fox social organizations are characterized by exceptionally loose organizational structure. Power and authority are widely distributed. The most important organizing principle is kinship, including fictive ties, as well as the ties of marriage and descent.

Kinship networks are a primary component of the Fox social fabric. These networks are expressed in the minutiae of day-to-day life, and perhaps most clearly in the context of the clan ceremonies. The clan ceremonies are described by Gearing:

Each year during the summer months there was a round of ceremonial feasts in which each of the several Fox clans took its turn being the host to the remaining clans; the host clan sang while the others danced, and the host prepared a feast for others to enjoy. This was the traditional Fox religion. (Gearing 1970:80)

All but a few families participated in the clan ceremonials. Therefore it was an important manifestation of the community's organization while it expressed certain Fox conceptions of the supernatural.

To the observing anthropologist, the ceremonies were clear manifestations of the operating importance of the kinship system. The kinship system is a system of mutual obligations. Gearing suggests that these obligations were "more clear and more imperative" than what one would expect in the American setting (1970:82). The kinship system has endured, structurally, but has become significantly less potent. The logic of the system still exists, but its spectrum of uses has declined to those areas of human concern that are least related to the practical considerations of everyday life. In addition to the kinship system, Fox society is characterized by clanlike groups, a tribal council, and various factions.

Many Fox are organized in terms of a nuclear family pattern. There are a significant number of "large, bilaterally extended family groups" (Peattie 1960a:44). These groups form the basis for extensive community factionalism. The factions consist of alignments of both large and small family groups. While these families serve as the basis for conflicting factions, they are also linked through various other social institutions, such as marriage and clanship.

The traditional tribal political system of the Fox was displaced in 1937 by an elected council organized under the provisions of the Indian Reorganization Act. This movement was associated with the efforts of a "group of young progressives" who worked very closely with the Indian Service (Peattie 1960a:47). This council was established in conflict and was legitimized narrowly in a well-contested election. As Peattie notes: "The council came into existence, thus, under a shadow, and it has not tended to fulfill the hopes of its founders as time has gone on. In fact, the council, officially the government of the tribe, does not govern" (Peattie 1960a:47).

The functions of government have been carried out by organizations outside the community, such as the Indian Service, as well as special-purpose organizations within the Fox community, such as the Powwow Committee, which oversees the preparation for the annual powwow, with its public dance performances and food sales. The success of this committee is largely based on its narrowly defined purpose and the fact that the committee does not have to compete with any organization like the Indian Service. The Powwow Committee serves a number of uses in Fox society in addition to the obvious one of planning and executing the powwow. The powwow itself is an important group-focused event. It provides a variety of opportunities to participate. In spite of its commercial overtones, it is an important community activity, a situation where "Foxness" can be acted out and expressed with both individual and group benefits.

Fox social activities are further channelled by various other types of organizations. In the realm of religion there can be found a number of organizational types. For a community of such small scale there is a surprising diversity in the organizational expressions of religious life. In addition to the clan-focused ceremonial activities that can be characterized as traditional, there are a number of new cultural forms that have become part of the religion of the Fox community. The new religions include two Christian forms, the Presbyterians and the Open Bible Mission. In addition, two American Indian forms have come to be part of the Fox religious life. These are the Oklahoma-derived Peyote Cult, and the Drum Society, derived from the Potawatomi of Wisconsin.

The organizational inventory of the community is also augmented by various secular organizations, such as a veterans' group and a women's club.

The original conception of the University of Chicago–Fox encounter did not include the idea that the group would engage in purposive attempts to change the Fox. The project began more or less as a loosely structured field school, more likely to change a handful of would-be anthropologists than the Fox community. The collective focus of the group turned to Fox problems rather than scientific problems; or more precisely, Fox problems became the scientific problems.

Fox Problems

It was true that the Fox manifested a range of problems that are typical of conditions found in many American Indian communities. These included low income and low labor force participation. While these conditions were recognized, the action anthropologists of the Fox Project focused on problems in cultural rather than economic terms. They were particularly concerned with the problems that grew out of the relationship between the Fox and their white neighbors. They tended to see problems in abstract cognitive terms. The proposed solutions were of course concrete, but conceived as being linked to the abstract problems. Project participants also conceptualized problems internal to the Fox community.

The internal problems were of two interrelated types. These were the problem of factionalism and the problem of diffuse political authority. In a sense these two problems were both causes and effects of each other. That is, the division of a community into informal, contentious subgroups tends to limit a political leader's capacity to establish a power base in that he does not have equal access to the entire community. The diffuse nature of authority can create an atmosphere in which factions tend to develop, there being little power to mobilize the entire community across lines of contention. Further, it might be stated that in the absence of centralized political authority, factions may provide an important social control function, creating a kind of order generated out of the playing off of opposing forces. Both the issues of factionalism and diffuse authority were dealt with by Fox project participants.

Fox Factionalism

It is apparent that factionalism among the Fox dates from the earliest periods of contact, during which it was possible to identify both pro- and anti-French bands. The tribe existed as an expression of tribal identity, but not as a concrete planning and action group. There was a village council and a chief that seemed to rarely initiate action. "They could, through appeals to traditional values, adjudicate disputes, but had no authority to enforce commands through the exercise of coercive sanctions" (Fallers 1960:80). In this early period of Fox factionalism there were numerous attempts by whites to "bind the entire tribe to a course of action" (Fallers 1960:80). However, because of the powerlessness of leadership roles, these attempts failed. This pattern was encouraged because of the competition among the whites, as represented by various fur trading companies and various national interests.

As the fur trade matured and then declined, the purposive involvement of the American government increased. The economy of the Fox became more and more based on annuity payments derived from lands sold to the Americans. These annuity payments were channeled to the Fox through certain selected chiefs, and thus these chiefs developed a basis of authority and power. Government attempts at acculturation through these leaders caused conflict between the leaders and the rest of the Fox. This conflict was a cause of Fox separation and subsequent settlement in Iowa. In 1896, the Iowa Fox were again made the targets of concerted white attempts at acculturation. This took the form of educational activities that called for the enrollment of Fox children in schools. There developed in response to this movement an opposing faction.

The factions that existed during the Fox Project were historically derived from the factions that were operating in 1890s. In the intervening six decades a great deal of acculturation had occurred in the community that influenced both factions, yet the factions still existed and could be labeled pro-white and anti-white, or conservative and traditional. Both factions had allies among whites. It might be said that the balance of power among the factions of the Fox was maintained through affiliation with sympathetic whites.

It is clear that the presence of the dominant white cultural system in the Fox environment contributed to both the creation and the maintenance of Fox factionalism. As Fallers notes,

when a cultural group finds itself in an inferior power and status position to another cultural group, certain lines of tension appear in the society. Those members of the inferior group who find favor in the superordinate group tend to press for the acceptance by their fellows of the values of that group. The members of the subordinate society who have not found such favor tend to oppose such acceptance. (Fallers 1960:83)

Both groups perceive themselves as acting in the interests of the community and therefore become more and more persistent in their complementary contentiousness. In the face of a political system that is based on diffuse power relations, there are few ways of resolving the conflict internally. Among the Fox, the intransient nature of the situation was further enhanced by the ready availability of white allies to support each faction. The result was conflict that was seemingly unresolvable. Further, the conflict inhibited the establishment of institutionalized ways of achieving Fox group and individual goals.

Authority and Leadership

Prior to white contact, the Fox manifested a pattern typical of societies at the tribal level of sociocultural integration (Service 1960). Tribal societies are egalitarian. There is little internal economic or political differentiation. Families are the basic units of production and consumption, and political power is diffusely distributed.

Traditionally, the Fox tribal council was an important source of authority. It consisted of the head men of the constituent clans of the Fox. The council was a representative body that was highly committed to deliberative, consensus-based decision making. The consensus principle was at times applied to mass meetings of the community. The political system had relatively few formal roles. These tendencies were complemented by the general-purpose nature of the basic kin groups, which inhibited the formation of special-purpose organizations that might have accumulated power. Special-purpose organizations, such as they were, were temporary and fleeting, playing a small role in the life of the Fox. Neither was there a high degree of stratification.

Authority or power was a scarce and diffuse resource in Fox society. Yet given the nature of traditional Fox life, this pattern of distribution seemed appropriate. Most activities were carried out among small family groups. Larger-scale activities were familiar and repetitive, and therefore did not require a great deal of coordination. Leadership usually consisted of merely signalling the next phase of a familiar routine.

As the leadership of the community acted, the citizens made judgments. If the people disagreed with the leadership they could choose not to follow. There was no unquestioning respect for authority or fear of repercussion for the unresponsive follower. The system provided sufficient leadership to deal with the familiar and simple, but was insufficient to deal with the changing white-dominated environment. In the face of the need for leadership, the Fox strongly resisted any tendencies to accrue power. Individuals who attempted to increase their authority were subject to severe sanctions. The constraints seemed also to increase the reluctance of individuals to participate in political leadership positions.

These patterns of leadership and authority were consistent with certain organizational patterns. The Fox had some success with native-derived organization, while white-derived organizations were often unsuccessful. Some white-derived organizations had developed, but tended to collapse with the withdrawal of white support. The more persistent native pattern was characterized by a number of key features, including consensus-based decision making and diffuse authority patterns.

The fallout of this problem was that the Fox were more or less unsuccessful in using nonnative organizational models. This means that these organizations tended not to work effectively without significant white participation. This produced a sense of inadequacy in the Fox. This of course limited the range of possible effective Fox organizational alternatives, and thereby limited Fox developmental alternatives. These conditions were intimately related to the Fox problem, identified by Gearing as structural paralysis.

Structural Paralysis

It was, of course, possible to identify a functioning Fox social structure; Gearing, however, raised certain questions about how well these structures worked. As Gearing suggested, these structures no longer seemed to work very well, and therefore participation in these structures was neither satisfying nor rewarding. This may be regarded as the most significant problem faced by the Fox. This condition, termed structural paralysis, was defined as "a state of chronic disarticulation in the community-wide webs of influence and authority which form a small community" (Gearing 1970:96). The condition was caused by the nature of the historical relations between the Fox and the federal government. Historically, these relationships generated conditions of dependency in which the federal government slowly preempted Fox responsibility for the day-to-day management of community affairs (Gearing 1970:96).

It is possible to class Fox activities into two categories: one category, including the clan ceremonials, the annual powwow, and various other activities, could be characterized by a certain competence and assertiveness; the second category, including "school affairs, matters of health, and law and order," was characterized by "mutual hostility, fear, ignorance, self-pity and a feeling of incompetence" (Gearing 1970:96). It was in this area that the term structural paralysis applied.

Gearing and the others consistently argued that Fox problems were generated in the conditions of culture contact. Structural paralysis was causally linked to the nature of the relationship between the whites and the Fox. Gearing also identified problems that grew out of the differences between the mutual conceptions of the Fox and the whites. Gearing viewed the Fox problem primarily in terms of white beliefs concerning the nature of the Fox, Fox self-conceptions, especially as these related to white action, and the dynamic interrelations between these elements.

The approach used by Gearing emphasized the differences between the Fox and whites. Whites, in contrast to the Fox, are in a "becoming" process, described as "a ceaseless effort to make the real self coincide with that ideal self" (Gearing 1960a:296). According to Gearing, the Fox do not have such tendencies. As Gearing notes, "The Fox individual does not seem to create such an ideal self; he does not see himself as becoming at all; he is" (1960a:296). This contrast expressed in terms of the day-to-day behavior of the Fox leads to a negative evaluation.

The Fox individual is committed through enculturation to harmonious relations with his fellow Fox. In contrast, the white is much more independent of group pressures. The problem arises in the perceptions of these behavior modes by representatives of the other culture. The harmonious relations of the Fox yield a behavior mode that is interpreted by the whites as laziness and unreliability. The Fox perceive the whites as selfish and aggressive. The laziness interpretation is carried further, and provides the whites with a basis for the belief that the Fox are a "burden on honest, hard working taxpayers." (Gearing 1960a:296).

Whites conceive of the Fox as temporary; that is to say, they are viewed as under an inevitable, unstoppable process of acculturation that will result in assimilation. The white imputation of impermanence has certain effects on the Fox. They tend to resist change. They view their life positively and want to continue living as Fox. And further, they are threatened by the changes proffered by the whites as they act out their view of the Fox as temporary. As Gearing notes,

They want their lands to remain in protected status. They are instantly opposed to any suggested changes—in their school system, in their trust status, in the jurisdiction of their law and order. They oppose the idea of change, irrespective of the substantive details which never really get discussed. They do this because they fear failure—generically. (Gearing 1960a:297)

The fear of failure is simple to understand, for in a white-dominated world the game is white, as are the rules. Success is more frequent when the Fox are in control. Yet in these situations there are limitations to the kinds of activities in which the Fox can successfully engage. The Fox have an especially difficult time with activities that require hierarchical organization of authority. The Fox, as discussed above, mistrust authority and invest much effort in social control to resist its accumulation in the organizations in which they take part.

Gearing depicted these conditions of beliefs and misperception in systemic terms; he referred to the system as "the vicious circle in Fox-white relations" (Gearing 1960a:295). It was a system of problems to be acted upon as a system of interlocking causes. We will consider some of the "treatments" prescribed by the project later in our discussion. In any case, the "treatments" were multiphasic and were for the most part educational in nature.

Project Objectives

Clearly, the project viewed Fox problems as being largely cultural. The treatment specified tended to be cultural in nature. The project did not place primary stress on the physical or economic development of the Fox community, except as such developments were regarded as treatments effective in the cultural realm.

A major problem in value-explicit applied anthropology is the difficulty of linking conceptions of problems and prescribed concrete activities as mediated by the values that guide the project. Problems can be identified and actions can be specified. The problem of determining the extent of instrumental relationship between action and goal is difficult. This is complicated by the fact that some problems are not subject to control, and that other problems are caused by factors outside the community. The action anthropologist "has the problem of influencing not only the community but whatever forces impinge on the community" (Tax 1960b:171). In Fox society, the achievement of positive impact was further complicated by the general lack of ways for the Fox to achieve group goals.

The project considered a large number of projects during its history. Many of the projects were implemented. These projects were of three general types: economic development, white-stereotype modification projects, and Fox training projects. Each project was considered in terms of how it would impact the overall set of problems manifested by the Fox and identified by the project. It should be reemphasized that the project attempted to carry out these programs in terms of the encompassing goal of Fox self-determination.

Economic Development

It was thought that economic development strategies should result in increased economic activity on the Fox reservation so as to allow increased material well-being in a context that did not necessitate increasing the rate of assimilation. The economic development projects that were proposed were all on the reservation. All projects were small in scale so as to allow groups to be formed of workable size.

The first economic development project was a small truck farm using land owned by the University of Chicago. It was not a success. The Fox seemed to have difficulty activating the required leadership roles.

The most successful of the economic development projects involved craft production and sales. The idea appeared very early in the history of the project. Although ostensibly an economic development project, planners thought that such a project could have a major impact on the relationships that existed between the Fox and the whites.

Though, as an economic institution, its primary function will be seen as economic, perhaps, its most important value for Fox and whites will be educative, assisting toward the clarification of certain major [Fox] goals, aiding in redefinition of the general Fox situation in terms more acceptable to both Fox and whites, and providing a new and important opportunity for citizenship education for the Fox through actual participation in local social and economic affairs. (University of Chicago 1960:335)

The response to the project was rapid and positive among both Fox and whites.

The objectives of the arts and crafts project grew out of the contact between the project staff and the Fox Indian artist Charles Pushetonequa. Pushetonequa had returned to the community, and while it afforded him an opportunity to reactivate relationships with the Fox, it meant that his involvement in art had to decline. Pushetonequa was a major force in the development of the project.

Through these efforts a group emerged called Tama Indian Crafts. They produced a number of products for sale, drawing upon the designs of Pushetonequa and financed through the project. The products included home painting kits based on traditional Fox life. Later, the group sold lithographed greeting cards and ceramic tiles, all with Pushetonequa's designs. Other items were added later. The sales of such products were good, and the number of participating Fox increased.

The Tamacraft products were of good quality. The whites of Tama County seemed impressed, as they always are with new locally made products. They also valued the "Indian-ness" of the products, which seemed to be "visible evidence that Fox culture itself has something to offer" (University of Chicago 1960:338). Further, it should be noted that the Fox were perceived in a new role, namely, that of producer. This new perception was viewed as important in terms of changing the vicious circle of opinion and belief of the whites and Fox. Gearing suggested:

To some small, but important degree the Fox have been located squarely within the Iowan community as fellow producers, as it were, mitigating somewhat another negative white impression of the Fox as a dis-articulated passive group which needs to be integrated through assimilation; i.e., the fact of a settlement industry is a fact of integration. (University of Chicago 1960:338).

Gearing further argued that Tamacraft allowed the Fox to participate effectively in regional life without being made to give up their identity. The project was viewed as an opportunity for the Fox to act out their desire not to be assimilated, to demonstrate a future at variance from that expected by the whites, with its implied assimilation.

Education Projects

One of the key Fox problems was the white conception of them as impermanent. White conceptions of the Fox as temporary were the first target of the project's educational activities. It was decided that the first treatment would consist of providing accurate information about the Fox through the mass media, directed at both the Fox and the white. The material was initially prepared by Frederick Gearing, and then commented upon by other anthropologists and Fox community members. The message was delivered in the form of articles prepared for local newspapers. The articles were based on a complex of assumptions. The core assumptions were that the Fox community and way of thinking were not likely to disappear, and that whites judged the Fox negatively.

The articles appeared in the *Tama News-Herald* and expressed a number of elements of the cognitive view of difficulties of the Fox. The action approach used knowledge of cultural systems to modify the belief systems relevant to the problems of the Fox. This is a recurring theme in the action approach and is consciously cultural in nature. The project also carried out similar activities on broadcast media and other publication media.

The education needs of the Fox were dealt with more specifically by attempts of the Fox Project to develop funding for university fellowships for Fox students. After some conflict with certain Fox factions, the project was reexamined and placed on a somewhat firmer basis. Plans for a four-year project were developed. One of the key components of the newly reconstituted project was a major effort to increase the rate at which the Fox attended and graduated from college. The goal of this project was not to equip individual Fox with a means to escape their Foxness, but to increase the overall capability of the Fox by increasing their "education capital." Tax cites cultural data to support the contention that ties would be maintained between the Fox community and the newly educated Fox (1958). If the contention was not borne out in reality, it was felt that nothing would be lost because of the positive effect of education on the individuals of the community. The potential benefits were thought to be great, affecting both the Fox and the nearby white community. It was felt that this effort would make higher education an integral part of the community. The project entailed the acquisition of money from a foundation as well as certain tuition concessions from the State University of Iowa. The Fox responded to this project very well; by the second year, ten Fox students were attending various Iowa universities. The number of students assisted tended to run about twice the projected rate.

The major achievements of the Fox Project were Tamacraft and the scholarship program. The anthropologists assisted in a number of additional areas. These included engaging as a third party in negotiations with the Bureau of Indian Affairs concerning the future of the Fox government school. The Fox Project personnel, especially Tax, came to be identified clearly on the side of the Fox in these deliberations. In addition, others worked in conjunction with the American Legion organization in the Fox community, although these projects seemed to have little impact.

The project of course had a research output as part of the twofold goal of action anthropology—self-determination and scientific truth. The project resulted in a number of ethnographic studies. These studies included studies of ethnohistory, kinship and genealogy, Fox leadership and authority, and studies of Fox teenagers. These studies were viewed as an essential component of the action strategy. That is, program tactics were based on knowledge discovered through conscious and thoughtful anthropological inquiry. There was another motivation, however. Tax notes:

I have said that the corpus of knowledge that may be applied to a situation always falls far short of the needs of effective action. Application of what knowledge there is, one takes for granted. Not to turn about to replenish the common pot seems almost immoral. Every situation has its unique elements and should be reported. (Tax 1960b:169)

Research results are an inevitable product of the activity of action anthropology.

Outcomes

The literature on action anthropology, though extensive, does not systematically review the effects of a program in a concrete sense. A review of the basic Fox Project documents does indicate, here and there, assessments of the individual treatments in terms of "how they came off." We are told that the truck farming venture was a failure. The scholarship program and Tamacraft project seemed to be quite successful. Yet the Fox Project was not systematically evaluated. This is consistent with both the action approach and the institutional context in which the Fox Project occurred. The low emphasis on evaluation of impact also seems to be consistent with the absence of an intervening agency. The project was not carried out for a third party and therefore it was presumably unnecessary to spell out explicitly the accomplishments of the project. It should also be clear that the general goals of the project were highly abstract. How does one measure goals clarification and self-determination? Reporting of success and failure is inhibited by the reluctance to engage in activities that might limit success of the total strategy.

Retrospective accounts of the project, such as *The Face of the Fox* by Frederick Gearing (1988) do not inventory success. Gearing's study is critical, yet suggests that the Fox Project can serve applied anthropologists as a prototype of a socially useful procedure. Gearing has his doubts about the impact of the project on the quality of Fox life. Given the identified causes, the solutions to problems proposed by the action team were probably appropriate as to form but insufficient as to scale. This raises an issue of concern for all applied anthropologists as problem solvers. Anthropologists may conceive of "treatments" to alleviate or solve problems, but what of the scale of the problems identified and the "dosage" of the treatment? This issue was particularly striking in two realms associated with the Fox Project. These were the vicious circle of Fox-white relations and structural paralysis. It is apparent that neither problem was easily correctable or even reversible given the time, techniques, and resources of the Fox team.

SUMMARY

Action anthropology represents a useful set of ideas for dealing with research and development tasks in a number of different kinds of communities. Action anthropology is highly interactive. In this aspect, action anthropology represents a workable alternative to the more typical linear approaches to development planning often used. That is, in most development efforts there is significant investment in the specification of concrete, measurable goals early in the development process. Often development funding is contingent upon the capacity to document convincingly these kinds of goals.

In action anthropology goals unfold in the complex process of interaction between community and researcher. The research process is in fact focused on the discovery of goals and means of achieving them. This approach works best in small-scale communities and organizations. It is a mechanism for maintaining community control and fostering the growth of community adaptability. The approach is limited in that it requires substantial investment in the process of discovery, and because the difficulties inherent in evaluating a development effort that has changing goals. For these reasons, it is most workable where the relationship between the anthropologist and the community is independent of agency restrictions. One might also say that the action anthropology approach is indicated where the community has experienced what might best be called a dependency-generating history. It is important to remember that action anthropology is also a means of doing research.

FURTHER READING

Gearing, Frederick O., Robert McC. Netting, and Lisa R. Peattie, eds., 1960. *Documentary History of the Fox Project*. Chicago: University of Chicago, Department of Anthropology.

Anyone who is interested in using the action anthropology approach should carefully read this book. Most of the utility of the approach relates to the evolution of the relationship between the anthropologists and the community. This book, which is a collection of many different types of documents, shows this process quite clearly. One cannot just do action anthropology; the relationship with the community that makes it possible must evolve. In this volume, study the articles by Gearing ("The Strategy of the Fox Project") and Peattie ("The Failure of the Means-End Scheme in Action Anthropology") very carefully.

Gearing, Frederick O. 1970. *The Face of the Fox*. Chicago: Aldine, Publishing.

This elegant book takes a retrospective look at the results of the Fox Project from a critical perspective. Out of print for some time, the book has been reprinted by Waveland Press (Gearing 1988).

5

Research and Development Anthropology

Research and development is a value-explicit, extended role approach to applying anthropological knowledge. Coupled with action anthropology it exemplifies the post–World War II shift from the more or less exclusively value-implicit approaches that had dominated applied anthropology previously. The approach, which was developed by Allan Holmberg, was first used in the context of a highland Peruvian hacienda community in the Cornell-Peru or Vicos Project.

Like action anthropology, the process has both scientific and developmental goals, but its basic concepts and strategies are somewhat different. The primary focus of the strategy is a value attainment process, around which other aspects of the activity revolve. Defined technically, research and development anthropology is a means of bringing about increases in the net amount and breadth of distribution of certain basic human values through research-based participant intervention in a community. The focus of research and development is values. Holmberg clearly recognized the value implications of all science. It is from this recognition that the research and development approach emerged.

DEVELOPMENT OF THE APPROACH

Holmberg recognized the inevitability of the influence between social scientists and their subjects. He thought that this influence should be understood, and perhaps controlled and guided for the good of science and the community. As Holmberg notes:

By its very nature the social process is an influencing process among individuals and social groups, one upon which the very existence of society depends. It is no less a necessary condition for the study of social life. Even the most "pure" anthropologist imaginable, conducting his research with "complete" detachment and objectivity, cannot avoid influencing his subjects of study or in turn of being influenced by them. (Holmberg 1958:12)

Research and development anthropology is based on the idea that some communities are better places within which to live than others. The approach implies that better communities can be designed and achieved. The view seems idealistic, yet case study material indicates that above all it is a practical process, a process stimulated by a defined goal: the wider sharing of positive human values. The utopian tendencies suggested by this goal are tempered by the research component of the approach. As the reader will see, the technique is relatively precise. The precision is brought to the process by careful research and methodical documentation. The tendency to document is manifested in the substantial number of papers and reports written and produced by program participants.

The specific events that led to the testing of the research and development approach began in 1949. Mario C. Vazquez, a Peruvian anthropologist trained at Cornell, engaged in basic research in the highland Peruvian community named Vicos as part of a major comparative study of modernization. This project was part of Cornell University's major research effort that involved studying social change cross-culturally.

Although it is clear that the essential aspects of the approach were identified prior to the initiation of the project, the project had a somewhat accidental cast to it. The original and motivating goal was basic research in cultural change in a number of Peruvian communities of various types within the Callejón de Hauylas. One of the primary reasons for selecting this area was that a major hydroelectric dam was going to be constructed. It was thought that the Cornell team would carry out a state-of-the-art "before-and-after" research project in the area that was to be affected by the dam. Although the research team had done a good job of documenting the "before," the "after" never happened; a flood washed out the partially constructed dam.

Mario C. Vazquez suggested that the project focus on the Vicos hacienda community. It was regarded as representative of a hacienda community subtype. Vicos was a type of community called a public manor, which are common in Peru. Often, charitable societies hold title and rent them out for five to ten years to the highest bidder (Holmberg 1971:34). The lease for Vicos was coming due. It was suggested by Vazquez that Holmberg and Cornell take over the lease. The prior tenant had gone bankrupt raising flax, when European flax came back on the market at the end of the war. Holmberg seemed to share Vazquez's belief that somewhere between the Peruvian Ministry of the Interior and the Cornell Board of Trustees the idea would get turned down.

KEY CONCEPTS

The goal of research and development anthropology is the wider sharing of basic human values. These values are not defined by science, but are *discovered through* science. As will be apparent later in this chapter, knowledge of values is essential for the operation of the process. The process is, in its most general sense, a process of value achievement in which persons work to obtain certain desired ends. This is based on certain key assumptions made by Holmberg. These assumptions are, "(1) that human traits are such that progress can be made towards the realization of human dignity," and "(2) that the natural order (physical nature) is such that with greater knowledge and skill, human beings can turn it progressively to the service of social goals" (Holmberg 1958:13).

The later work of Holmberg and the political scientist Harold Lasswell deserves our attention here. These two social scientists attempted to develop what they referred to as a general theory of directed social change (Lasswell and Holmberg 1966:14). They conceptualized social change as "a process in which *participants* seek to maximize net value outcomes (*values*) by employing practices (*institutions*), affecting *resources*" (Lasswell and Holmberg 1966:15). The social change process as the two described it involved goals, interaction contexts, and the environment. At the core were the PREWSWAR Values, which were regarded as sufficiently precise and universalistic to allow systematic cross-cultural comparison. Further, the authors felt that the eight values and their related practices were the focus of specialized research disciplines. PREWSWAR is an acronym based on the initials of the eight values. The PREWSWAR Values are power, respect, enlightenment, wealth, skill, well-being, affection, and rectitude.

Human beings are viewed as maximizers; in Lasswell and Holmberg's terms, "Participants in the social process are seeking to maximize their net value position" (Lasswell and Holmberg 1966:17). To return to Holmberg's discussion of Vicos and values:

The wider sharing of such values among members of the Vicos community was essentially the overall basic value position and policy goal to which we subscribed. In other words, everyone, if he so desired, should at least have the right and the opportunity, if not the responsibility, to participate in the decision-making process in the community, to enjoy a fair share of its wealth, to pursue a desire for knowledge, to be esteemed by his fellowmen, to develop talents to the best of his ability, to be relatively free from physical and mental disease, to enjoy the affection of others, and to command respect for his private life. (Holmberg 1958:13)

The intervening social scientist works to increase the sharing of these values. In order to do this, it is necessary to identify the base values in a community, and with this knowledge intervene in the community so as to help achieve value goals.

The knowledge required goes far beyond mere identification of the base values. It is necessary to investigate and understand the contexts within which the values are produced, exchanged, and shared. These contexts are referred to as institutions. Institutions are the social interaction patterns guided by more or less stable practice patterns that are to an extent focused on certain value outcomes.

The foundation of the research and development approach is knowledge. It is, in spite of all of its action involvement and change-producing behavior, research-based. It shares with all of the other applied anthropologies a base in research. This is fundamental and will be reemphasized in our discussion of the process. It is this firm basis in research that separates this approach from political action. It is also the source of the strength of the approach. It is through research that the "contextuality" of the process is understood. This is consistent with the total view of system stressed in anthropology, that is to say, the holistic approach.

Before considering the process specifically, it is necessary to review the relationship between the conception of values associated with the research and development approach, and the traditional concern in anthropology for cultural relativism. Although it is true that the approach does focus on a specific value orientation, generally stated as a "wider sharing of positive human values" as represented by the specific value categories included in the PREWSWAR list, further study of the approach indicates that the conceptual scheme recognizes the importance of local institutional variability. The values take different forms and exist in different institutional settings. As Holmberg states the principle:

I have not meant to suggest that movement towards these goals can occur only through a single set of institutional practices. Like most anthropologists I subscribe to the doctrine of the relativity of culture and I firmly believe that people have the right of self-determination, as long as they respect that right in others. (Holmberg 1958:13)

Thus at the general level, Holmberg and his associates possessed a vision of the potential of human groups to change progressively. This vision was given substance by the act of research, and was guided by the conception of values developed through cross-cultural analysis.

RESEARCH AND DEVELOPMENT PROCESS

Research and development anthropology is not based on the discovery of a secret strategy or mechanism, nor is it based on a single bright idea. Instead its strength is thoughtful, anthropological conceptualization of an encompassing understanding of culture appropriate to the goal of stimulating the "right" kinds of culture change. This conception would be meaningless without the detailed research necessary for understanding the substance of total context. The value scheme seems, in isolation, utopian and impractical. With basic research and the logical specification of reality, the construction of an effective overall action design is possible. With the recognition of possibilities and goals, practical action can be specific.

The key to success using the research and development approach is adequate research and documentation. The research makes the development work, and development efforts provide an opportunity for further research. This is, as Holmberg notes, not unlike the interdependence between natural science and related technology. As Holmberg suggests, "A great strength of, if not a necessary condition for, natural science is feedback through development" (Holmberg 1958:14). The process is based on continual feedback. Each element may be rather minor. The total effect, however, may be quite significant. The significance is derived not from a few decisive acts but from a large number of small acts that are guided and mediated by an overall design, a theory, and ideology. This guide increases the total impact of the intervention. The persistence, coupled with the feedback loops, which constantly result in corrective behavior, can result in a powerful total effect.

As the technique was applied at Vicos, Holmberg and his staff charted large numbers of potential interventions in the community. These interventions were laid out diagrammatically. At Vicos these were put on large bulletin boards. The diagrams, depicted below schematically, became a representation of the process of research and development.

The Research and Development Approach:

An ideological goal or end point

A corresponding institutional goal or end point

Program plans for probes, pretests, interventions, and appraisals

Present ideological situation with respect to above goals summarized

Present institution situation with respect to above goals summarized

Record of past interventions

Baseline ideological situation

Baseline institutional situation

CASE STUDY: THE CORNELL-PERU PROJECT AT VICOS

The Community

Vicos was a typical mountain hacienda community of Peru. It was about 250 miles from Lima, the capital city, and consisted of a tract of over thirty thousand acres. Only about twenty-five hundred acres were cultivated while sixty-seven hundred acres were used for grazing. Somewhat less than one-tenth of the hacienda was exploited through cultivation. In 1952, the population was revealed to be, through a project census, 1,703 Quechua-speaking Indians.

These people were tied to the land, which was owned by the Public Benefit Society of Huaraz. The society rented out the land to the highest bidder for periods of five to ten years. The money paid in rent was used, along with the money from fifty-six other properties, to support the only hospital in the administrative district of which Vicos was a part. The estate was largely managed for and by the regional Latino elites. The key authority figure in Vicos political life was the *patrón* who had rented the property. The *patrón* was never an Indian. The *patrón* possessed extensive power and authority and could profoundly influence a person's life. The *patrón*'s agent on the estate lands was another non-

Indian, an overseer or administrator. It was his task to maintain the daily operations of the hacienda with its seventeen-hundred-person work force. Augmenting hacienda management were a number of non-Indian foremen who directly supervised the work force and dealt with such problems as absenteeism, fertilization, irrigation, and harvest. This small group of outsiders held power over the Vicosinos, who were bound to a community over which they had very little control.

The non-Indian managers were linked to the labor force through Vicosino straw bosses (*mayorales*). These men supervised the 380-man work force of the hacienda, who worked three days a week for the manor for about a penny a day. On occasion, the Vicosino laborers were hired out to other farming operations in the region, in which case their pay was taken by the *patrón*. Further, Vicosinos were bound to provide domestic services for the maintenance of the manor house. In addition to the labor exploitation hierarchy, there existed an organizational structure within the Vicos community itself. There were seventeen *varayoc* who formed the local decision-making body. The *varayoc* system had been created by Spanish colonial administrators as part of an indirect rule system. Through the years, the *varayoc* system had become highly involuted, presumably because it was one of the few organizations in which Vicosinos could participate at a decision-making level. Through the *varayoc* institution Vicosinos gained prestige and status.

Although their primary function was the planning and management of the religious ceremonial life of the community, the *varayoc* also served to mobilize labor for public works and to resolve conflicts within the community concerning land and animals. In addition, the *varayoc* were responsible for carrying out the punishments specified by the *patrón* in response to infractions of the rules. This included floggings, public denunciations, and incarcerations.

The Vicosinos were peons, social inferiors with little control over their destiny. The relationship that existed between the Vicosino farmer and the *patrón* was brutal and exploitative. It served as a model for virtually all relationships between Vicosinos and non-Indians. It was assumed that the non-Indian was inherently superior to the Indian, the latter being a slow-witted, ignorant drunkard, almost subhuman. The role expectations that the non-Indian held for the Indian were well sanctioned. Indians who did not play their role were subject to tremendous abuse from both the non-Indian and the Indian. The "successful" Indian manifested the stereotypical behavior that reduced sanctions but also placed him in a subservient position. Proper role behavior made the Indian a powerless exploited dependent.

The Vicosinos were organized into a somewhat different kinship system than the non-Indians. Instead of a bilateral system, they were born into a type of patrilineal descent group, termed locally a *casta*. Males dominated as family leaders. Marriage was often established on a trial basis, and then, if accepted, formalized in a church ceremony. Childhood for Vicosinos was a difficult time. School attendance was noncompulsory and rare. Children were involved in a substantial number of chores at a very young age and interacted in few affectionate relationships.

The material well-being of the Vicosinos was limited. Adults usually had no more than a single set of regionally distinctive clothes, with the children being dressed in little more than rags. The cost of the costume in labor and materials was equivalent to a year's wages for a Vicosino (Alers 1971). Housing available to the Vicosinos was deficient: dirt floors and no windows were the standard.

The health and nutrition status of the Vicosinos was poor. Their diet was limited largely to what they could produce in their small garden plots and what they could glean from the fields. Their limited diet was buffeted by success and failure in the harvest. Very few of the families had significant amounts of animal protein in their diets. Dietary surveys indicate that the Vicosinos consumed only about 76 percent of their daily needs of calories and protein. Associated with the nutritional deficiencies were certain health problems of high frequency. Fifty percent of the population were infested with parasites of various kinds. Given the diet and high incidence of parasite infestation, there was an expectedly high rate of gastrointestinal infection. The community was periodically subject to epidemics of measles, influenza, and whooping cough.

The anthropologists of the Vicos Project deviated from the traditional analyst and consultant roles. To use Holmberg's term, they used participant-intervention as opposed to participant-observation. They became both observers and designers. The Peruvian government's Institute of Indigenous Affairs, which is a semi-autonomous agency of the Ministry of Labor and Indigenous Affairs, gave its full support to this major field experiment.

Project Goals

The plan of intervention was framed in terms of the PREWSWAR values of power, respect, enlightenment, wealth, skill, well-being, affection, and rectitude. The overall goal was twofold. The anthropologists would work for wider sharing of values. Certain goal values were viewed as strategically more important than others. Consequently, the project invested greater efforts in intervention in the realms of power, wealth, enlightenment, skill, and well-being. It was hypothesized that the other values could be treated as dependent variables. That is, these values could be regarded as responsive to changes in the other values. These values derived their shape from the other values. Rectitude, affection, and respect were regarded in this way as derived values, best modified through interventions in other value domains.

The general goals of the project thereby came to be:

1. Devolution of power.
2. Increases in the production and sharing of wealth.
3. Improvements in health and well-being.

4. Increases in organizational complexity.

5. Improvements in the opportunities available in the community for enlightenment.

These goals became the development priorities for the anthropologists. The selection of these priorities was based on the values of both the anthropologists and the community, and the theoretical idea that some values are derived from others. They accepted as a guiding principle the notion that innovations would be accepted where the people felt the most deficiency.

The primary area of intervention in the initial stages of the project was the power domain. The goal was power devolution, that is, a reduction of the amount of control the *patrón* had over the Vicosinos, and an increase in the amount of control the Vicosinos had over their own lives. This began on the first day of project operations. The Cornell staff decided quickly to work not with the *varayoc*, but with the former straw bosses who, while being experienced in hacienda affairs, were not so tied to the religious life of the community. In spite of the age of this group and the fact of their preferred position under the old system, they represented an effective transitional organization. Older members were later replaced by persons more committed to modernization.

In preparation for the interventions, Cornell quickly resolved some of the problems that contributed to the bitterness of the Vicosinos. For example, Vicosinos strongly resented the practice of required unpaid service to the manor household. This requirement was immediately abolished. Instead, these services were provided by paid community members. It had been the practice to pay a small amount to each farm laborer. However, the previous *patrón* had failed to carry out this responsibility. Cornell made the payments and charged the cost to the transfer fees. These acts, as well as the rapport that existed between Mario C. Vazquez and the Vicosinos, contributed greatly to the developing new *patrón-*Vicosino relationship.

Paralleling the initial "therapeutic" and political interventions were activities in other areas, particularly in agricultural production, health, and education. These will be discussed later.

The power devolution process proceeded along three fronts. Cornell attempted to overhaul old organizational forms and to create new ones so as to facilitate a meaningful transfer of power. There was a concerted effort to increase Vicosinos' knowledge of democratic practice through discussion and other instructional efforts. And finally, largely outside the context of the Vicos community, advocates for the community were working to help the Vicosinos overcome political resistance to their purchase of the land. The advocacy work was crucial and occurred at the highest levels of the national government.

Effort was invested in developing the skills of *mayorales* as decision makers. This took place in weekly meetings and in the traditional *mando*, the weekly gathering of peons to receive work orders. This strategy was designed by Holmberg, who was very successful in teaching Vicosinos to "think about Vicos as a whole, to consider issues in terms of a common good as well as individual and family interest, and how to arrive at group decisions upon a basis of open discussion'' (Dobyns 1971:147). The *mayorales* met with Holmberg every week. After great efforts, the "timid and fearful" foremen were drawn into policy discussions. Ultimately, the *mando*, or labor shape-up, in which representatives of all the families participated, came to be more democratic. Dobyns notes: "Slowly the serfs learned to discuss manorial activities in the shape-up meetings until they learned to make community-wide decisions in what became a sort of town meeting" (1971:147).

The overall effect of the transformation was remarkable. Soon these people were directly influencing the direction of their lives. The devolution of power occurred by providing an organizational context within which the Vicosinos could slowly activate power prerogatives, while the Cornell group consciously refrained from the use of power. The first stage of the power devolution process lasted five years and was concluded by the transference of the *patrón*'s role from Holmberg and Cornell to the collective community of Vicos, as represented by the community council that evolved out of the Cornell seminars.

When the Cornell rental agreement was to end, the Cornell staff attempted to identify the community's future wishes. The identified goal was the purchase of the lands and the establishment of Vicos as a free and self-governing community. Vicosinos advocated that they continue to farm the lands collectively and that the proceeds go to pay for the land itself. The achievement of these goals required the establishment of more complex organization. The hacienda was subdivided into ten zones based on the distribution of population. Each zone was to send a single popularly elected delegate to the Communal Directive Board (*Junta de Delegados*). The officers of the newly elected board made contact with the Peruvian Indian Institute, which assisted in beginning the process of expropriation. The passage of an expropriation resolution was not enough; the process of acquiring the land took four full years. The board rather quickly evolved in terms of more workable democratic practice.

Much of this development was made possible by Cornell and other project supporters external to Vicos itself acting on behalf of the Vicosinos. The Cornell Peru Project had a national power base. Because of this, the Vicosinos were no longer under the influence of the non-Indians of nearby towns. The Cornell-Peru Project served as a protective umbrella while development occurred. The presence of the Cornell people gave the Vicosinos much better access to extracommunity resources. Ultimately, the Vicos community had the benefits of government teachers, health care workers, and various technical assistance personnel.

The Cornell power umbrella was most crucial in regards to the final disposition of the land. As the rental agreement ended the project advised the Peruvian government to expropriate the land from the Public Benefit Society of Huaraz to be given to the Vicos communty. As this possibility developed, fierce local opposition emerged. The Public Benefit Society of Huaraz precipitously raised the price of the land tenfold, including in their appraisal facilities built by the

Vicosinos as part of the development project. The Rotary Club of Huaraz accused project personnel of being communists. The resistance of the non-Indian establishment rather quickly developed at the national level. Later, the Prime Minister of Peru, Pedro Beltran, advanced the opinion to representatives of the American Embassy that sale of the land at any price would not be approved because of the precedent it would set for land reform in the country. The uncertainty that this resistance caused among the Vicosinos slowed the course of development in the area of capital investment.

The Vicosinos grew tense as the Public Benefit Society of Huaraz prepared to lease the land to the next *patrón*. These tensions increased when peasants on an adjoining hacienda were killed by national police. The Vicosinos were taking up arms themselves. From this high level of frustration the course of struggle shifted to the national level. Intervention at a high level from outside the country was required. The United States's ambassador to Peru worked to obtain the approval of land sales with the aid of Edward Kennedy. Finally, success was met.

Economic Development at Vicos

A major component of the development effort was an attempt to improve the economic well-being of the Vicosinos. Virtually all of these efforts were focused upon the farming system. The Vicosinos were subsistence farmers for three days a week and unpaid agricultural workers for the remaining work days. In return for their labor they received the use of a homesite and a small plot of land to farm to support their families. These one-half to five-acre plots were planted primarily with potatoes, maize, various Andean root crops, wheat, barley, rye, beans, and pigweed. Many families owned cattle, which they grazed in scrubby upland pastures. Families supplemented a protein-short diet by raising guinea pigs and chickens.

The transformation of the technology of Vicos agriculture was given a high priority by the Cornell-Peru Project. At the time of Cornell's assumption of the *patrón* role, the hacienda lands farmed for the market were planted with flax. This practice was uneconomical. The project received technical assistance from the Inter-American Cooperative Food Production Service, which suggested that the project take up potato raising. Potato raising, as the technical assistants identified it, required the acceptance of an entire complex of practices, which included new mountain varieties, anti-rot fumigation of seed potatoes, fertilization at various stages, and spraying against insects and mosaic infection. The potato complex had to be introduced all at once in order to be successful. This broad spectrum substitution was in fact accomplished. The transfer of technical knowledge was facilitated by Cornell's identification as a *patrón*.

Later these technical improvements were augmented by improvements in the economic arrangement associated with the potato. Vicosinos became eligible for a crop loan program. Initially these funds were used to improve farming on communal lands. By this time, Vicosinos understood banking practices sufficiently so that they could manage their loans properly. In addition to the communal loans, individual Vicosino farmers were able to borrow for their farming operations. The Vicos farming operation remained in two parts: the communal lands and individual plots. The communal plots were farmed commercially and thereby served as a source of funds to maintain the farm operation. In addition, because these lands were under the control of Cornell as *patrón*, they were also used as demonstration plots for higher technology farming practices. The Vicosinos could observe the improved practices when they performed their three days of required labor. In spite of favorable credit arrangements and demonstrations few Vicosinos engaged the new practices. Virtually all 17 of 363 families who adopted the innovations, however, made big profits. Over the next few years the innovations spread steadily. After Cornell ceased being the *patrón* the Vicos Community Board took over the lending role.

In addition to the interventions in the political and agricultural realms, there were significant interventions in education, leading to a wider sharing of enlightenment. Control of knowledge and skill sources were a primary means of maintaining the status quo in the highland communities. Consequently, enlightenment was given major emphasis by the project. Vicosinos, like other Andean peasants, were dependent on traditional knowledge. As part of the adaptation to the complex system of dominance and submissiveness, the Vicosinos, like other oppressed Andeans, actively resisted what little educational opportunities there were. Part of this was motivated by fear of the non-Indian teaching staff. Education programs had been so ineffective that at the beginning of the project only 2 percent of the population could speak Spanish, and only five persons could read and write.

Improvements in enlightenment were essential for significant changes in other realms to occur. The first major educational efforts were informal and were related to knowledge of potato farming and political development. Knowledge of potato raising techniques led to a wide variety of changes in Vicosino life. As Vicosinos produced more potatoes for the market, their relationship of dependency on non-Indian merchants declined in importance while they became better integrated into the national market. This allowed them better prices. Their remarkable increases in disposable income led regional merchants to send goods to Vicos to be considered for purchase by community members. Again, this served to improve the Vicosinos' integration into the national economy. Vicosinos ultimately were able to reverse economic roles to the extent that some even hired skilled non-Indian workers.

In addition to the remarkable effects of training in potato raising, the Cornell project also attempted to improve local knowledge of construction techniques. This was done by hiring a non-Indian journeyman-instructor to assist the Vicosinos in constructing buildings. A similar arrangement was developed by Mario C. Vazquez in terms of sewing instruction for women. Later, the sewing classes were coupled with Spanish classes.

Perhaps the most important thing taught at Vicos was democratic decision making. This "instructional event" represented the most essential transformation at Vicos. It was the ultimate expression of the project's values and the best evidence of the utility of the research and development approach. The success of the project was based on enlightenment domains, yet it was something more than education; it was education guided by a theory. That is, in the enlightenment domain as well as others, Holmberg and other members of the project were able to create a link between their theories of development and practical action. This perhaps is what is most remarkable about the entire Vicos enterprise: the capacity to link up ideas with direct action.

The educational strategy that the project followed was simple and direct. The first interventions for enlightenment were informal, carried out independently of whatever formal educational institutions existed at Vicos. The knowledge transmitted was directly related to immediately useful activities. The enlightenment process is instrumental and therefore can be judged in terms of its here and now impact on the community and the project. These interventions were not to make the Vicosinos ready for change, they were to change the Vicosinos directly. It was not until later in the project that general education was given a significant emphasis.

SUMMARY

Research and development anthropology is an approach to development intervention that is clearly focused on values. This focus is expressed in a generalized procedure that requires that the anthropologist understand the institutional framework of the distribution of valued "things." This feature of research and development anthropology gives it a holistic but systematic quality that makes the approach useful in a variety of situations. The approach provides a means of ordering and displaying information in support of the planning and implementation of interventions. The use of an institutional framework in conjunction with values gives the approach a somewhat greater potential for considering major structural transformations as development goals, along with the community needs focus of the approach.

Potential interventionists within anthropology might consider using features from action anthropology and research and development anthropology to develop a composite approach. Both provide ideas that may serve a variety of development situations well. Both schemes provide useful concepts for community-based development planning. Perhaps there is some potential for combining the value category planning techniques associated with research and development, with the interactive planning orientation characteristic of action anthropology. While it appears that the two approaches contain features that could be usefully combined, it is important to point out a fundamental contrast between the two approaches. That is, as these approaches were operationalized in their prototypical projects, they took very different positions on the extent to which the anthropologist assumes power. The action anthropologist *avoids* it. The research and development anthropologist *assumes* it, where appropriate, and then "devolves" it. Looking beyond this fundamental opposition will result in awareness of substantial similarities between the two approaches.

FURTHER READING

Dobyns, Henry F., Paul Doughty, and Harold Lasswell, eds. 1971. *Peasants, Power and Applied Social Change: Vicos as a Model.* Beverly Hills, Calif.: Sage Publications.

Contains many of the articles that describe the research and development approach. In addition, it contains descriptions of some project outcomes and characteristics of the Vicos community. Unfortunately, there is no single comprehensive description of the project, but this volume is an excellent substitute.

Doughty, Paul L. 1986. "Vicos: Success, Rejection and Rediscovery of a Classic Program." In *Applied Anthropology in America*, 2d ed. E. M. Eddy and W. L. Partridge, eds. New York: Columbia University Press.

———. 1987. "Against the Odds: Collaboration and Development at Vicos." In *Collaborative Research and Social Change: Applied Anthropology in Action*, Donald D. Stull and Jean J. Schensul, eds. Boulder, Colo.: Westview Press.

These two articles provide an excellent update and assessment of this classic project.

6

Community Development

The origins of the community development model are more complex than the other models for intervention that we are considering in this text. The approach developed out of an uneasy and largely unplanned cooperation between academics and practitioners. Anthropology is only one of many disciplines that have contributed to the development of community development theory and practice.

Although the community development approach has been widely used by many different kinds of people, there is substantial agreement as to its essential features. Content analysis of fifty-nine policy articles, carried out by the anthropologist Charles J. Erasmus, reveals some of the conceptual uniformities that can be found in definitions of community development.

Erasmus attempts to identify the recurring stress given concepts that appear in the definitions. The most frequently stressed attribute is " 'self-help' group action via community participation and voluntary cooperation,'' which appears in 60 percent of the definitions (1968:65). Forty percent of the definitions mention as "ideal goals" such concepts as self-determination, democracy, self-reliance, or local self-government; the articles deemphasize material goals, "such as better living standards, improved housing, health, and diet.'' These things appear in only 10 percent of the definitions. Fifteen percent make reference to "the development of self-confidence in backward groups suffering from apathy, limited expectations and distrust of government'' (1968:65). Further, the "felt needs'' of the people to be aided and the need for "technical help'' from agencies providing aid are each mentioned by approximately 30 percent of the authors (1968:65).

There are a number of definitions in the literature that accurately reflect the nature of the model. The one that was used by the program we will consider as a representative case study was developed by the International Cooperation Administration, an agency of the American government.

Community development is a process of social action in which the people of a community organize themselves for planning and action; define their common and individual needs and problems; make group and individual plans to meet their needs and solve their problems; execute the plans with a maximum of reliance upon community resources; and supplement these resources when necessary with services and materials from government and non-governmental agencies outside the community. (1955:1)

DEVELOPMENT OF THE APPROACH

Community development has a rather complex history. Special meanings became attached to the phrase in 1948 when the Cambridge Conference on African Administration, sponsored by the British Colonial Office, used "community development" to replace the phrase "mass education" (Mezirow 1963:9). Mass education was a term coined in the British Colonial Office to signify an educational focus on the entire community with concern for getting people involved in their own development.

Influenced by diverse disciplines, community development received its major impetus from education and social work. The influence of education was especially important in Great Britain's colonial development policy. The influence of social work on community development has been more apparent in the United States than Great Britain. Community development has affinities with a subspecialty within social work called community organization practice. This field represents a major source of community development thought in the United States. The similarities are quite fundamental. Professional competencies in both areas are based on knowledge of community, the capacity to assist people in problem identification, the ability to identify and foster community leadership, the capacity to stimulate planning, and the techniques of resource mobilization. The differences between the two fields are subtle and unimportant.

KEY CONCEPTS

Community is a focal concept in the community development process. The process in its original formulation was largely directed at "little communities" in rural, Third World settings. Increasingly, however, a broader applicability was asserted and used by practitioners. Roland Warren suggests that "it applies to the needs of remote villages of traditionally agricultural countries and to those of turbulent metropolises of highly industrialized countries" (1970:32). More and more the technique was applied in a wider variety of contexts.

The concept of community as it is used in community development is quite variable. The anthropologist Ward Goodenough defines the concept broadly, focusing on the relationship between professional and client. "We shall use the expression 'community' broadly, referring to any social entity in a client relationship with a development agent or agency. It may be a rural village, a metropolitan government, a tribe, an industrial organization, or a nation state" (1963:16). Goodenough defends his choice by noting that "the human requirements for getting the cooperation of the members of a power elite in helping them to develop an effective national public health service are not unlike those for getting the cooperation of a group of villagers in helping them to improve agricultural production or to develop a local irrigation system'' (1963:16).

A second perspective on community is apparent in the work of William Biddle, and Loureide J. Biddle. In their terms, "Community is whatever sense of local common good citizens can be helped to achieve" (1965:77).

These definitions are not so disparate as it may appear. Both implicitly or explicitly suggest that a community is a unit of real or potential interaction in a spatial or residential framework. Goodenough identifies the community as client while Biddle suggests that community may in fact be the goal. The community concept must be broadly defined so as to reflect the wide variety of behavior called community development. Community development specialists have worked to achieve the goals of existing communities, and to create communities.

Another focal concept in community development is *process*. Process has come to be a term subjected to a heavy load of meaning. It is a code word, often used to signify the whole of community development ideology. Its concrete foundation is based on the various conceptions of procedure. Various procedural schemes are to be found in the literature.

In *The Community Development Process: The Rediscovery of Local Initiative*, William and Loureide Biddle describe "major stages" of the "flow of process" (1965:90-91). The six stages are derived from an examination of "numerous case studies of community development process" (1965:90-91). Biddle and Biddle emphasize the process approach in their work. They define community development as a "social process by which human beings can become more competent to live with and gain some control over local aspects of a frustrating and changing world" (1965:78).

Physical development of the community, which may be implied by the phrase community development, is absent from Biddle and Biddle's definition. The desired end of the process is not physical improvement, but the increased ability of a community to deal with its environment. The process approach continually stresses "what happens to *people*—socially and psychologically" (Sanders 1958:407; see also Sanders 1970:19).

The actions of community developers are often thought to be contingent upon the discovered *felt needs* of a community. Orthodox community development was thought to discover the felt needs of a community and then stimulate action in response to them. This orientation is the product of other factors. It might be stated that the community development strategy emerged in reaction to the failures of more autocratic approaches—the so-called development-from-above strategies. Because of the grass roots orientation of the community development movement, a target had to be developed that allowed programmatic involvement in small-scale communities by representatives of national or international agencies in a way that was acceptably democratic. Community felt needs came to be that target.

The community development strategy requires intense local involvement. Involvement is most easily achieved when the community defines the goals of the activity as high priorities. Stated simply, the proposition might be, communities will work for what they want. The concept is appealing but, nevertheless, has its problems. For example, all participants in the development process—agents, community members, and community political leadership—have their own felt needs. The community as a composite has felt needs that are somewhat different from those of its individual participants. And further, a community's "best interests" may not be its felt needs.

Lack of recognition of the felt needs of a community is often stated as a cause of failure in development programs. Often the technical expert assumes that his or her understanding of the community's needs is virtually identical with that of the community (Goodenough 1963:59). It is in this context that the special skills of the social scientist are so useful. Goodenough suggests that there are at least four relevant perspectives on community needs that must be accounted for in the program implementation process. These are: 1) the agent's assessment of community needs in terms of his or her own goals; 2) the agent's assessment of needs mitigated by his or her understanding of the community's goals; 3) the community's assessment as mitigated by their understanding of the agent's goals; and 4) the community's conception of its needs (1963:59).

It is through the needs concept that the culture of the developing community becomes incorporated into the process of development planning. Goodenough infers that "customs, as shared habits, must be gratifying in some way to the majority of a society's members if they are to persist" (1963:64). One might say that the achievement of developmental goals would be facilitated if the community perceives them as a potential source of gratification. The saliency of the felt needs concept in the community development literature is derived from this fact.

Cultural systems rarely exist in isolation. That is to say, in virtually all human groups, one.can detect evidence of adaptive change that was stimulated by intergroup cultural borrowing; cultural diffusion is a fact of human life. The community developer is oriented toward facilitating adaptive change in a focused and accelerated manner. This often involves conscious attempts to provide, in a discriminating manner, alternative and perhaps improved means of meeting cultural needs.

Because of the seeming inevitability of cultural change, one might ask whether community development is necessary. That is, if it is truly based on a community's felt needs, wouldn't the community act purposively without the stimulus of the professional practitioner? Given the nature of things, this question is not readily answered. There have been few really critical assessments of specific projects to appear in the literature.

VALUE SYSTEM

Perhaps the most fundamental value orientation represented in community development is the belief in progress. Biddle and Biddle notes: "Most community developers are optimistic about people. The belief in human potential for favorable growth is necessary to the process they hope to inspire'' (1965:58). Rooted in this positive view of human potential is the understanding that in order to apply the community development approach in a particular community, the community members must have a positive view of their own potential. It might be stated that the value orientations of the practitioner are projections of his or her desires for the community.

Biddle and Biddle have stated their position on the human potential value quite clearly. Their discussion will serve as representative of this characteristic value of community development. They assert that "each person is valuable, unique, and capable of growth toward greater social sensitivity and responsibility" (1965:60). They suggest further that "each person has underdeveloped abilities in initiative, originality and leadership [and that] these qualities can be cultivated and strengthened" (1965:60). Further, "these abilities tend to emerge and grow stronger when people work together in small groups that serve the common (community) good" (1965:60).

This introduces a fundamental component of community development ideology: the process can result in two types of success, just as the process can result in two types of failure. That is, the process as it is usually implemented involves the definition of tangible goals. These may include such things as a new water system or a school. In addition, the community development process has abstract goals, which to the practitioner may be more important than the concrete goals. These goals relate to increasing the community's capacity to change purposively. This implies the creation of representative, competent community organization, and leadership that can instigate and control adaptive community action. The practitioner therefore often focuses on intangible "results in the mind" rather than the physical results of projects. We will consider this in our critique of the approach. The benefits of citizen participation in the community development process are viewed as extensive.

In spite of its importance, participation has not been adequately conceptualized in the community development literature. Frequently it seems to exist as a goal unto itself. We should emphasize that the goals of participation are manifold, ranging from the economic to the political. The quality and extent of participation expected is quite high, but in fact exceedingly variable. The variation is related to a number of factors. These include the size of the community, the extent of factionalism and stratification, the community's functional complexity, the nature of the problem faced, and previous experience in organized, change-directed participation.

COMMUNITY DEVELOPMENT PROCESS

As suggested above, the concept of community development process carries a very heavy semantic load. Biddle and Biddle (1965) provide one of the most widely used and thorough analyses of the nature of the community development process. As noted above, they define community development in terms of process. Community development is viewed as a group process in that it encompasses "cooperative study, group decisions, collective action, and joint evaluation that leads to continuing action" (1965:78). It is thought to result in improvements in facilities, but the primary focus is on increasing human capability.

Biddle and Biddle define process as "a progression of events that is planned by the participants to serve goals they progressively choose. The events point to changes in a group and in individuals that can be termed growth in social sensitivity and competence" (1965:77). Although it may be initiated by a community development professional, process is motivated by its participants. The locus of process activity is a primary group of citizen-volunteers who manifest interest in the development of their community. Initially, the nucleus may be small, with limited goals and resources. The active nucleus may expand as they are able to identify new problem areas. Initial project success may provide a feedback of rewards, which may lead to increases in group size and capability.

The role of the practitioner is envisioned, by Biddle and Biddle, as that of researcher, encourager, and enabler. As such the practitioner discovers the existing processes in the community and the local culture and uses this knowledge to facilitate his or her invited participation. The research orientation is viewed as essential for the successful performance of the role. The primary research method might be labeled participant-observation in the initial stages, but may develop into community self-survey and community self-evaluation strategies. The accumulating findings are used to guide and correct the continuing process. Participants contribute to research in the manner that their increasing abilities will allow.

The process also emphasizes the education of the community, especially in terms of the range of developmental alternatives. The professional is usually not thought to be an advocate of a particular problem solution. It is his or her professional responsibility to assist the community in discovering all possible alternative paths to their goals, and to help stimulate the development of an organization that can legitimately and skillfully select from among the alternatives.

Community development programs are often evaluated in terms of whether or not they result in sustained developmental action following the withdrawal of the community development professional. The process-based scheme under examination here also stresses this orientation in the new projects and continuation phases. The goal of the process is to encourage and foster the emergence of a community development tradition in the community. Through the activities of the community development specialist, the community's capacity to sustain development action should be increased. Developmental competence is based on three components: organization, knowledge, and resources. Organization is largely an intracommunity matter, whereas knowledge and resources are often derived from outside the community. This requires that relationships be developed between the community and the world external to it.

All three requisites for developmental competence imply increases in power (i.e., the capacity to control). Organizations serve as frameworks to concentrate and direct political power. This requires knowledge of the community's power brokers and their resources. In this way knowledge serves as a basis of power. The process sequence identified by Biddle and Biddle implicitly recognizes that power is a primary means for effective developmental action. They suggest that what they call pressure action is sometimes necessary "if the milder approaches to authority prove ineffective" (1965:101).

It should be recognized that the primary orientation of community development is toward cooperation rather than power. Yet community developers must be aware that in the face of an intransigent or oppressive political system, forceful political action is sometimes a necessity. Certain community development strategies, such as those designed by Saul Alinsky, are largely contingent on the development of a community power base and the "creative use of conflict" (Alinsky 1946). Biddle and Biddle suggest that the process should proceed as far as it can on "assumptions of good will" (1965:101). Also, as M. K. Gandhi so convincingly demonstrated in the Satyagraha movement, morally right conflict can be an effective way to achieve political power. Conflict should not be precluded, nor should it be viewed as a requisite for developmental success. It is just another tool.

To summarize, process is a focal concept in community development. It is viewed as having two ends: the *achievement of community goals,* and *the improvement of the community's capacity to change purposively*. This is to occur with the minimum of professional intervention and the ultimate withdrawal of that intervention. Further, the process is research-based. The professional must know the community and the community must know itself.

CASE STUDY: THE TOHONO O'ODHAM COMMUNITY DEVELOPMENT PROGRAM

This case study will describe and evaluate the results of a program that was organized to stimulate development in the Tohono O'Odham Indian communities, located on the Gila Bend, San Xavier, and the Tohono O'Odham reservations in southern Arizona. The Tohono O'Odham Community Development Program began its operations in July of 1967 with the selection and training of the first workers.

Context of the Program

There are approximately eleven thousand Tohono O'Odhams, about half of whom live in the on-reservation villages that were the primary target of the program. The reservations are part of the Sonoran Desert, which forms a major portion of the southwestern United States.

The basic unit of settlement is the village, of which there are forty of various sizes. Traditionally, the Tohono O'Odham village's political deliberations have taken place in a village council, which can be characterized by its commitment to consensus-based democracy. The councils remain a vital force in many villages. However, it should be recognized that both the structural complexity and capacity for problem solving in individual villages is quite variable. The most thoroughly integrated communities may have the benefit of several specific organizations, such as stockmen's associations, water committees, and feast committees.

The community's organizational focal point is usually the village council, which deals with a range of problems. An important component of the village political organization are the individuals who link the village to higher-level Tohono O'Odham political organizations, such as the district and tribal councils. There was no formal pan-Tohono O'Odham political organization until the creation of the Tohono O'Odham Tribal Council in 1937, under the provisions of the Indian Reorganization Act of 1934. There are now district councilmen and tribal councilmen, who serve, in theory at least, to communicate the desires and decisions of the village people to the tribal and district councils. In addition, contemporary Tohono O'Odham communities may have the benefit of a number of special-purpose organizations made up of differing segments of the village population.

The current Tohono O'Odham economic adaptation consists of three major strata. The first stratum consists of residual elements of the traditional economic system, which was based on flash-flood farming of corn, beans, and squash; hunting of desert game such as whitetailed deer and javelina; gathering the edible portions of plants such as cholla, mesquite, and saguaro; and the production of craft items. The second stratum, derived from Spanish sources, consists of major augmentations to traditional farming, such as wheat and barley, and the use of various domestic animals, such as cattle and horses. The last stratum, associated with Anglo-American contact, includes increased monetization of Tohono O'Odham economic life through wage labor, welfare programs, cattle sales and, in some places, lease income payments. Currently, elements from all strata make up the Tohono O'Odham economic system. Individual Tohono O'Odhams are differentially committed to various parts of the system. The importance of the first stratum is limited.

Development Strategy

In response to conditions of need, and the opportunity afforded it by the federal government through its Office of Economic Opportunity, the Tohono O'Odham Tribal Council requested support for the community development program, which they thought would meet some of their developmental needs. The cutting edge of the program were to be multipurpose community-level workers selected by the communities within which they were to work. The program was to use the community development approach as its basic strategy. The program used the International Cooperation Administration's definition of community development in the initial training sessions. This definition was cited above.

The program was to operate in terms of the *felt need concept*. It was considered necessary to involve the people in the process of realizing their needs, and to develop a community-based strategy for achieving goals predicated on those needs. This was to be done with a minimum of reliance on resources from outside the community. Therefore, one of the program's responsibilities was to "encourage discussion in the villages and to focus on the real concerns of the people, define and rank the needs, develop the confidence and the will to work at these needs before aid is solicited and provided to them" (Tohono O'Odham Community Action Program Staff 1966:2).

The program was to work within the context of existing Tohono O'Odham social organization. The workers were interested in "developing individual feelings of worth and dignity [as well as] community pride [while they were attempting to] significantly raise living standards within existing social organization" (Tohono O'Odham Community Action Program Staff 1966:6). There was a realization that the existing organization might not be adequate for the new developments. Therefore, the project staff noted that development could be in terms of "community organization which may, or may not, already exist, or by helping to create that organization where it does not exist" (Tohono O'Odham Community Action Program Staff 1966:2). It was realized that new needs would develop within the community, that a "whole series of problems may develop for which new mechanisms to provide for the economic and psychological needs now taken care of by family organization may have to be developed" (Tohono O'Odham Community Action Program Staff 1966:2). There were no specific recommendations for the creation of new community organization.

One of the major concerns of the program was the stimulation of community independence. The concept of cooperative self-help was seen as basic to this concern. Communities engaged in development were to improve their competence in dealing with their own problems. "The possibilities envisioned are limitless but the self-help, working together, and awakening to the potential of a community are necessary attributes of the program. A learn by doing approach is a prerequisite to its success" (Tohono O'Odham Community Action Program Staff 1966:6).

The planners were very much concerned that Tohono O'Odham communities learn how to make use of their own resources as well as resources from outside the community. One of the products of increased community independence was to be increased problem-solving ability. This was to come from increased cooperation, new organizations, new technology, and increased knowledge of available resources. The proposal states: "It is anticipated that the community development program . . . will make it possible to extend the range and scope of the problems with which communities can deal successfully'' (Tohono O'Odham Community Action Program Staff 1966:3).

The community development program was to serve as the connecting link between Tohono O'Odham communities and the other tribal programs. Through these linkages the chances for success of the other tribal programs—Head Start, parent and child centers, administration, and legal services—were expected to increase. The workers were to coordinate all programs of the Office of Economic Opportunity at the local level. The workers were also to increase the communication between all government programs and Tohono O'Odham communities.

There was a very strong commitment not to impose the program on the people. The communities were to choose voluntarily to participate. This is related to a desire not to disrupt the Tohono O'Odham way of life. Discussing technological innovation, the proposal notes that ''many aspects of life in a Tohono O'Odham Community relate to customs, beliefs, ceremonies and rituals which may be affected in a fundamental way by the introduction of these new ideas and subsequent technical changes'' (Tohono O'Odham Community Action Program Staff 1966:1).

Goals of the Program

The thrust of the program was to be the achievement of the developmental goals of the traditional Tohono O'Odham villages. The planners disavowed direct planning of specific development projects for these villages, although the original program proposal indicates some of the potential areas of development. The most fundamental concern was with ''basic living conditions,'' including a desire for improved basic technology rather than large-scale economic transformations. The planners also desired ''that the Tohono O'Odham communities be stimulated or helped to adapt new techniques that will lead to greater economic productivity and provide them with better food, housing, health, education'' (Tohono O'Odham Community Action Program Staff 1966:2).

More specifically, there were aspects of Tohono O'Odham community life that the program staff regarded as ''crucial gaps.'' These were to be the foci of concentrated effort. These foci included adult education, pre-school education, community recreation for all age groups, improved community sanitation programs, citizenship and leadership training, agricultural development, improved marketing techniques for livestock, stimulation of arts and crafts production, training in the building trades, improved house construction, and programs to preserve Tohono O'Odham culture.

Selection of Workers

The worker selection policy stressed community control. The communities were to select their own workers, with minimal guidance from the administrative staff. As a corollary to this, few job requirements were specified, except those stipulated by the Office of Economic Opportunity as conditions of the grant (i.e., all employees were to be at least twenty-one years old). The workers needed to be able to speak English and Tohono O'Odham.

The community development concept was not something with which Tohono O'Odham communities were conversant. Therefore, the program staff had to provide communities with information through the tribal political organization upon which a rational selection decision could be based.

The various administrators associated with the program did little to influence the selection process. The communities themselves established requisite qualifications for community development workers as the program matured. One requirement that was often insisted upon was the possession of a high school diploma. Another community-defined job requirement was the ability to cope with drinking.

The basic attributes of the community development workers selected are as follows: the median age was thirty-four, with a range from twenty-two to fifty-two years. Only two of the workers were female, whereas fifteen were males. The median educational attainment was a relatively high ten years, although the range was from zero years to two years of college. All the workers were active in Tohono O'Odham religious life; fourteen were Roman Catholic, one was Sonoran Catholic, and two others were Protestant. Five workers were also traditional Tohono O'Odham religious practitioners. All but one worker spoke English; all spoke Tohono O'Odham. Many of the workers participated in a wide range of activities in their districts, communities, schools, and their places of employment.

The Tohono O'Odham Community Development Program was committed to a set of abstract goals, which are clearly stated in the original proposal and training plans. The staff attempted to execute policy and administer the program with these goals in mind. However, it remained the responsibility of the individual community-level worker to translate his or her understanding of the role as a Tohono O'Odham community development worker into daily actions that were appropriate for achieving program goals. The Tohono O'Odham Community Development Program workers were able to do this with varying success. Some were able effectively to stimulate development projects that were responsive to both concrete community-defined goals and the abstract goals of the program. Others tended to routinize the service component of their jobs and did not actively stimulate change.

The program did have some success in achieving certain development goals. In addition, it is possible to point to a certain number of goals that the program failed to attain. Furthermore, the program had effects that were largely unanticipated. We will discuss the effects of the program in terms of four areas. These are the effects on community facilities, the effects on the economy, the effects on sociopolitical milieu, and the effects on the bureaucratic context.

Effects on Community Facilities

One of the program's most significant successes was in terms of housing development. Virtually every community in direct contact with the program had some success in solving its housing problems. During the period of study the workers assisted in the construction of approximately 250 units (i.e., remodeled houses, expansions, and new construction). The housing constructed by the program was based on traditional housing concepts. The basic house was small and rectangular, made from adobe blocks. The improvements incorporated in program-constructed housing included concrete floors (instead of dirt), framed-up plywood roofs (instead of desert-grown materials), and plastered external walls (instead of bare adobe).

In addition to housing development, the workers were successful in constructing or remodeling a number of community buildings, such as feast houses and meeting halls. This type of construction was a high priority in some communities. In addition, workers participated in the construction of community water systems, community sanitation systems, and community recreation facilities. As the program matured, there came to be development activities within the local cattle industry, such as pastures and community corrals.

Economic Effects

The program produced various economic effects; none of these could be construed as real economic growth. There may have been some flaws in the program strategy, but the major problem was lack of investment in economic growth at the village level. Where specific "job-creating" entrepreneurial projects were attempted, they failed. Among the villages directly participating in the program, only two initiated programs that were entrepreneurial in nature. One was an attempt to manufacture roof trusses with material, equipment, and technical assistance supplied by the Bureau of Indian Affairs. The project was abandoned after two preliminary planning meetings. The other project involved the manufacturing of burnt adobe bricks for local construction projects. This idea was abandoned after a few trips to a town in the adjacent Mexican state of Sonora to observe brick manufacturing techniques.

Virtually nothing was accomplished in the area of improving cattle and basketry marketing, because the economic exchange relations were strongly entrenched. There seemed to be little concern with the problem on the part of the community, and developments in this area would have affected only a portion of the community. In addition, there were other organizations that had established an interest in these areas.

One of the few planned economic effects that was realized was increased access by Tohono O'Odham villages to information concerning employment opportunities. This was based on the working relationship that was established between the Community Development Program and the Arizona State Employment Service. The relationship was encouraged by welfare eligibility policies that required that all applicants go to the State Employment Service to see if there was available work. Community development workers came to refer community members routinely to the employment service.

An unanticipated effect of the program was the increased participation of Tohono O'Odhams in various programs of government subsidy. There were increases in social security payments, Veteran's Administration benefits, and in various welfare programs. The most dramatic increases occurred in the Bureau of Indian Affairs General Assistance Program. The most important aspect of the bureau's general assistance payments is the Tribal Work Experience Program, in which an individual who is qualified for welfare accepts a job assignment in either his or her village or an agency. The grants are issued to him or her weekly on a *pro rata* basis for time worked. There was a fivefold increase in the local BIA welfare case load.

The massive increase in general assistance was largely due to the efforts of the community development workers. Prior to the inception of the program, individual enrollees in the Tribal Work Experience Program were always placed in job training situations in government agencies. Individual community development workers successfully established community-based work crews subsidized by the General Assistance Program. Because these crews worked on community projects, such as housing improvement, there was a great deal of community support for participation in this program. In response to this support, community workers actively recruited program enrollees.

Sociopolitical Effects

The program had little effect on the quality of traditional community leadership, in spite of the fact that this was a major goal of the program. The ostensible cause of this shortfall was the lack of any useful strategy to fulfill the goal. Such a strategy would have been difficult to develop given the immense variation in leadership competence levels, and the animosity that sometimes existed between community-level workers and traditional leaders. In spite of this program shortfall, there were significant increases in the number of community organizations that would serve community needs.

One of the other planned goals was increasing the integration between the tribal administration and the villages. In general there was improved access to information concerning tribal administrative affairs. The communication link between the community development workers and staff paralleled and reinforced the link that existed between the tribal chairman and the tribal council representatives. This served to make the tribal council communicate to the villages more effectively. It made it more difficult to withhold information.

The integrative communication function of the Tohono O'Odham Community Development Program was not without its problems. The minor problems included unfair distribution of information, inaccuracy, and overly literal interpretations of messages. In spite of the benefits of the communication, it was at times obvious that there was inconsistency between tribal government goals and village goals. Some Tohono O'Odham leaders assumed that community workers were to be regarded as extensions of the tribal administrators. Some tribal administrators assumed that there was a "line relationship" between the tribal administration and the village-level workers through the community development director. This would cause community workers temporarily to set aside community-defined, goal-oriented activities while tribal-administration-defined, goal-oriented activities were carried out. When this occurred it would delay the achievement of community goals as well as increase in the minds of community members the identification of community workers with the political establishment.

The program had unanticipated sociopolitical effects. These unanticipated effects included the formalization of regional intervillage alliances that focused on program activities. The focus of these alliances included the selection of the program workers, as well as specific development projects. Regional projects included a major pasture development and a community center construction project for a group of villages.

Another unanticipated effect was the tendency for communities to elect community workers to formal political roles in village, district, and tribal organizations. A primary function of the community development worker's role is communication. In this project, important sources of information included: community development worker meetings, training sessions, staff counseling, staff memoranda, tribal council meetings, district council meetings, and officials of tribal government. Information obtained from these sources was communicated to workers' communities through home visits, community meetings, district meetings, and meetings that the worker himself "put up."

It is clear that in communities having a rather high dependence on extracommunity resources, information relating to resource exploitation is crucially important. In the Tohono O'Odham case, its importance was increased by the general lack of access to information resulting from the language barrier, illiteracy, the almost total absence of relevant mass media, such as newspapers and radio, and the lack of numerous parallel political communication links. The political power of community development workers increased because they had superior access to politically significant information, such as welfare program enrollment requirements, or deadlines for applying for BIA housing subsidies.

Ten of the original twelve community workers were nominated for political office, ranging from village chairman to vice-chairman of the tribal council. This phenomenon can best be explained as a community attempt to superimpose formal political roles on individuals who were acting out behavior appropriate to those roles.

Bureaucratic Effects

In the initial program plans, coordination of existing tribal programs at the village level was stated as a program goal. Effects were rather mixed in this area. There was fairly successful coordination with programs that had limited field staff, such as legal services and the emergency food and medical services program. In the case of other tribal community-level worker programs, such as the Public Health Service–sponsored Community Health Representative program, there was a substantial amount of conflict and jealousy. In some cases workers from both programs invested time and effort in bad-mouthing their counterpart in the other program. In certain cases, the directors of both programs had to meet and establish "truces" between workers.

One of the program's goals that was more uniformly achieved was the increase of development resources available to the Tohono O'Odham villages. These resources included various programs and departments of the federal bureaucracies, such as the Domestic Water and Sanitation Program of the U.S. Public Health Service, and the Tribal Work Experience Program of the BIA. The various programs supported by charitable organizations, such as the Save the Children Federation Community Program, the Red Cross Emergency Relief Program, and the Saint Vincent de Paul Used Clothing Program, had a role to play in village-level development. In addition, there were numerous state, county, tribal, and village resource-providing institutions. These included the Arizona State Cooperative Extension Service, the Pima County Adult Education Program, and the Tohono O'Odham Tribal Well Maintenance Department, as well as Tohono O'Odham stockmen's associations.

In addition to increasing broadly the number and impact of resources provided to Tohono O'Odham communities, the workers often came to act as administrative extensions of some of those programs. This was particularly important in the BIA housing program and the water system development program of the Public Health Service.

SUMMARY

The depth and breadth of the use of community development as a development strategy is much more extensive than for any other approach treated in this text. The community development approach evolved with contributions from mass education, extension work, and social work, as well as anthropology. The use of the approach was very extensive in the immediate postwar period, with use being curtailed somewhat in the 1970s. With its more broadly based use, it is much more diverse than any of the other approaches considered here.

It is difficult to identify the factors that led to the reduction of its use. Some relevant factors include its strong commitment to local input in planning, and its heavy reliance on the use of local resources, which caused national-level politicians to lose control. The pendulum seems to have swung, however. Increasingly, the development literature is expressing disenchantment with big picture, top-down projects in which local initiative is ignored. Thus one would expect that community development experiences and ideas will be put to use again. The names may change, but the practices will remain the same. Many community development ideas will be useful in the context of the increased commitment to decentralization in development planning and the appropriate technology movement.

The approach seems to be more typically used by the development staff of private voluntary organizations rather than by government-sponsored international development agencies. These days, organizations such as the U.S. Agency for International Development seem to support community development work through private voluntary organizations. In this framework public-sector international development agencies express their residual grass roots tendencies. One problem with the grass roots approach to development is that development efforts tend to be too localized when viewed from the standpoint of host country governments and the politics of international public agencies. Local development efforts are hard to evaluate except on a case-by-case basis. They are often based on narrow views of needs, which tend to ignore large infrastructure development projects such as roads or irrigation systems.

The approach is useful in situations where there are existing, functioning communities that can benefit from improved integration with regional and national governments. Often the key task of development is to bring to bear culturally appropriate technical assistance and resources with local organizations and plans. The approach can be used to stimulate the development of local organizations so as to allow further self-sustained development or to provide a means of increasing national integration through development.

The important concepts are felt needs and the so-called process approach. The felt need idea is perhaps self-explanatory. The process idea is more cryptic. Process refers to the notion that both the means and ends of development must be considered. Ends are to be determined locally, and the means used for achieving them must be designed to increase community adaptability. This orientation is not inconsistent with the action anthropology and the research and development approaches. It should be noted that the means-ends conception found in action anthropology communicates a different but complementary idea.

FURTHER READING

Biddle, William W., and Loureide J. Biddle. 1965. *The Community Development Process: The Rediscovery of Local Initiative*. New York: Holt, Rinehart and Winston.

Presents a classic account of the process-based approach. Many readers may react negatively to its naive politics, but if you can read through that, you will find some ideas that are in fact practical. The approach specified here is oriented toward rural America. The idea of class struggle and revolution is not part of the approach.

Brokensha, David, and Peter Hodge. 1969. *Community Development: An Interpretation*. San Francisco: Chandler Publishing.

A useful, although dated, textbook on the topic.

Goodenough, Ward H. 1963. *Cooperation in Change: An Anthropological Approach to Community Development*. New York: Russell Sage Foundation.

This comprehensive work can serve as a handbook for the community-focused development administrator. It offers a good review of effective change agent practice, as well as an extensive discussion of issues relating to cultural appropriateness. The ideology of the text is adjusted to conditions that do not exist any longer. Much of the text is useful.

7

Advocacy Anthropology

Anthropologists such as Sol Tax and Allan Holmberg operated on unfamiliar ground when they developed research and development anthropology and action anthropology. They were operating under the limitations of an assumption of a value-free social science. Their approaches contrasted with existing patterns of application that did not include the role of change agent. The value-explicit nature of these new approaches allowed the anthropologist to become involved in producing change.

Community advocacy is a kind of value-explicit applied anthropology useful in certain types of communities. Like action anthropology, research and development anthropology, and community development, community advocacy anthropology is a values-in-action process. In advocacy anthropology there is a distinctive relationship between the anthropologist and the community.

Community advocacy anthropology is a value-explicit process by which the anthropologist as researcher acts to augment and facilitate indigenously designed and controlled social action or development programs by providing data and technical assistance in research, training, and communication to a community through its leadership. Although community advocacy is primarily a research activity, the anthropologist is also involved in change-producing action. The anthropologist serves not as a direct change agent but as an auxiliary to community leaders. This contrasts with the more direct involvement of anthropologists as change agents in both action anthropology and research and development anthropology. The community advocacy anthropologist does not work through an intervening agency. His or her relationship with the community is direct and intimate.

DEVELOPMENT OF ADVOCACY TECHNIQUES

A kind of community advocacy anthropology was developed by Stephen Schensul within the context of a community mental health program in Chicago.

The approach developed by Schensul emerged out of a community research unit that was a component of a mental health program. As an approach, it developed as an adaptation of the factors extant in this situation. These included the values of the researcher, the needs of the client community, and the nature of the initial sponsoring organization.

Program specifications indicated the research unit was to serve the direct informational needs of the program's administration and thereby, indirectly, the community. This proved unworkable. Research team members felt that the health program staff "were neither open to new information nor flexible in their ideas concerning program development and provision of services" (Schensul 1973:107). It seemed inevitable to the team that "no matter how good" the data acquired was, it would not have a significant impact on the community. Members of the research team tended more and more to identify with the community rather than the clinical program.

"Thus," Schensul notes, "we began to withdraw from intensive involvement in the clinical activities of the program. We turned to a search for new situations in which our research data could make useful contributions to positive social action. We found those action situations *directly* in the communities themselves" (Schensul 1973:107). The research efforts developed most intensively in the Chicano barrio in Chicago, where the relationships between team and community developed quite intensively.

KEY CONCEPTS

The primary reference group of the community advocate anthropologist is the community. It is through an understanding of this relationship that we can best understand the nature of community advocacy anthropology. A key concept is collaboration: collaboration between anthropologists and community leadership focusing on the former's research skills and the latter's information needs. Community advocacy anthropology is an involved-in-the-action process. It is based on two fundamental assumptions. First, "Anthropological research should provide information to the population under study which contributes to the development of the community and the improvement of community life" (Schensul 1973:111). The research effort is focused on short-term research needs, with provisions for "direct, immediate and localized" feedback. Further, the research is not intended to make a contribution to the generalized pool of scientific knowledge, because the "pay-off" to the community from this type of research is limited.

A second basic assumption is that "programs for community development and improvement are most successful and effective when they are conceived and directed by knowledgeable community residents" (Schensul 1973:111). This assumption indicates a belief that an anthropologist's potential for success in assisting a community to achieve its goals is enhanced by working in collaboration with the community rather than an external agency. Based on these assumptions,

Schensul notes that "it should be the goal of our applied anthropological research unit to facilitate indigenous social action programs by supplying data and results which can make significant contributions to the effectiveness of their efforts" (Schensul 1973:111).

The collaboration occurs in the relationships that develop between the researcher and community activists. The activists are those community members who are regularly involved in community planning and action. This group is a changing network of individuals with various degrees of commitment, areas of specialized knowledge, and ideological orientations. These people often exist as the natural leaders in a community. They are proficient at mobilizing members of the community.

The activist role calls for a very broad range of skills and a high level of commitment to the community. They must effectively communicate with the power structures of both the establishment and their own community. They must be able to mobilize their community to achieve community goals. Often their success produces as much criticism as praise. It is this group that forms the principal constituency of the community advocacy anthropologist. The activists' view of community needs shapes the content of the research process. Their importance in shaping the research effort is based on a number of factors. They have significant knowledge of the community and participate in situations that have potential for useful research activities. Further, they often serve as "gatekeepers" by controlling access into the community. Researcher-activist ties are often facilitated by the need for the activists to develop alliances with persons who will assist in their work for the community. However, it should be noted that the activist can serve as either facilitator or limiter of research.

The nature of the specific advocacy project grows out of the relationship developed with the activists. This relationship is multistranded and contingent upon many of the rapport-building skills characteristic of anthropological fieldwork. A substantial period of time is necessary to develop effective collaboration because of the need to develop trust and understanding in the context of complex political activities. A key to effective collaboration is the manifestation of commitment on the part of the researcher. The researcher has to be prepared to allocate a significant amount of time to the process. It is suggested that something more than a year is necessary. Collaboration is also facilitated by the residence of the anthropologist in the community, much like traditional fieldwork. Community residence may signify for the community the commitment of the researcher to the community. Additionally, it allows the researcher to develop intense knowledge of the community. This knowledge develops through the increased opportunity for participation.

There are real limits to the extent to which rapport can be developed in a community. The limitations are most striking in complex, politicized urban situations. In these settings, the anthropologists may come to be affiliated with certain factions in the community. Neutrality is not aggressively maintained. Advocacy means being on someone's side and, of course, being in opposition.

Although the anthropologist will inevitably become aligned with certain community factions, he or she must attempt to maintain an open and flexible stance for the purpose of maintaining contact with the whole community. The anthropologist should not actively participate in the internal conflict between community organizations. In fact, the advocacy anthropologist needs to maintain working relations with all parties to the development situation.

Community advocacy anthropologists are primarily researchers. They need to avoid displacing the activists as representatives of the community. Nor should they foster the role of the outside expert. Advocacy anthropologists need to avoid competition with community leaders. The activists must retain their positions as community organizers and leaders.

COMPONENTS OF SUCCESSFUL COLLABORATION

For successful collaboration to occur, a number of principles should be followed. The relationship between researcher and activist must be symmetrical and coequal. The activists must work as coinvestigators on advocacy research projects. The *principle of parity* is based not so much on democratic values, but on the fact that the activist knows the community and its needs, which is essential for meaningful advocacy research. Further, it is through parity that the research and data utilization skills are most effectively conveyed. It is intended that through collaboration the activist becomes a better producer and consumer of research results.

Success in collaboration is also enhanced by *community control of research operations*. Community representatives must determine if a specific research project and its related methods are appropriate to community needs. Community control implies an informed and involved constituency. Community control also implies a substantial amount of reformulation of the research effort during implementation.

The effectiveness of research collaboration is enhanced by wide sharing of the research effort. The sharing of effort helps insure that research will be useful to the community and its action plans. Sharing also increases the research skills of the community.

The recipients of research results are the activists and the community members. Dissemination of results through traditional academic channels is a secondary consideration. The primary function of the research effort in collaborative terms is the furtherance of the developmental and political goals of the community. Communication of research results outside the community can only be done if it is in the interests of the community. Review of research results by community activists prior to dissemination in public contexts is advisable.

A major factor relating to the success of the collaborative research effort is the extent to which the research is an expression of community goals. Thus, real collaboration is only possible where there is substantial ideological sharing and agreement between anthropologist and activist. The quality of the collaboration is evaluated through analysis of its positive impact on the community, not its impact on the discipline of anthropology.

Community advocacy researchers are above all parsimonious. They must be able to identify research goals in such a way as to allow quick satisfaction of community informational needs. This means that research techniques must be time-effective. The community advocacy anthropologist should be a master of the "quick and dirty" study. This is not to disparage the approach, but it does recognize that theoretical elegance and justification back to the theoretical literature, which do not serve the goals of the community, are viewed as unproductive in community advocacy. Community advocacy research makes use of various techniques that contribute time economies. These include large research teams, highly focused research instruments, and clear conceptualizations of research purposes. Consistent with both time-effectiveness and the basic ideology of community advocacy is direct community participation in the research effort. In fact, most instructional activities in community advocacy relate to making community members into competent researchers. The developers of the community advocacy approach have clearly conceptualized the contrast between applied and theoretical research, and have through their efforts made a significant contribution to the development of anthropological methodology.

COMMUNITY ADVOCACY PROCESS

In an article dealing with the Chicago project, Schensul identifies an idealized conception of the action research process. The article, entitled "Action Research: The Applied Anthropologist in a Community Mental Health Program" (Schensul 1973), indicates nine steps that are thought to be part of the action research process. The following discussion is based on that article.

The Nine Steps

I. *Development of Rapport and Credibility of Applied Research*. The process is based on rather intimate involvement of the researcher in the life of the community. He or she is advised to live in the community and is thought to have greater potential for success if he or she works in close conjunction with community activists.

Traditional anthropological fieldwork approaches are very useful for developing working relationships and rapport. Fieldwork also serves to develop in the researcher an operational understanding of the total setting of a problem. Feedback of research results is important early in the process because this clarifies the researcher's role and "demonstrates to community people that the information gathered can be of value to their action programs" (Schensul 1973:112).

II. *The Identification of Significant, Indigenous, Action Programs*. The participant-observer, anthropologist-as-advocate attempts to establish a preliminary understanding of community priorities as they are related to the organization of existing and potential programs. This understanding will provide a basis for decisions that the anthropologist must make concerning involvement. The involvement process is, of course, based on some value-explicit decisions. Schensul notes:

Unlike the traditional fieldworker, the researcher's own value system plays an important part in the kind of action he will seek to facilitate. Rather than avoid this issue, the researcher must balance the values and attitudes of the people in the community with his own ways of looking at the world before he commits himself to any program (Schensul 1973:113).

In these settings it is often difficult to resist pressures. Because of this, the anthropologist may not be able to plan and control the nature of his or her involvement to any great extent. Pressures from the discipline are unimportant. As Schensul notes, "localized action has become the prime molder of our research operations and goals" (1973:113).

III. *The Negotiation of Cooperative and Reciprocal Relationships between the Applied Researchers and the Action People*. This process is most successful when the potential contribution of research to the community is quite well understood. Associated with this is the need for a clear identification of the motives of the researcher. The researchers and activists must both participate in the negotiation process. This process is calculated to produce a clear indication of the communities research needs. Additionally, the process, which increases community sensitivity toward the utility of research, can result in increased access to information in the community on the part of the researchers.

IV. *Initial Participation in Specific Action Programs*. This step often results in the collection of case study material relevant to specific programs. The researcher should stress rapport development and program assessment in this period. Baseline data is also collected, which is useful for long-term program evaluation.

V. *The Identification of Specific Informational Needs of the Action People*. Schensul makes a recommendation concerning this part of the process: "We have found that research results have a higher probability of being useful when people in the community who are involved in programs play an important role in the development of research concepts and strategies, and when community and program people help in the collection and analysis of data" (Schensul 1973:114).

VI. *Meeting the Needs of Long-Range Research Plans*. In addition to meeting the short-term informational needs of the community, the community advocacy anthropologist should develop a set of long-term research goals. These goals are more closely identified with the type of operations typical of the theoretical anthropologist, yet these long-term operations are also important to the goals of the community. Through these efforts the researchers create a data base that may meet the short-term informational needs of the community. Short research projects often serve as practice for the long-term research projects.

VII. *Formalized Research and Data Collection Operations*. As the process continues less reliance is placed on the informal research strategies, such as participant-observation and key informant interviewing. As specific informational needs are identified, research operations become more structured and formal. As community members come to participate in the research effort, the process becomes more highly structured.

VIII. *Analysis of Data*. Analysis techniques must be time-effective. This is a crucial attribute of the process. Schensul notes:

Unlike more academically based research, the time within which research results are produced is vitally related to their usefulness. The "involvement in the action" strategy requires the development of procedures for the rapid analysis of data utilizing simple and easily manipulated techniques. At the same time, more sophisticated techniques are used to serve less pressing action needs as well as the long-term research goals. (1973:116)

IX. *Data Dissemination, Evaluation, and Interpretation*. The results of the research are rapidly disseminated. If the information is not effectively communicated, even the most "significant" results will not have significant impact on the situation. The researcher can increase communication effectiveness by increasing the number of media of presentation. Results suggest that the least effective means of communicating is the typical technical report. An anthropologist who is concerned with communicating with his clients should use a variety of presentation techniques. It is suggested that the anthropologist be an aggressive and innovative communicator. The dissemination process is thought to influence the outcome of the process significantly, in that "disseminating data to community groups allows criticism, evaluation and assessment of the results to be rapidly fed back to the researcher" (Schensul 1973:116). The results of research, good or bad, are "exposed to scrutiny" in the community.

The two key components of the community advocacy process are research and communication. These two processes are used to achieve a number of objectives, which include:

Communicating community goals and understandings to persons and agencies outside the community.

Assisting community-oriented programs in being appropriate to the needs of the community.

Evaluating community-oriented service programs.

Evaluating community-run programs.

Decreasing divisiveness between community factions.

CASE STUDY: THE COMMUNITY MENTAL HEALTH PROGRAM AND EL BARRIO

The Community Mental Health Program was developed to serve the needs of a large population of blacks, Mexicans, and Middle Europeans on the lower

West Side of Chicago. The activities of the research team primarily focused on the Mexican portion of the population. The population resides in an east-west oriented corridor clearly marked by physical and ethnic boundaries. The corridor is characterized by substantial population movement. It extends six miles, east to west, and six to nine blocks, north to south.

The area served by the mental health program clearly manifests its culturally plural nature. This area, in the jargon of community mental health programs, is called the *catchment* area. The black portion of the population is segregated from the rest of the population by a railroad underpass. The Middle Europeans and the Mexicans live in close spatial association, each maintaining a distinctive physical presence in the community. The Middle Europeans are leaving the area, whereas the Mexican population is expanding. This shift commenced in the 1950s with the movement of Mexican families from other parts of Chicago. The flow of people into the corridor was augmented by immigrants from Mexico, who were largely concentrated in the eastern portion of the corridor. According to Schensul, this area "has taken on an overwhelming Mexican cultural orientation. Restaurants, taverns, groceries and supermarkets providing Mexican foods and services dominate the entrepreneurial activity" (1973:108). The intensity of Mexican residence makes it possible for persons to be employed in Spanish-speaking contexts. The resident Mexican population represents three types of individuals: immigrants from Mexico, and *Tejanos,* that is, Chicanos from Texas, as well as Chicago-born Chicanos.

The research team concentrated their efforts on the eastern section of the corridor, which had a higher concentration of individuals of Mexican origin.

Initial Program Context

The Community Mental Health Program was established to bring alternative mental health services to various portions of Chicago's population. Based on federal funds, the program was to provide psychiatric services to the ethnically diverse population of the catchment area. Program strategy was based on community "outpost" clinics in the black, Mexican, and Middle European neighborhoods. The clinics were to be staffed by a full complement of professionally trained staff, including psychiatrists, psychologists, psychiatric social workers, psychiatric nurses, and vocational counselors, who were to increase access of low-income populations to professional mental health care. From these centers patients were to be referred to the "parent" mental health center. The outposts were also intended to make available a wide range of community social services to people in the neighborhood. It was assumed that outpost staff would develop a more intense familiarity with the neighborhoods so that preventative programs could be more easily developed. Prior to the development of this community-focused approach the local ethnic population had made little use of the services of the supporting hospital.

The professionals of the centers came from the hospital staff. At the new centers they were faced with a different assortment of mental health problems. This change was related to substantial staff turnover. The services actually offered in the program were far from being innovative, and there was a relatively small number of Mexican participants. The staff of the outposts seemed frustrated and the potential client population seemed apathetic. An anthropologist was brought in. The anthropologist was to be involved in the community and to systematically tell the "community's story" for the benefit of the various staff members. Initially, Schensul interpreted the role as an ethnographer. He was to collect data that would lead to improved program structures and new treatment styles, and to provide data about the community to program administrators.

The research team attempted to activate the more traditional role, but found that the community situation took them in another direction. Schensul found that it was possible to conceptualize the research task at hand, yet difficult to carry it out. One of the major difficulties seemed to be that program administrators had little understanding of what potential contribution the anthropologist would make to the program. As a result, no specific responsibilities were assigned. This situation was complicated by Schensul's lack of knowledge of the community itself. His previous research experience was among rural Minnesotans and Ugandans. Because of limited experiences, his initial inputs were limited to general statements about the nature of culture and cultural relativity. In addition, Schensul attempted to develop a set of research strategies that would serve the needs of the program. Schensul indicates that both research and instructional strategies were failures. He felt that new inputs did not provide the program staff with any useful or problem-solving information. The response was one of hostility. The staff, it should be noted, had had negative experiences with previous researchers.

Schensul felt that his efforts in activating the traditional role were consistently unsuccessful. He tried various strategies to improve his positive impact on the program, but nothing seemed to work.

The short-run adaptation to the situation was to spend more and more time in the community. The team's knowledge of the community increased as they had more time to follow their natural tendencies to discover the community. This both reduced stress and increased their skill and knowledge. Because their role was not well understood by the staff, their withdrawal from daily involvement in the program was not difficult. As their knowledge of the community increased, so did their "contacts." This tended to legitimize them in the eyes of program staff and they became increasingly free to participate in the affairs of the community.

The relationship between the community research unit and the community steadily improved. The unit was able to get involved in its first survey project, which involved identification of certain characteristics of the school population. The school project, which was developed in conjunction with school staff, was to provide information that would lead to improvements in parent–school communication. Specifically, the project intended to determine through parental interviews the nature of family social and economic life in a specific neighborhood and to discover the parents' attitudes toward the school. In addition, the research intended to determine the nature and attitudes of the teacher population in terms of teaching Mexican-American children, and to determine the basis of the students' responses toward the school situation. The research procedure used interviews, home visits, and student records applied to a random sample.

The research produced a number of interesting results that improved the researchers' understanding of the community. Through the survey they found that they had grossly underestimated the size of the Mexican-born population of the total Chicano population. The research indicated that the parents had strong preferences for bilingual and bicultural education. Although the research had little impact on school administrators, the researchers learned some lessons about effectively conveying data to program administrators.

The school survey was followed up with a similar study of a Catholic school that served the same neighborhood. The research found that the Catholic school families had lived in Chicago longer and were more bilingual. They also seemed better off socioeconomically and educationally. The Catholic school's administration offered the researchers greater opportunities to communicate to the parents. This included a session in which the researchers were allowed to address a meeting of the parents' association. The researchers used a number of different techniques, including hand-outs of summary tables, Spanish translation, overhead projections, and parental feedback. The parents were especially interested in the demographic aspects of the study.

For a number of reasons, the research did not have any significant impact on the community or the school. The researchers felt the schools were unresponsive to this type of research because of control from outside the community, nonindigenous staff, and little interest in orienting programs toward the community. The school research left the research team frustrated and dissatisfied.

The team's energies came to be directed at the research needs of a settlement house funded by the Presbyterian church that served one of the neighborhoods in the corridor. Preliminary research indicated that the settlement house played an important role in the community as a meeting place for various community groups. The research for the settlement house was to focus on the "block clubs" that the settlement house was attempting to develop in their service area. Relations with the settlement house were quite good, based on the interaction with persons at the center that occurred during the initial period of participant-observation. Without any specific goals in mind, the research team began negotiations with the staff of the settlement house to determine the nature of the research. The team was to interview residents and perform the necessary work to carry out a census survey. Significantly, the anthropologists were to be in contact with the block team leaders and residents in order to provide feedback of research results to decision makers.

The researchers assigned to each block were quickly drawn into the action of the block club development teams. The researchers assisted in getting community improvement petitions filled out, organizing community activities such as street dances and fiestas, and doing attitudinal research concerning community needs. The researchers also carefully documented residents' participation. The initial efforts improved researcher understanding of the community. This, coupled with the high-quality interpersonal relations that developed, did much to facilitate the application and development of the action research or community advocacy model.

As the research progressed there was a shift in emphasis from general, area-wide research for the purpose of generating basic demographic data to problem-focused, block-specific research. There were a number of issues examined. One block was faced with a problem characteristic of many American neighborhoods, a zoning change. The research team assisted in the collection of data that was useful in the resistance process. The team worked to communicate the nature of the threat to the community. They also documented the nature of the participation, which was useful for further projects. They were able to give group leaders some idea of the identity of the most effective community members. They found, for example, that the Mexican portion of the area was more predisposed to continued participation in action programs.

Initially, the group seemed successful in resisting the change. A large group attended the zoning commission meeting in which the key decision was to be made. Community opposition was strong and articulate, and the decision was deferred, temporarily. Unfortunately, the zoning change was approved at a meeting held by the zoning commission that was not announced in the community. Some months later the new construction took place. The anthropologists were somewhat disillusioned by this. In any case, it was a lesson in big-city politics.

The experience with the zoning project led to further decreases in the participation of the research team in the community mental health program. The team was no longer concerned about the utility of their efforts to the clinical staff. They were concerned with the research needs of community groups, and justified their approach in terms of the preventative component of the community mental health approach. At this point they "discovered" the advocacy anthropology approach. Although community mental health programming was intended primarily to provide mental health care directly to patients, a certain portion of resources could be allocated to alleviating community-based causes of mental health problems, such as bad schools or little economic opportunity.

The approach was successfully applied in a number of different contexts following the somewhat fortuitous "discovery" of the approach. A selection of these projects will be reviewed here. The projects selected were related to community needs and the developing data base of the research team. Additionally, the team came to be more and more tied to formally established community organizations. One of these organizations was ALAS (Alliance Latino-Americano para Adelante Social), which was one of the first and most active community action groups. ALAS dealt with a number of crucial issues that faced Chicanos nationally and locally. More specifically, this meant increasing the quality of bilingual and bicultural programming in the Chicago school system. They were especially interested in augmenting the Teaching English as a Second Language (TESL) program. The action research team supported the efforts of ALAS in this and other realms.

Commando Anthropology

Initially, involvement in the bilingual education issue took the form of an ALAS-organized "commando raid" to assess the quality of TESL programs in the schools of the area. With no forewarning, eleven separate research teams entered the schools of the community at precisely eleven o'clock in the morning. Each team was equipped with a data collection schedule. The teams attempted to identify the extent and quality of the TESL programs. The investigators discovered that TESL classes were limited in time and were often not held. Additionally, TESL classes were often run by untrained substitutes or non-Spanish-speaking teachers. The space allocated to the program was determined to be of low quality. The general conclusion was that the TESL program did not meet program guidelines.

The data derived from the process of "commando research" was organized and used to support the filing of a suit with the Illinois Civil Rights Commission. The "raid" showed that it was possible to do good research under severe time constraints, if speed was planned into the research project.

The Community Research Unit and El Centro de la Causa

The staff of the Eighteenth Street settlement house in the barrio had become increasingly concerned with the quality of recreational, social, and educational services that they offered. The situation had become critical because of the physical deterioration of existing community facilities. To improve the situation the settlement house staff attempted to develop a new youth program to deal with what the other social service agencies called "hard-core kids." These individuals were simply not welcome at the existing social service programs. The situation called for an alternative kind of facility. This alternative was to take form under the name of El Centro de la Causa. The key organizer was a street-worker who developed a following among local gang members.

The group found an old parochial school that was not fully used. With a group of volunteers the building was cleaned and renovated. A recreation program was organized and soon a group of Chicano students were able to offer some classes on various Chicano topics. Various local businessmen were able to make contributions. Some clinical services were also offered at the center. The center drew a number of new participants. As participation increased, so did the services offered.

El Centro began its first fund-raisers in 1971 with a community fiesta and carnival. Three years later, El Centro had a $400,000 budget. The staff had been successful in acquiring funds from outside the community. Their fund-raising success was related to their skill as well as the changing relationship between Chicanos and the federal government. In the case of El Centro, these grants took the form of a drug treatment program and a mental health para-professional training program, as well as various other education, youth and other social service programs. Increasingly, El Centro became a focal point for the political activism that was to sweep the Chicago Chicano community.

It was in conjunction with the program at El Centro that the community advocacy was most effective. The research team's activities grew, expanded, and increased in complexity. Their relationship with El Centro was multifaceted in that it included a wide range of activities and responsibilities.

While the ultimate goals of community advocacy must be in the hands of the community leaders, the researcher has to be involved in all phases of the action. This implies that the community advocacy anthropologist activates a number of roles beyond that of researcher. El Centro project made use of the anthropologists' research skills very early, but soon these activities were supplemented. Members of the research team participated with activists in strategy planning and policy making. The team was also given the responsibility of providing historic documentation, and a major role in "facilitating communication with outside groups" (Schensul 1974:205).

The team's involvement included "identifying potential sources of funding, participating in meetings with representatives of a number of institutions and funding agencies, using research data on health, mental health, drugs, drug use, youth organizations, community structure, and demography in reports and discussions in which the community 'case' was presented," and "collaborating with community activists in writing formal proposals for funds to private institutions and federal funding sources" (Schensul 1974:206). Through the research team, El Centro was better able to present its case to relevant agencies. The developing data base of the center collected by the team was useful in preparing proposals, which served to legitimate the presence of the research team.

The data that proved useful was quite variable, including such things as ethnographic studies of Mexican folk medicine found in the literature, data relating to evaluation of local health care facilities, and information dealing with sources of additional grant funds. Although research skills are important, they can only be made useful through an ability to communicate. The researchers were the means by which the community could express its ideas and plans. "The applied researcher must demonstrate the ability not only to describe the research results, but also to write effectively and economically about program structures, treatment plans, training schedules and other components of community programs" (Schensul 1974:206).

Increasingly, the team was drawn into all aspects of program operations and management. This related to a general tendency of the researchers and the activists to become more and more alike. The researchers were taught action skills in organization of the community and bureaucratic manipulation. The activists learned to be competent researchers. Ultimately, they could develop research protocols and analyze research data.

As the program at El Centro increased in complexity, the team was called upon to carry out more focused research. Often a staff member would communicate a specific research problem in conjunction with a program development need.

For example, the youth service staff decided that, before developing a program that would be based on their own preconceptions, they needed a survey of youth attitudes and behavior. Together, we constructed an extensive questionnaire that was eventually administered to over eight hundred youngsters (aged thirteen to fifteen) in the community. (Schensul 1974:206)

Similar activities developed in association with a program of treatment for Chicano drug addicts.

Research skills increased and the team developed a good workable understanding of the advocacy process. The team discovered that a key to research success was to negotiate research methodology with staff and activists. According to Schensul, negotiation ''can increase the relevance of the information collected, make activists more receptive to the resulting data and create more sensitivity to the inevitable problems and delays in data collection'' (1974:207). The team also attempted to carry out research both in terms of long-term and short-term needs so that each short-term project would result in an increase of their data base. The effectiveness of this approach increased as the team learned how to better predict future information needs. The team discovered that the well-designed, methodologically clean project often did not meet the needs of the situation. The results were often not available at the correct time. At times, in order to be effective, the researchers had to go into a ''quick and dirty'' mode.

As the relationship between the researchers and the El Centro activists improved, there came to be an increasing focus on internal research activities. This grew out of a need to institutionalize the research effort of El Centro. In response to this, an internal research unit was created. The unit engaged in a number of significant research problems.

The team continued to work through El Centro. Their efforts became directed at a wide range of increasingly concrete action programs. Each was addressed to specific needs identified within the Chicano community. These programs were diverse and included drug treatment, community education, and mental health training.

SUMMARY

Advocacy anthropology represents a set of anthropological activities that are well adapted to working in direct relationship with community organizations as opposed to working through an intervening agency. The role of the advocacy anthropologist is limited to the expressed needs of the community, usually expressed through its leadership. Usually this involves work as aa researcher, research trainer, and proposal writer. Advocacy relations do not usually call for the anthropologist to be directly involved in change-produciing decision making. The advocacy anthropologist is, as Schensul says, involved in the action, but as an auxiliary to community leadership. The advocacy portion of the name of this approach simply means using one's research skills to support the attainment of community goals.

This simple, but very useful idea can be expressed in many ways. The case presented here represents a good model of the advocacy role. It is clear that the advocacy anthropologist must be able to reduce somewhat his or her use of the discipline as a reference group. The reference group is the community. Professional achievement is measured in reference to the community's achievement of its goals. This is not an easy task, but when it occurs it can yield powerful satisfactions on the part of the anthropologist, while increasing community capabilities. Although there are a number of skills that are useful to the advocacy anthropologist, proposal writing often is crucial. This can both help achieve the goals of the community, and provide the means for the continued involvement of the anthropologist.

FURTHER READING

Stull, Donald D., and Jean J. Schensul, eds. 1987. *Collaborative Research and Social Change: Applied Anthropology in Action*. Boulder, Colo.: Westview Press.

Contains good documentation on a number of advocacy projects.

Weber, George H., and George J. McCall, eds. 1978. *Social Scientists as Advocates: Views from the Applied Disciplines*. Beverly Hills, Calif.: Sage Publications.

Contains chapters that discuss advocacy from the standpoint of social work, law, psychology, urban planning, sociology, and anthropology. The chapter on anthropology was written by Stephen L. Schensul and Jean J. Schensul. Their article includes reference to the Chicago work discussed here, and the use of the same technique in Hartford, Connecticut.

8

Cultural Brokerage

Hazel Weidman first described in 1973 (Weidman 1973) her conception of culture broker applied in the "health care context" (Lefley and Bestman 1984:120). Her idea was based on a concept developed originally by Eric Wolf to account for those persons who served as links between two cultural systems (1956), but was modified and extended by Weidman to serve socially useful purposes.

Wolf's view of culture broker was conceptualized in the context of his research into the linkage between peasant communities and national life in Mexico. Wolf suggested that "we can achieve greater synthesis in the study of complex societies by focusing our attention on the relationships between different groups operating on different levels of the society, rather than on any one of its isolated segments" (1956:1074). The broker provides the individual link between sociocultural units. In the case of Mexico, the units are peasant communities and various national systems. Specifically, Wolf suggested that the study of brokers would be a useful first step in studying the integration of large-scale, culturally plural systems. Brokers are important because

they stand guard over the crucial junctures or synapses of relationships which connect the local system to the larger whole. Their basic function is to relate community-oriented individuals who want to stabilize or improve their life chances, but who lack economic security and political connections, with nation-oriented individuals who operate primarily in terms of complex cultural forms standardized as national institutions, but whose success in these operations depends on the size and strength of their personal following. (Wolf 1956:1075-76)

It is this concept of role that forms the basis of the cultural brokerage model. The concept of the broker role is supplemented by other ideas that are essential to the approach. Cultural brokerage is an intervention strategy of research, training, and service that links persons of two or more coequal socio-cultural systems through an individual, with the primary goals of making community service programs more open and responsive to the needs of the community, and of improving the community's access to resources. While other types of intervention affect the community in substantial ways, cultural brokerage substantially affects the service providers. In other words the focus of change processes are the agencies themselves. The cultural brokerage approach to intervention is a way of restructuring cultural relationships not so much to resolve cross-cultural conflicts, but to prevent them.

DEVELOPMENT OF THE APPROACH

The development of the approach started with a research project focused on "health systems, beliefs and behavior" begun in 1971 by the Department of Psychiatry of a large, county-owned general hospital in Miami, Florida (Lefley and Bestman 1984:120). Called the Health Ecology Project, this research made use of a variety of different data collection techniques, including in-depth interviewing, survey questionnaires, a symptoms and conditions list, values scale, and health calendar (Lefley and Bestman 1984:121). These and other techniques were used in collecting data from a sample of five hundred families over a period of time. This data was supplemented by interviews with "folk healers and their patients from each ethnic group" (Lefley and Bestman 1984:121). As a result of the research, the team thoroughly documented the health culture of a major segment of the service area of the hospital.

The hospital's service area was ethnically diverse. Within its area it was possible to find Cubans, Puerto Ricans, black Americans, Haitians, and Bahamians, as well as whites. In its massive scale and impersonal nature the hospital was similar to most large, public, and urban hospitals. Weidman notes: "Even if the services are provided in a sympathetic and compassionate manner, they are seldom appropriate in the cultural sense. Examined largely by white middle-class health professionals or professionals in training, the patients were evaluated and labeled according to white middle-class criteria, and treated with middle-class therapies" (Sussex and Weidman 1975:307).

The psychiatric patients were often critically ill. This factor and the heavy case load caused the care providers to emphasize control of inappropriate behavior through drugs. Unresponsive patients were transferred to a state hospital for custodial care. Although the program was under review, no major improvements were forthcoming. It was thought that a major limitation to more effective service was lack of understanding of the cultural differences among the ethnic communities in Miami.

The research field staff had fostered good working relationships with community members as part of the community research effort. Through the efforts of community research assistants who were the same ethnic background as community members, the demand for improved mental health care services increased. The practice of brokerage grew out of these relationships.

Using ideas that developed out of the research and the interaction with community members, the cultural brokerage approach to mental health care delivery was formally implemented in the Miami Community Mental Health Program, funded in 1974 by the National Institute of Mental Health, under provisions of the Community Health Centers Act of 1963 (Lefley and Bestman 1984:122).

KEY CONCEPTS

According to Weidman, there are five concepts that are essential to understanding the cultural brokerage approach (1975:312). These concepts are culture, health culture, coculture, culture broker, and culture mediation. The conceptualization used for culture is "the learned patterns of thought and behavior characteristic of a population or society—a society's repertory of behavioral, cognitive, and emotional patterns" (Harris, in Weidman 1975:312). The project was very strongly committed to a cultural relativism position. The concepts used in the project provided a means by which project personnel could think about the cultural complexity in the community without necessarily engaging in an evaluative comparison of the alternative systems. This represents an important conceptual innovation that is an essential aspect of Weidman's transcultural perspective. This perspective places the anthropologist at the margins of the cultures of both the health care providers and the community (Weidman 1982:203; 1979:86).

The project's conceptual structure is quite well developed and internally consistent, and rather more explicit than some of the other conceptual schemes discussed in this text. Importantly, the health care providers were able to respond well to these ideas because they made sense to them.

Coupled with the culture concept is the health culture concept, which is defined as "all the phenomena associated with the maintenance of well-being and problems of sickness with which people cope in traditional ways within their own social networks" (Weidman 1975:313). Health culture encompasses both "the cognitive and social-system aspects of folk therapies." Cognitively, this includes health values and beliefs, guides for health action and the relevant folk theories of "health maintenance, disease etiology, prevention, diagnosis, treatment and cure" (Weidman 1975:313). The social component of the concept deals with the structural-functional aspects of health-related social statuses and roles.

An essential aspect of cultural brokerage is the concept of *coculture*. Coculture is a conceptual substitute for "subculture," though it is different in very important ways. Most importantly it stresses parity. Cocultures are equal in value to their participants. As expressed by Weidman, the concept of subculture implies that one group is subordinate to another. The role of the culture broker is introduced to accommodate the link between cocultures. The role concept is appropriate to the "parity of cultures" notion. To quote Weidman, "The label seems applicable whenever there is need to recognize the existence of separate cultural or subcultural systems and to acknowledge a particular person's role in establishing useful links between them" (1975:313). The parity idea, and the responsiveness, respect, and support that it produces, contributes to the acceptance of the approach to community members. Parity does not mean that the cultures are the same. As Weidman states, use of the concept results in the juxtaposition of cultural systems, which "provides the basis for comparison of congruent and non-congruent elements in them" (1982:210). This perspective is consistent with the comparative method of anthropology as a research science.

The concept, as noted above, developed out of research and teaching activities at the hospital and was ultimately expressed in project organization; that is, persons were hired as culture brokers. The culture broker's linkage activities occurred in two frameworks. The broker served to link the community health culture and the orthodox health care system so as to facilitate the provision of orthodox care that is "coculturally informed." The second arena for linkages was between the community and the "broader social, economic, and political system" (Weidman 1975:314).

The process of linkage is labeled *culture mediation*. In practical terms this means the provision of culturally appropriate services. Effective mediation facilitates better interaction between representatives of the cocultures represented in a community. The basis for cultural mediation is the culture broker's knowledge of the involved cultures. This requires a strong commitment to synthesis of various health traditions as well as various scientific disciplines. The process of mediation will be discussed below.

THE CULTURE BROKER'S ROLE

The culture broker is to be viewed as an important player in the interactions between two parts of a larger cultural system. In the scientific literature on brokerage, the broker links traditional and modern, national and local, or European and "native" (Fallers 1955; Wolf 1956; Geertz 1959). In the Miami project these distinctions were rejected to the extent that they implied cultural dominance.

The broker role as conceptualized by Wolf attributes a certain self-interested quality to the role. Wolf notes:

They must serve some of the interests of groups operating on both the community and national level, and they must cope with the conflicts raised by the collision of these interests. They cannot settle them, since by doing so they would abolish their own usefulness to others. Thus they often act as buffers between groups, maintaining the tensions which provide the dynamic of their actions. (1956:1076)

This component of meaning associated with Wolf's conception was not part of the use of the concept in the Miami project. Weidman and the others stressed the buffering and mediation that serves to facilitate harmony and equality between cocultures, while they recognized that their approach restructured community services. Their conception of the broker role included a purposive and intentional aspect that does not appear in the original conception (Weidman 1985).

The application of the cultural brokerage approach is motivated by the need to increase accessibility of basic medical care in the United States. There exists in every complex society a range of alternative health care systems that typically are in competition. Different viable health cultures are found throughout the world in isolated rural areas and in dense urban settlements. In one way or another, the therapeutic practices that are part of these health cultures are in competition with each other and with modern medicine.

The position of Western medicine in this competition is unique. As Weidman notes, "Since it emerged in the Western world, that social institution called 'scientific' or 'modern' medicine has been sanctioned internationally as being ultimately responsible for the health of national populations" (1979:85). In the total scope of human history this is a relatively recent event. Throughout the world much health maintenance behavior is based not on "scientific" medicine but on traditional health culture. According to Weidman, "Our field of inquiry is a culturally plural one. In every urban center in the world today we must recognize a 'pluriverse' of health cultures, one of which is our own or that of Western medicine, all of which are interacting or inhibiting from interacting on the basis of reciprocal images of each other" (Weidman 1973:8).

In these settings the culture broker links alternative systems that are equivalent. This, of course, relates to the discussion of coculture indicated above. The relationship between the systems is thought to be symmetrical. The parity concept is what distinguishes the culture broker from the more common outreach worker. This more typical role is consistent with the view that Western medicine is dominant and the cultural alternatives are to be aided, displaced, or changed, because of their impotence. Typical outreach workers are usually agents for the dominant culture and often work in an inherently compromised political position.

Because the culture brokers are thought to operate between two systems at parity, the broker's function calls for substantial knowledge of the two systems involved. Therefore brokerage requires ongoing research. In the prototype project in Miami, there was an extensive research effort. The Health Ecology Research Project, briefly described above, attempted to obtain data on the health culture of the different ethnic groups of the area. Some of the areas researched included patterns of symptoms, categories of illness, folk etiologies, nature of self-care, health care use patterns, healer roles, referral patterns, value orientations, and world view (Weidman 1982:209). It is important to remember that the research often compared the traditional and orthodox health cultures, and that it was ongoing.

PROCESS OF CULTURAL BROKERAGE

The process of cultural brokerage includes the establishment and maintenance of a system of interaction, mutual support, and communication between cocultures expressed through the culture broker's role. The process of mediation protects the cultural values of the involved ethnic groups. It is within this framework that change occurs. Change is toward increased cultural appropriateness, access to resources, better health, and more compliance with medical regimens (Weidman 1985). The potential for change goes much beyond health; social and economic conditions may also be positively influenced. The basic process can include a variety of strategies that benefit community members, including many of the strategies discussed in this section of the book, such as advocacy.

Phases of the Process

I. The compilation of research data on the health culture of all the cocultures in the community. This includes both the traditional and orthodox health systems.

II. The training of brokers in aspects of community life. Culture brokers are usually members of the ethnic group being related to, as well as being trained social scientists. The primary reference in the training is health culture. The training may involve participation in the initial research.

III. Early activation of the culture broker role usually involves collaboration with institutionally based health care personnel to assist in providing culturally more appropriate health care. In addition, the broker fosters referral relationships with traditional health practitioners and trains community people to assume broker roles. These activities are associated with continual involvement in research to increase the project's data base and support community action projects.

IV. The brokerage efforts cause change in both the community and the orthodox health care system. These include increased knowledge of the culture of the community on the part of the health care providers, and improvements in the community's resource base. Overall improvements in mental health levels occur.

Prior to implementation of a culture broker program, interactions between community members and the health care facility are based largely on decisions of the individual community member. There are no outreach or other efforts at linkage. The institution does not possess any significant knowledge about the patient's way of life. This way of life is conceptualized in subcultural terms, that is, inevitably changing to the pattern of the institutional or dominant culture. The little information that is gathered about patient subculture is obtained on a nonsystematic, *ad hoc* basis. Encounters between health care institutions and the community are almost always between therapist and "sick person." That is, the interactions are single-stranded.

In the early phase of implementation a new formal role is created, the culture broker, and the culture parity concept is asserted. The parity concept is an ideological commitment to be operationalized programmatically. Parity may not be manifested in the relationship between the two cocultures in the larger political realm. Later, the culture broker comes to be more throughly integrated into both cocultures, serving as a knowledge resource for both.

CASE STUDY: THE MIAMI COMMUNITY MENTAL HEALTH PROGRAM

The Miami Community Mental Health Program was designed to serve the mental health needs of a large, ethnically diverse area of Miami (Lefley and Bestman 1984:122). The service area, so-called catchment area IV, was a low-income area inhabited by five major ethnic groups: Bahamians, Cubans, Haitians, Puerto Ricans, and American blacks. Ethnically diverse, this population exhibited many of the stresses typical of low-income, inner-city populations. The area had higher rates of crime and unemployment and much substandard housing. Program designers felt that the standard ''medical model'' approach would be inadequate for achieving mental health improvements. It was felt that the traditional approach would not produce culturally appropriate health care. The diversity of causes of ill health and the cultural complexities of the community would not yield to the orthodox treatments available in the hospital.

The Miami model, as suggested above, was built upon a thorough community research base provided by the research component of the Miami Health Ecology Project, which had been established earlier. The primary finding of the project was that each of the five ethnic groups had distinctive knowledge and behavior vis-à-vis mental health. The diverse conditions under which they lived produced culturally patterned health conditions, including ''culture-bound syndromes not recognized by the orthodox medical profession'' (Lefley 1975:317). In the community, ''alternative healing modalities were widely used, often in conjunction with orthodox medical treatment'' (Lefley and Bestman 1984:121). ''Differential perceptions of causation and remediation of illness'' were identified (Lefley and Bestman 1984:121). The most fundamental and far-reaching conclusion from the research was that ''culturally specific therapeutic interventions were needed to deal with ethnic variables in these diverse groups'' (Lefley 1975:317). Research results were documented in publications and ''ethnic libraries'' for use of the project (Lefley and Bestman 1984:121).

Basing their approach on the existing mental health services of the hospital, the project attempted to develop a culturally appropriate approach. The county-owned hospital was a 1,250-bed general hospital serving an area of Dade County populated by 200,000 persons. This economically depressed area manifested significant numbers of mental health problems. Although the hospital seemed to be in the middle of things it was somewhat inaccessible to the residents of the catchment area. Public transportation, for example, was inadequate for getting patients to the clinic. The service was impersonal and culturally inappropriate. The diagnosis procedure was based on white, middle-class conceptions of symptoms. Patients tended to come to the hospital only when they were desperate— when ''they have been stabbed or shot or otherwise injured, when they are critically ill, or when they are so behaviorally deranged that the police deliver them to our doorstep'' (Sussex and Weidman 1975:307).

The hospital's psychiatric service had operated as a disease-focused mental health service that viewed health in terms of the medical model (Fabrega 1972). That is, care was based on

the assumption that a given *disease* should be treated in a certain generally accepted way because it always has the same cause, . . . and always responds (or should respond) to a particular type of treatment. So the standard nomenclature is used, the usual signs and symptoms of the mental-status examination are duly elicited and recorded, and the customary therapeutic procedures are prescribed. (Sussex and Weidman 1975:307)

The psychiatric service had a rather high case load, largely derived from a busy emergency service. The goal of the service was behavior control, mostly through the use of drugs. Patients who did not respond were typically sent to a state hospital. Case management was made more difficult by limitations in after-care treatment.

In 1974, the action component of the project was funded. The proposal emerged directly from the work of five field teams that were ethnically identical to the different communities. As is often the case with ethnographic fieldwork, the teams developed good rapport with community members. Although not necessarily intended, the teams' efforts resulted in increased sensitivity to the possibilities for improved mental health services for the community. As an outgrowth of this, there was increased demand for appropriate services. The funding for action allowed the placement of the five ethnically specific teams. The five teams were ultimately supplemented by teams that dealt with the substantial elderly Anglo-American and black populations. The efforts of each of the ethnically specific teams were supplemented by a community advisory board that assisted in defining program goals and team personnel recruitment. Each team was directed by a social scientist with training, in most cases, to the Ph.D. level. These directors were the culture brokers referred to as the key component of this approach.

One important role of the culture broker was to serve as a bridge between the community and the hospital. This effort included acting as liaison between community leaders and the hospital. There was to be a special effort at serving as a link between the different kinds of physicians and the community members who faced particular health problems. The broker was to serve as both a researcher and a teacher in the program. As teachers, the brokers were engaged in augmenting courses in various hospital training programs, instructing in community orientation classes for hospital staff, consulting on the health problems of individual patients, and assisting students on projects. Further, the culture brokers were to act as trainers of community representatives in various areas, as well as training various health professionals as culture brokers. For an excellent review of the development of the role of the anthropologist in clinical settings in Miami, one should read Weidman's "Research Strategies, Structural Alterations and Clinically Applied Anthropology" (1982).

The other important aspect of the broker role developed in the community, where they organized community groups with social action goals. These efforts often started with assessments of community needs, which were used for community planning and proposal development. The brokers could be thought of as social change catalysts that acted primarily through their research. Research was done in support of many different goals that the community related to mental health problems. These included research in support of such things as day care centers, hot lunch programs, and changes in housing policy. These community involvements also included acting as resource specialists to bring consumers together with service providers in Miami. This helped community members to act when agencies were lacking or inadequate (Lefley 1975:318).

Each ethnic community had its own pattern of program development, although each team provided "essential psychiatric services" (Lefley and Bestman 1984:127). Much of the content of program activities was based on advice given by community advisory boards. Some of the early efforts included research done on behalf of community groups (Lefley and Bestman 1984:127). It is important to remember that the teams functioned both in the hospital and community frameworks.

Teams at Work: Some Examples

The black American mental health unit worked in two communities within catchment area IV. These were Model City, with eighty thousand persons, and Overtown, described as a "transitional" community of fifteen thousand blacks. Each posed a different and complex set of problems. Overtown was fragmented by ill-planned urban renewal and freeway development, although it had a history of community life. The community had lost much of its organizational coherence. Overtown came to be the focus of the program efforts. The black American mental health unit attempted to achieve program objectives by "the creation of a comprehensive services center," and "the development of a dynamic communication network system for educating, informing and organizing the Overtown residents" (Carroo 1975:321).

Based on needs assessment research carried out with a sample of community residents, the mental health unit focused upon housing, education, employment, mental problems, and after care (Carroo 1975:321). The unit worked toward collaborating with existing social service agencies in order to create a comprehensive service center in the midst of the community. This cooperative effort came to be the focus of much of the unit's efforts. The center offered a range of important services, such as a mini-clinic that offered both clinical and social services. There was an emphasis on "the principles of self-help and collective action" (Carroo 1975:322). The unit, in conjunction with a nearby community college, offered community workshops on aspects of social service. The clinic also was involved in "building and strengthening support systems for high-risk groups" (Carroo 1975:322). This included work with the school system. The cultural specialist worked with school counselors in group therapy sessions, and also facilitated the development of a tutoring program to treat one of the causes of stress among students.

Housing problems were addressed through an arrangement with a tenant organization and a local poverty law group. In this context the mental health unit determined community sentiments through survey research, developed a community forum for review of the housing problem, and contacted individuals in the community who were having significant difficulty. In addition to these efforts, the mental health unit also served to coordinate and focus many of the diverse community groups. This took a special effort because of the diverse and transitional nature of the Overtown community.

The Cuban unit began operations in early 1974, in the Edison-Little River region of Miami. Initial mental health unit operations were research-focused. Over 620 families were interviewed to assess needs and to begin to determine action goals in Edison-Little River. The research indicated some of the needs of the low-income and elderly population. Out of this initial research certain preliminary goals were identified. These included a shopping assistance and hot lunch program for elderly residents. The need for day care and after-school care was also identified in the community. Shortly all these problem areas were addressed programmatically. Soon the mental health unit had geared up a shopping assistance program for elderly residents of Edison-Little River. Somewhat later, hot lunch and day care programs were established. Parallel to these action projects, the team offered social services to an increasing number of people.

During the early stages of the Edison-Little River work, the Cuban mental health unit went through substantial in-service training. This training was directed toward improving the team's knowledge of social research techniques, Cuban culture and its relevance to service delivery, social services available in the community, and basic techniques for dealing with mental health problems at an individual level.

The Edison-Little River project seemed to be good training for the work in the section of catchment area IV called Allapattah, with its very heavy concentration of Cubans. The southern half of Allapattah is about 68 percent Cuban (Sandoval and Tozo 1975:329). The Allapattah community was marked by a very limited sense of identity.

The Allapattah Cuban community had very few appropriate programs available to meet its substantial social, health, and mental health needs. Many Cuban-focused services could only be obtained by going to nearby Little Havana. This included public schooling and Cuban *clinicas* for outpatient health care. According to Sandoval and Tozo, the Cuban population was characterized by substantial intergenerational conflict caused by the fact that the old and the young Cubans were raised in two different cultural settings. Further, it was also felt that the Cuban extended family had weakened (Sandoval and Tozo 1975:329).

In Allapattah, the Cuban unit carried through a basic demographic census. This was coupled with an attempt to contact various leaders in the community. Through this procedure, the team came to be "aware of the lack of cohesiveness within the different ethnic groups in the community, the lack of power structure within the Cuban community, and the lack of communication between the various ethnic groups'' (Sandoval and Tozo 1975:330). The unit was also very much committed to improving the capacity of the community to assess its own needs. Much of the strategy was oriented toward increasing community awareness in Allapattah. This awareness was built upon the growing data base on the community that was developed by the members of the team.

This effort resulted in the development of a community social service agency called La Norguesera. The agency delivered a substantial range of services, including food stamps, legal counseling, and medical services. These general efforts were coupled with a specific program for mental health treatment that resulted in the establishment of a mini-clinic. This operation was similar to the project developed in Overtown. La Norguesera mini-clinic staff found cases and provided initial treatment and follow-up within a Cuban neighborhood. People in need of services could drop in for recreational, social, and therapeutic activities. All this was oriented toward rehabilitation in the community itself rather than outside (Sandoval and Tozo 1975:331).

The mini-clinic's mental health services were designed to be culturally appropriate. All staff members were Cuban and, of course, the research team continually provided relevant data. Action was taken that accommodated Cuban culture at a number of different levels.

A somewhat different orientation was used by the Puerto Rican mental health unit (Bryant 1975). The team focused its efforts on Wynwood, a section of the catchment area that had the highest concentration of the twenty thousand Puerto Ricans living in Dade County. It manifested many of the same difficulties and stresses characteristic of the other catchment areas: "low incomes, high rents, a plethora of health and mental health problems, and an underutilization of health, mental health and social-service agencies'' (Bryant 1975:333). The Puerto Rican team's approach was conceptually related to that of the other units. Led by an anthropologist, the team was committed to "building support networks" in the community, facilitating "indigenous social action and community development," and acting as "systems linkers or culture brokers between psychiatric personnel and Puerto Rican patients in the Psychiatric Institute" (Bryant 1975:333). Further, the strategy called for participation in the hospital's training programs for mental health staff who were to work with the Puerto Rican community, and the provision of research data and other information about the community to social service agencies (Bryant 1975:333).

The Puerto Rican mental health unit used the culture brokerage approach in two ways. The unit attempted to make significant use of community mental health resources such as the extended family, churches, clubs, and traditional curers (*espiritistas*), thus bringing community resources directly to bear on specific patient needs. The brokerage efforts were also directed at creating new community organizations to help meet community needs. Often this meant initiation of an organizational effort and the subsequent reduction in involvement as community members took on the responsibility. These efforts included recreation and athletic programs, and activities more clearly related to mental health programs.

The cultural brokerage program started by dividing the Wynwood community into four areas, each with one or two neighborhood workers. Area workers were initially involved in researching the basic community characteristics and needs. The field staff continued to work as community information sources. As research questions came up, these workers collected appropriate information. The workers also did basic mental health assistance work with afflicted individuals in their neighborhoods. Bryant notes: "By working on a neighborhood basis in all activities—a consistent and comprehensive contact is maintained between community and [the] program" (1975:335).

The linkage effort was further served by having the workers regularly participate in community organizations. This linkage was replicated at the leadership level; the leader of the Puerto Rican mental health unit met with leaders of other programs regularly in order to facilitate coordination of program efforts. This led to the development of an incipient coalition between the program and community activists.

The mental health unit served the community's leadership in three ways. The team provided community leaders with data on various community problems and the use of social services outside the community. One of the projects that illustrates this activity was a community survey that helped identify, in cooperation with a local community action group, housing needs and problems in the community. This information was used in dealing with the Department of Housing and Urban Development. The team also assisted community leaders in the proposal development that would lead to more community-based programs. In one case the mental health team member was able to facilitate the development of day care facilities in the community. The third aspect of the team's community collaboration strategy was the evaluation of existing community programs at the request of the community leadership.

The Puerto Rican mental health unit also worked to assist agencies serving the community with their research needs. One agency was concerned about the perceived underutilization of their services by the Puerto Rican community.

SUMMARY

Cultural brokerage is a useful strategy for applying anthropological knowledge to a wide range of contexts. It, quite obviously, has had its utility demonstrated in health and medical programs. It has begun to be used in other settings as well. Its primary purpose is linking two culturally different groups with the intent of increasing cultural appropriateness of services and increasing the resource base of the community.

The ideological program of cultural brokerage is quite simple. It is the programmatic operationalization of intercultural parity. It does not have the elaborate values-in-action factor characteristic of research and development anthropology, nor does it have a strong concern for the bifurcated goals of scientific truth and community self-determination, as does action anthropology. Its conceptual structure provides an excellent means for providing culturally appropriate services.

The goals of cultural brokerage contrast significantly with some of the other value-explicit approaches. The others are largely up-front change programs, in which the anthropologist is actively seeking changes in the behavior of a target community. The goals of cultural brokerage are different. While change is an intended product of cultural brokerage, a primary target of the change-producing activities is the health care or other service-providing system. If that system changes so that it effectively deals with cultural pluralism, then the task of the broker is over. He or she will have worked him or herself out of a job. A health care system that was truly "transcultural" would have no use for the culture brokerage role. The care providers would be the brokers.

Cultural brokerage functions have long been a part of the applied anthropologist's role. It was not until more recent times that there emerged an entire strategy based on cultural brokerage.

Cultural brokerage could be used in many different kinds of situations. It seems especially useful when there is a need to link a service-providing organization with an ethnic community where there is a commitment to cultural pluralism. Commitments to cultural pluralism seem to be based upon emerging equality of power. In other words, the approach seems very well adjusted to contemporary American urban ethnic politics.

Further Reading

Lefley, Harriet P., and Evalina W. Bestman. 1984. "Community Mental Health and Minorities: A Multi-Ethnic Approach." In *The Pluralistic Society: A Community Mental Health Perspective*, Stanley Sue and Thom Moore, eds. New York: Human Sciences Press.

A recent, comprehensive account of the approach and its development.

Weidman, Hazel H. 1982. "Research Strategies, Structural Alerations and Clinically Applied Anthropology." In *Clinically Applied Anthropology*, N. J. Chrisman and T. W. Maretzki, eds. Dordrecht: D. Reidel Publishing Company.

Excellent discussion of aspects of the cultural brokerage role, with emphasis on the in-hospital function.

———. 1976. "In Praise of the Double-Bind Inherent in Anthropological Application." In *Do Applied Anthropologists Apply Anthropology?*, M. V. Angrosino, ed. Proceedings of the Southern Anthropological Society no. 10. Athens: University of Georgia Press.

Presents Weidman's view of cultural brokerage as she contrasts it with other kinds of applied anthropology. Also discusses the key concepts of cultural brokerage.

9

Social Marketing

Social marketing is a social change strategy that combines commercial marketing techniques with applied social science to help people change to beneficial behaviors. Some examples of the issues targeted by social marketing are contraception (Schellstede and Ciszewski 1984), blood cholesterol screening (Lefebvre and Flora 1988), heart disease prevention (Maccoby et al. 1977), safer sex (BEBASHI 1990), high blood pressure reduction (Ward 1984), oral rehydration therapy use (Clift 1989), and smoking reduction (Altman et al. 1987).

Used in both the developed and developing countries (Manoff 1985:221), social marketing represents a synthesis of "marketing, mass communication, instructional design, health education, behavioral analysis, anthropology, and related social sciences" (Academy for Educational Development 1987:67). While commercial marketing is an organizing concept in social marketing, as it "provides analytical techniques for segmenting market audiences, product development, pricing, testing, and distribution," the core of social marketing practice is "a commitment to understand consumer needs and to produce products, programs or practices to enable them to better solve their problems" (Bryant and Lindenberger 1992:1). Social change is promoted through culturally appropriate messages carried through mass media. These efforts are highly coordinated, working cooperatively with local agencies and community groups.

Social marketing requires skills and viewpoints that are part of being an anthropologist, and therefore increasingly we find anthropologists working in all stages of the social marketing process. The anthropologist's primary role in social marketing is research. Social marketing uses qualitative and quantitative research during all phases of planning, implementation, and administration. Good ethnographers bring many useful skills to the process, including the "creative interpretation of research into ingenious message design" (Manoff 1988:4). The attitudes of social marketers about research are highly consistent with those of ethnographers. Both have a strong commitment to the "native" viewpoint and skepticism about survey research.

In this chapter social marketing is illustrated by the BEST START project. Directed by anthropologist Carol A. Bryant, this project is directed at increasing the number of low-income women that breastfeed in the southeastern United States.

While social marketing draws heavily from commercial marketing, there are differences (Academy for Educational Development 1987:70). First, the changes called for in commercial marketing are often less complex than those aspired to through social marketing. For example, it is less complicated to persuade people to switch cigarette brands than to stop smoking. Second, the new behavior or product may be more controversial. The promotion of safer sex practices is made difficult because of public modesty standards. Third, the new products or practices advocated in social marketing may be less satisfying to people. In the case of smoking, for example, present gratification is exchanged for future health improvements. Fourth, often the intended audience of social marketing has fewer resources and cannot easily act on their new information. Many times the target population is poor. Fifth, the politics of social marketing often require high levels of success. In the commercial realm a small increase in market share may justify substantial marketing investment, while in the public arena large, sustained increases are demanded.

DEVELOPMENT OF THE APPROACH

The use of the term social marketing dates from the late 1960s and grew out of discussions between Philip Kotler and Richard Manoff (Kotler 1975; Manoff 1985). Kotler was a professor of marketing from Northwestern University and Manoff was director of a marketing firm that had begun to approach nutrition and health education as a marketing problem. The term social marketing was used to distinguish between marketing commercial products and marketing better health practices.

The early 1970s saw increased academic interest in the idea; there were more publications on it and, of course, considerable debate about the "but is it marketing" question. During that time social marketing approaches were used in many different areas, mostly relating to promoting ideas, practices, and products in health and nutrition.

KEY CONCEPTS

There are a number of concepts that are fundamental to understanding the process. *Marketing* involves those activities that result in the movement of goods and services from producer to consumer in response to consumer demand, satisfying consumer needs, and achieving the goals of the producer. Increasingly marketing is seen as a process of communicating ideas rather than the movement of goods and services. This may involve informing consumers of products and services or the discovery and communication of consumer needs by producers. The goal of commercial marketing is a profit or increase in market share. In social marketing the goal is societal improvement or social problem solving, a process that often involves creating demand for a socially beneficial product and developing products or programs to meet consumer needs.

The people to whom social marketing efforts are directed are referred to as the *target audience*. The primary audience is the people you wish would accept the new behavior. This group may be segmented in various ways. There may be a difference between rural and urban people, rich and poor, for example. The secondary audience is an audience that influences the decision making of the primary audience. For example, the mothers and husbands of potentially breastfeeding women are a good example of a secondary audience. The tertiary audience may be opinion leaders in the community or the general public. These are people whom others look up to, or who in other ways influence decision makers. Effective social marketing is often based on identification and targeting of a large number of audience segments. In a Brazilian breastfeeding promotion project, eight distinctive target audiences were identified. These were doctors, health services, hospitals, infant food industry, industry in general, community, government officials, and mothers (Manoff 1985:48).

Communication channel refers to the media through which the message is communicated. Typically, mass media like radio and television are combined with print media and personal communication. An important task is the identification of available communication channels, or channel analysis. An important task in social marketing is to identify the most effective channels for communicating each message. In general, mass media are used to transmit short, persuasive, or informational messages and create a climate conducive for change. Print material is used for more lengthy, instructional messages, and personal communication is used for the more complex information that requires interaction and social support.

Resistance points are the constraints that prevent people from adopting a new behavior. Resistance points can be of "social, cultural, economic or religious origin, or the product of ignorance" (Manoff 1985:107). These constraints will vary between audience segments. The resistance points are very important to identify and overcome. This is a very important aspect of the social marketing process.

Social marketing has various functions. *Demand creation* involves letting people know about the availability of a particular service or product. This requires more than simple publicity: the people need to know the relative advantage of a particular innovation and the community itself needs to be motivated to act on a particular situation. *Appropriate use* is a more complex goal (Academy for Educational Development 1987:68), because often the new practices are complex and can be applied in a variety of ways.

SOCIAL MARKETING PROCESS

The social marketing process consists of a long-term program to produce sustainable changes in a clearly defined set of behaviors in a large population (Academy for Educational Development 1987:75). There are various conceptions of the process in the literature on social marketing (Manoff 1985; Kotler and Roberto 1989; Fine 1981). The following description is based on the discussion of process that was developed in the BEST START project (Bryant and Lindenberger 1992).

The social marketing process has five phases, according to Bryant and Lindenberger. These are formative research, strategy formation, program development, program implementation, and program monitoring and revision (1992). While there are five phases, in practice the different stages are repeated depending on the experience with the specific project. That is, if a part of the strategy is not working, the team will go through a phase of the process again. The process is iterative. You change what you do, based on what you learn.

Stages in Social Marketing

I. Formative Research
II. Strategy Formation
III. Program Development
IV. Program Implementation
V. Program Monitoring and Revision

The formative research stage starts with review of recent literature on the problem and examination of existing programs that deal with the problem. Often staff of exemplary programs are interviewed and materials produced by their program are reviewed. The formative stage includes the design of a research plan in which qualitative and quantitative data needs are specified, along with potential data sources and research objectives. Identification of program partners, including collaborating agencies, occurs in this phase. Research makes use of in-depth interviews, focus groups, and surveys of various types, creating a foundation for the project.

Formative research includes preliminary research on the community and agency context of the project. Social marketers need to know the nature of the organizations and persons with whom they will be working. These people need to achieve consensus on the nature of the problem. It is this consensus that makes things work. It is very important to identify the ''real players'' rather than the formal leadership as depicted in the organization chart. When the concerns of the cooperating professionals are not understood and addressed, projects fail.

Formative research identifies the target population's perception of the problem and the nature of resistance points. This research typically has a very large qualitative component, often based on the focus group technique. The strategy development stage also requires the identification of the primary, secondary, and tertiary target audiences, with the appropriate segmentations.

Staff identify media that are available for the project. It is important to find out what the target audience listens to, watches, and reads. In developed countries this information is often readily available; in less developed countries it may be necessary to research the question of media exposure. This information is necessary for the formulation of an effective media plan.

During this early phase the team carefully establishes network ties with organizations that may be interested in the project's problem. These can be private voluntary organizations, religious organizations, commercial organizations, and various governmental organizations. This collaboration will back up the media campaign. Organizational networking is done to multiply the impact of messages, to obtain feedback from stakeholders and to decrease interagency competition.

The second stage in the social marketing process, *strategy formation*, is done in planning sessions with staff and key advisors, who are often representative of stakeholders and program partners. The first step in strategy formation is to produce a definitive statement of the problem. Once the problem is defined, the social marketing team expresses it as project objectives. Objectives are described in measurable action terms that relate to the goals of the project. Objectives need to be measurable, expressed in terms of "required input, desired output, and a time frame" (Manoff 1985:106). Manoff warns that they can be "too broad, too vague, too unrealistic, or 'off-target' " (1985:106). It is important to have measurable objectives so that evaluation of performance is possible.

The strategy formation stage is concluded with identification of the elements in the messages that will be included in the campaign. This includes selection of message content, spokespersons, and tone. These decisions create the basis of a marketing plan.

The third stage is *program development*, a stage often carried out with the help of an advertising agency. Program development includes message design and materials development. The entire program development stage is directed at producing a written media plan, which describes the formation of the project strategy. The plan includes the messages, the target audience and its segments, media to be used, the products, the research design for tracking the project, and the plan for integrating the project with other organizations. Media planning includes "preparation of draft or prototype materials; materials testing; final production and program inauguration" (Manoff 1985:111). The actual media can be developed "in-house" or they can be purchased from advertising agencies. Prototype versions of public service announcements, pamphlets, instructional tapes, advertisements, and other messages are prepared, pretested, and revised. This pre-testing is to decide whether the developed messages are "comprehensible, culturally relevant, practical, capable of motivating the target audiences, emotionally appealing, memorable and free of negatives" (Manoff 1988:3). Product development includes decisions about product names, packaging, price, and supportive promotion and sales materials. All this requires the technical skills of persons trained in media. The anthropologist will bring skills in research that will support the development of the product through research.

After pre-testing, the materials enter final production. The team makes presentations of the project to public officials and community groups for approval and guidance. The presentation will include supporting research results that can guide their decisions about the effects of the materials.

Also part of the development stage is identification of "primary, secondary and tertiary audiences and their component segments" (Manoff 1988:3). As part of this process, resistance points that limit the potential for change in behavior are identified. Persons and institutions that can advocate the desired change need to be identified. The team looks for opinion leaders in the community or any person that would "enhance credibility" of the messages, thus increasing the chances for change in behavior. The last component of the strategy development stage is the determination of the media use patterns of the population.

Channel analysis continues as part of the program development phase. In channel analysis researchers identify the pathways through which messages, products, and services can be delivered to a population (Lefebvre and Flora 1988:305), and how these pathways complement and compete with one another. In the social marketing framework this can include everything from electronic and print media to social networks and opinion leaders. It is necessary to inventory all the places where a person encounters messages; these in turn become possible channels to use in the marketing process. Lefebvre and Flora speak of the identification of "life path points," which they exemplify from an American urban setting as laundromats, groceries, restaurants, and bus stops. In channel analysis the researcher not only knows which channels the population is exposed to, but which ones are most influential and important. For example, for certain health behavior changes the mass media do not present credible information, while personal networks do.

The fourth stage is *program implementation*. This includes implementation of policy changes, training of professionals, and distribution of educational materials. Also the public information program may be launched.

The last phase of the social marketing process is *program monitoring and revision*. This has two components, formative and summative. The formative evaluation determines strengths and weaknesses of project components so that the project can be improved. The team introduces improvements in the process to increase effectiveness. Summative research finds out the actual impact of the project. Much of the summative research consists of studies to identify knowledge, attitudes, and practices of the project's products by potential consumers. These are repeated, with uniform measures and sampling, so that the results can be compared wave after wave to answer questions such as what the target audience knows and does because of the project. These may be supplemented with qualitative data collection to get at meanings that cannot be investigated with surveys.

SOCIAL MARKETING AND FOCUS GROUPS

A research technique often used in designing the social marketing plan is the focus group, or group depth interview. Sociologist Robert K. Merton developed the focus group technique while doing research on German propaganda films done during World War II. Merton wanted to provide an interpretive framework for quantitative data collected with propaganda film viewers to try to find out why they answered questions the way they did about their psychological responses to propaganda films (Merton and Kendall 1946; Merton, Fiske, and Kendall 1990). Examples of use of focus group research in social marketing can be found in many areas, including social action programs (Schearer 1981), family planning (Folch-Lyon, Macorra, and Schearer 1981), vitamin supplement use (Pollard 1987), and educational evaluation (Hess 1991).

A focus group is a small group discussion guided by a moderator to develop understanding about the group participants' perceptions of a designated topic. While it can be argued that data collection efficiency is improved because you are increasing the number of interviewees being interviewed at one time, more important are the effects of the interaction of the participants being interviewed. Morgan states this clearly: "The hallmark of focus groups is the explicit use of the group interaction to produce data and insights that would be less accessible without the interaction found in a group" (1988:12). While the interaction deals with the content specified by the moderator, the interaction should be informal and lively. Morgan describes it as being like a conversation between neighbors or friends.

The composition of focus groups is carefully planned to produce representative information about the population. The difficulty and cost of recruiting participants can vary considerably with the nature of the research problem. When a highly specialized population is being researched it may be expensive to find qualified participants. The number of group participants is typically between six and eight, although sometimes the groups are larger (Morgan 1988).

Smaller groups involve more interviewee participation and are more susceptible to the impact of domineering persons. Larger groups require more moderator participation. Unless you are investigating the life of a small organization it is unlikely that your research results will be statistically generalizable. It is best to overrecruit participants so that persons that are inappropriate can be easily replaced. The sessions usually do not last more than two hours.

It is important to be very aware of the problem of bias in participant selection. It is also important to screen the participants carefully so that you are sure they do share the relevant attributes. As Morgan states, "participants must feel able to talk to each other, and wide gaps in social background or life-style can defeat this" (1988:46). Gender, ethnicity, age, and class may influence willingness to discuss a topic. While participant similarity is important, it is better if the interviewees do not know each other.

The number of focus groups to be completed is an important consideration both methodologically and practically. The increase in the number of types of participants of course will lead to an increase in the number of groups. For example, if urban and rural differences are important you will need groups for each type.

An important part of quality data collection is the creation of a permissive, nonthreatening atmosphere, conducive to revelation and disclosure. Moderator skill and group homogeneity are important factors in establishing these conditions. Moderator involvement varies with the purpose of the research. As Morgan states, "if the goal is to learn something new from participants, then it is best to let them speak for themselves" (1988:49). High moderator involvement may be called for when it is necessary to get the discussion back on the topic, when the group loses energy, when minority positions are stifled, when domineering individuals need to be shut down, and when some participants need to be encouraged (Morgan 1988:51).

Morgan encourages low moderator involvement through a process he calls group self-management. To a large extent this involves simply giving the focus group participants expectations for their own behavior through instructions that will lead them in the desired direction. For example you might tell them to expect that if they get off track a member of the group will pull them back. Other practitioners of the technique may more directly intervene. It is also possible to intervene more at the end of the session to help make sure that the ground is covered. In any case the interviewer "must develop the practice of continuously assessing the interview as it is in process" (Merton Fiske, and Kendall 1990:11).

Like other techniques, focus group interviewing has both strengths and weaknesses. The technique is practical because it can be done quickly and easily. Morgan says that "when time and/or money are essential considerations, it is often possible to design focus group research when other methods would be prohibitive" (1988:20). A focus group–based research project does not require large teams of interviewers. Kumar estimates that a project based on ten to fifteen interview sessions can be carried out within six weeks under normal conditions (1987:6).

Focus groups are most useful for discovery, and less useful for hypothesis testing. When you are unfamiliar with the content or are potentially biased, focus groups offer real advantages. The approach may not work well on topics that are highly private, and it is sometimes difficult to get all persons in the group to participate equally. It is important to note that an important principle in ethical research practice is that the researcher does not share information obtained from one informant with another. While this is the essential feature of the focus group approach, people can choose not to talk. While this solves the ethical problem it raises considerable methodological issues. Privacy and confidentiality may go far to encourage talk.

CASE STUDY: BEST START—A BREASTFEEDING
PROMOTION PROJECT

The BEST START project was a joint effort of public health agencies in eight southeastern states to promote breastfeeding among low-income women by developing effective promotional messages and a workable strategy for communicating them. The developed materials and strategies were made available for use to programs around the country through a nonprofit organization called BEST START, Inc.

A team led by anthropologist Carol A. Bryant planned the project. Doraine F. C. Bailey contributed to the research and planning and subsequently served as the coordinator of the Kentucky state project and the local project in Lexington, Kentucky. Jeannine Coreil contributed to the formative research and strategy formation phases of the project by conducting focus groups among audience members and health professionals. The project was a collaboration between local health departments and three national organizations—the Healthy Mothers, Healthy Babies Coalition, the National Center of Education in Maternal and Child Health, and the National Maternal and Child Health Clearinghouse.

Breastfeeding offers considerable advantages over bottle-feeding. Mothers benefit because it offers a quicker recovery from childbirth, stronger bonding with the infant, and an emotionally satisfying activity. The infants are better off because it offers the best nutrition for normal growth and development, protection against disease, especially ear infections and gastrointestinal illness, and decreased risk of allergies. There are significant societal benefits. Breastfeeding results in stronger family bonds, increased self-esteem of women, decreased cost of infant formula in food subsidy programs, and decreased health care costs for infants (Bryant 1989:11).

Because of these advantages the U.S. Surgeon General, in his series of national health objectives for the year 2000 (U.S. Public Health Service 1991:379), included the goal of increasing breastfeeding to 75 percent of mothers at hospital discharge, from 54 percent in 1988. Increasing breastfeeding is a matter of national policy in the United States.

In spite of the advantages of breastfeeding, and considerable investment in public health education programs, the rate of breastfeeding among low-income women remained low. The rate of breastfeeding has increased among middle- and upper-income women.

The BEST START: Breastfeeding for Health Mothers, Healthy Babies Program is addressing these goals for a consortium of public health agencies in eight southeastern states, based on social marketing principles. Specifically BEST START's goal is to "enhance breastfeeding's image among economically disadvantaged women and the public at large" and "to motivate economically disadvantaged women, especially those participating in WIC [a federal mother and child food supplement program], to breastfeed" (Bryant et al. 1989:15).

Bryant's team used the social marketing approach because the traditional clinic-based health education directed at low-income women did not work (Bryant et al. 1989:642). Low-income women were not given the information they needed to make the decision to breastfeed. The messages used were culturally inappropriate. The clinical staff did not have the time for education activities. Further, the constraints faced by low-income women were poorly understood.

During the formative research phase, project staff completed forty focus group interviews with low-income women in Tennessee, Kentucky, Georgia, Florida, North Carolina, and South Carolina. Most of these women were recruited from public health programs. BEST START researchers conducted focus groups among black and white women, teenaged and older women, urban and rural women, and women that were bottle-feeding and breastfeeding. These interviews were conducted in health department conference rooms.

The location of the interviews was the place where the women usually received health services or their WIC support. Interviews involved from three to eight people, plus one or two moderators. The first moderator introduced topics and interjected questions and guided the discussion. The second person helped supervise audio or video recording and helped interpret questions. The interviews lasted from one to three hours. Often participants expressed satisfaction about participating in the process because it gave them positive feelings and they learned so much from their peers.

The analysis emulated Krueger's "chronological sequence of analysis" and made use of ideas expressed by various other researchers (Krueger 1988; Agar and Hobbs 1985; Glaser and Straus 1967; Miles and Huberman 1984). After each session the moderators prepared short summary statements on various topics. Focusing on each participant, they identified any problems with the recruitment criteria and considered "level of enthusiasm, strength of infant feeding preference, consistency of comments and reported behavior" (Bryant and Bailey 1991:30). Also identified were themes concerning breastfeeding constraints and motivational factors that might stimulate change. Differences between participants were noted. Researchers considered the way these women spoke about the topic; this information often influenced the questioning process in subsequent sessions. The moderator's techniques and the interview success were evaluated.

Researchers processed each interview with the help of a computer program called The Ethnograph (Seidel et al. 1988). This program allows the coding, indexing, and subsequent retrieval of portions of the interview transcript. Codes reflected questions in the interview guide and were expanded as analysis proceeded. Retrieval with The Ethnograph is done in terms of subsets of the sample so that comparisons can be made by ethnicity, parity, respondent age, residence, and other variables. For example, the statements made by black teenagers on a particular topic can be retrieved from the data base and read and written about. This software allows the nesting and overlapping of codes. Some might assume that the use of this software makes analysis a mechanical exercise. The software serves only as a more efficient and complete means for shuffling through and reading all the field notes. It is still necessary to think it through and interpret the meaning.

Through the focus groups, the BEST START team learned factors that were attracting women to breastfeeding. An important component of attraction was the mother's aspirations. Like other mothers these women hoped for a special relationship with their children; they wanted a closeness with the baby that would endure beyond childhood. Mothers wanted to give their children a better life than they had when they were young. Especially they wanted health, happiness, and a good education for their children. Participants saw breastfeeding as a means for establishing an exclusive relationship between mother and child.

Teenage participants viewed motherhood as an opportunity to come of age, to gain positive attention from friends and family, and to establish a long-term relationship with their child. They also thought that breastfeeding can indicate maturity and responsibility and a certain adventurousness that can set her apart from her peers. These mothers were also concerned about their children becoming too attached to the people that often provide child care. They felt that breast-feeding can help prevent the child from becoming too attached to these other caregivers.

Most of the focus group participants were aware that breastfeeding offers significant health benefits to the child, such as protection from infection, fewer allergies, and better nutrition. Breastfeeding mothers expressed these ideas with pride and said they felt they were giving their children the best. Many bottle-feeding mothers accepted these claims, but questioned their significance. Some challenged these claims, citing their own observations, and a few believed bottle-feeding is superior.

The breastfeeding mothers regarded nursing as a special time that only a mother can enjoy with her children. They noted that it makes them feel relaxed; some even reported falling asleep. Many women cherished the experience as a memory that makes motherhood worthwhile.

The research team identified several barriers to breastfeeding. The most important constraint to starting and continuing breastfeeding was many women's lack of confidence in their ability to produce good milk in an adequate supply. These women often did not understand how milk is produced. Often, in response to their fears of milk inadequacy, they would use formula supplements, resulting in a real reduction in the supply. These women felt that breastfeeding is a more complex, difficult to learn skill than it really is. Their lack of confidence made them more easily discouraged when they heard of other women's negative experiences.

An important constraint was the embarrassment that women might feel about breastfeeding when others are present. There were significant differences between breastfeeding and bottle-feeding women in this regard. Some saw breasts as sexual objects that would arouse men and make their husbands and boyfriends jealous. They thought breastfeeding would make other women jealous and that it might be viewed as disgusting. These women resented having to go and "hide" in a public rest room, their car, or the bedroom at home when they were breast-feeding. Others said they would feel comfortable in public if they could be discreet. Many said they feel comfortable breastfeeding in the presence of their husbands or boyfriends, mothers, sisters, or other female relatives or friends; others felt uncomfortable breastfeeding in the presence of these people. A small number of focus group participants felt that breastfeeding was not possible for them; for them breasts were strictly sexual and the idea of putting a baby's mouth on them was disgusting.

Historically, promotional materials have used women who are unusually at-tractive or well-dressed as models, and have stressed the importance of being healthy and relaxed. These messages reinforced the poorer women's fears that they might not be able to meet their health and nutrition needs and follow the practices needed to breastfeed successfully.

The women expressed concern that breastfeeding would cause them to lose freedom. They saw breastfeeding as incompatible with an active social life. Younger women thought that it would prevent them from having time for them-selves and their friends. Women expressed these ideas in various ways—breast-feeding will make it hard to leave the child with the babysitter, for example, and the breastfed child will cry when its mother is not nearby. These women tended not to know how to mix breastfeeding and formula use. Some thought the use of breast pumps was messy, painful, or a "hassle," and that school and work were constraints on starting and continuing breastfeeding. Some felt that they couldn't cope with breastfeeding while going to work.

The women were concerned about their ability to make life-style changes such as cessation of smoking tobacco and drinking alcohol. They also expressed concern about their ability to eat properly, to get enough sleep, and to be relaxed. Some women thought that breastfeeding might be more painful than they could tolerate and that breastfeeding would disfigure their breasts.

The formative research was used to formulate guidelines for design of messages and other aspects of the program. The development team concluded that the tone of the campaign should be strongly emotional, "to reflect the strong feelings women attach to their aspirations for their children and themselves as mothers" (Bryant and Bailey 1991:32). The messages themselves were to be succinct and easy to understand, in order to "counteract the mistaken belief that breastfeeding is complicated or difficult" (Bryant and Bailey 1991:32). The development team thought it was important that the women featured in the materials be of the same economic level, ethnic backgrounds, and ages as the targeted population. They concluded that images used in print and broadcast media should communicate modernity and confidence, and that celebrity spokespersons should be avoided.

The educational campaign was to emphasize that most women can produce enough good milk despite differences in diet, stress levels, and health status. The research showed there was a need for social marketing efforts that made use of various mutually supporting activities to change the image that lower-income women had of breastfeeding, and to help these women in overcoming the barriers to this behavior.

The project developed many educational materials based on the formative research that helped to overcome barriers to breastfeeding. These emphasized benefits identified in the focus groups as appealing to low-income women. Public information materials included five television public service announcements and seven radio public service announcements, in English and Spanish. Educational materials included videotapes featuring testimonials taken from focus group interviews with WIC food supplement recipients.

A pre-test of this tape revealed an interesting oversight that had to be corrected later. When pilot tested among clients, the tape was seen as highly motivational: women enjoyed seeing WIC clients discuss their fears and how they overcame them. The health professionals were less enthusiastic. They mistakenly believed that the WIC participants, who were more expressive and articulate in a focus group than a clinic setting, were actresses working from a script. Program designers had to revise the tape to explain that the women were, in fact, all WIC participants. This tape has also been produced using Spanish-speaking WIC participants.

Other educational materials included five posters, ten pamphlets in English, seven in Spanish, and ten pamphlets written for a low literacy population. For health professionals, a motivational videotape, training tape, and accompanying training manual have been produced to teach a new counseling approach. New and revised materials are being developed with proceeds from sales.

The team developed a counseling strategy for breastfeeding promotion based on what they discovered in the formative research. The team developed a three-step approach to breastfeeding promotion in order to "counteract the lack of confidence and lack of knowledge that are at the root of these women's fears and doubts" (Bryant 1990). The counseling steps are 1) elicit client's concerns; 2) acknowledge her feelings; and 3) educate.

The experience of the focus groups revealed that women need assistance with sorting out their feelings. The first step in the counseling process, therefore, is an open-ended exploration. Clients are asked about their feelings about breast-feeding, as opposed to direct questions about whether they want to feed with a bottle or breast. A typical question is "what have you heard about breastfeed-ing?" (Bryant 1990:C-4).

In addition to their feelings, the women's knowledge of breastfeeding is explored. Step one of the counseling process represents a kind of emotional and cognitive diagnosis that helps the counselor select materials to stress in further counseling. Inviting women to speak about their concerns validates these concerns and allows resolution.

In step two the counselor acknowledges the women's feelings. The most consistent problem is that the client thinks her response is unusual. With acknowledgment, the client's comfort increases as the encounter feels safer, especially if she receives positive reinforcement. It is important to respect her. As Bryant expresses it, "by laying this foundation of trust, you also build her self-respect and self-confidence, which is a prerequisite for successful breastfeeding" (1990:C–3).

The third step is education of the client with carefully targeted messages. The new information allows the woman to ignore misinformation that she has received in the past. Women tend not to understand the lactation process and therefore are easily influenced by fear-producing misinformation. The formula producers provide information about the quality of the product that is reassuring. Breast milk, on the other hand, does not come with an ingredient list.

It is important not to overload the women with new information, as the BEST START team found that can reinforce her fears. The counseling strategy can address women's lack of confidence, embarrassment, her concerns about loss of freedom, dietary and health practices, and the negative influence of family and friends. The counseling education strategy reflects the team's recognition that a major barrier to breastfeeding was lack of confidence, and that the foundation for the solution was listening to the women. Empowerment is very important.

The use of the focus group data was comprehensive. The whole fabric of the content of the campaign was based on these materials. In retrospect Bryant felt the educational materials should have been pretested with professional health educators. These people serve as gatekeepers, as they make the decisions about local program design and the purchase of media. It would have been very useful to know what their concerns were. It also would have been useful to have interviewed husbands and boyfriends.

The use of materials developed through this project is widespread. About thirty state programs are using the materials at one level or another. Ten of these programs have been funded by the Maternal and Child Health Bureau of the U.S. Department of Health and Human Services as part of an effort to build state-level programs. Evaluations have shown that the materials have a high impact: substantial increases in breastfeeding among low-income women have occurred at various sites.

SUMMARY

Social marketing is an approach to producing changes in people's behavior through the use of culturally appropriate education and advertising media, widely disseminated through communication channels, including mass media. Social marketing draws heavily from practices associated with commercial marketing although it is generally recognized that social marketing is more complex and difficult. The technique is most widely used in the area of public health and has had an impact on smoking, sexual behavior, and cardio-vascular problems, among other concerns.

The development of media with culturally appropriate content is an important part of social marketing. The media development process uses social science research to identify cultural and social constraints to behavioral change and to select communication channels that have the potential for high impact. Anthropological research skills are often used in social marketing because of the importance of understanding the viewpoint of members of the community.

Focus-group research techniques are an important data-collection technique in social marketing. Based on the work of sociologist Robert Merton, focus group technique involves a group interview process that is quite consistent with cultural anthropology research practice. A focus group's leader facilitates discussion among a small group of informants selected for their capacity to illuminate a particular marketing problem. The texts that document this discussion represent the primary product of focus-group technique. These materials are analyzed and help shape the research that is used to structure the media campaign.

FURTHER READING

Bryant, Carol, and Doraine F. C. Bailey. 1991. ''The Use of Focus Group Research in Program Development.'' In *Soundings: Rapid and Reliable Research Methods for Practicing Anthropologists*. NAPA Bulletin no. 10, John van Willigen and Timothy J. Finan, eds. Washington, D.C.: American Anthropological Association.

A detailed and concrete discussion of the formative research process in the BEST START project. It shows in remarkably clear terms how this process works.

Kotler, Philip, and Eduardo L. Roberto. 1989. *Social Marketing: Strategies for Changing Public Behavior*. New York: Free Press.

This comprehensive and straightforward guide shows how organizations can be more efficient using a social marketing approach.

Manoff, Richard K. 1985. *Social Marketing: New Imperative for Public Health*. New York: Praeger.

A readable, concrete account of the social marketing process.

Part III

Policy Research in Anthropology

10

Anthropology as a Policy Science

The purpose of policy science is to provide information to decision makers in support of the rational formulation, implementation, and evaluation of policy. Policies can be thought of as strategies of action and choice used to achieve desired goals. Mostly we think of policy in the context of various kinds of formal organizations like social agencies, educational institutions, business firms, and governments at all levels. There are many different kinds of policy. We use terms like public policy, social policy, food policy, employment policy, industrial policy, foreign policy, and others to designate the strategies of action and choice used by governments and other organizations in various aspects of life in complex societies. These terms reflect rather different situations in content and scope, yet all relate to the same set of basic issues. That is, all policy is concerned with values.

Policy formulation involves specifying behavior that is to result in achieving a valued condition. In a sense, a policy is a hypothesis about the relationship between behavior and values: if we want to be a certain way, we need to act this way. At a basic level, policies involve allocation decisions—decisions to spend money and time to achieve something. The "something" can be quite diverse, including increases in gross national product, decreases in unemployment, decreases in the relative cost of food staples in urban areas, decreases in the number of teenage pregnancies, or increases in fairness in the allocation of housing. These large-scale national concerns can be matched with smaller-scale, local concerns, such increases in public input in the planning of the construction of a dam, the determination of the usefulness of a particular development project, or the identification of local needs for a certain kind of educational program. Policy research can occur on both sides of a policy issue and can be adversarial. Community groups can carry out policy research as a political counterpoise to research done by the government.

POLICY PROCESS

Policy should be thought of in terms of a process. The policy process is very complex. Stating the process in the simplest possible terms, we can say that the process consists of the following stages:

I. Awareness of need.
II. Formulation of alternative solutions.
III. Evaluation of alternative solutions.
IV. Formulation of policy.
V. Implementation of policy.
VI. Evaluation of implementations.

This process is carried out in the political arena, in which there is much competition for resources. Thus what would appear in a schematic diagram as neatly rational and orderly in reality may be determined by compromise and blunt applications of political power. The basic problem is that everything can not be done at once. Competition forces more careful allocation decisions. The complexity of the competition creates opportunities for policy science.

Policy science includes a large variety of research activities that in one way or another support the process by which needs are identified and policies are formed, implemented, and evaluated. Each stage in the policy process is associated with research needs and opportunities.

The view of policy science taken here is unusually broad; basically it is synonymous with applied research. Much (probably most) policy is formed without the aid of specific research efforts. Then again, social science tends generally to inform participants in the policy arena so that it is continually brought to bear on policy problems without actually being commissioned for a specific policy formation purpose. In these cases we can speak of policy-relevant research. There are many different points in the policy process where research done by cultural anthropologists can be used. Most research by anthropologists in this arena is done because of an existing policy, rather than to determine what the policy should be. Program evaluation, a type of research commonly done by anthropologists, is a good example of this. Some may want to separate policy research from program research.

In any case, this is not new ground for anthropologists. In fact, one could argue that policy research needs accelerated the development of anthropology as a discipline in the nineteenth century. This view is argued in chapter 2 on the history of the development of applied anthropology. In many countries, anthropology emerged as an organized discipline to fulfill policy research needs associated with colonial administration, both internal and external. At the beginning, this took the form of doing basic ethnography in unknown areas or troubleshooting concerning intercultural relationships.

As early as 1895, James Mooney carried out research that had as its goal the determination of what the U.S. Department of War should do in response to the Ghost Dance as practiced among certain Plains Indians (Wallace 1976). The appointment of the early professors of anthropology at the great English universities was based on the need to train colonial administrators. In spite of this time depth, the use of anthropology as a policy science is quite recent. It was not until the 1970s that anthropologists became involved more extensively in policy research efforts. As stated in chapter 2, this involvement relates to both push and pull factors. The push factor is the collapse of the academic job market. The pull factor is the increase in policy research efforts because of federal legislation. This last factor, of course, is most important in the United States.

As a corollary to the policy research function, anthropologists have to some extent become policy makers. This function is rare and very poorly documented. One interesting example is the work of anthropologist Robert Textor in the Peace Corps. Textor participated in the development of the so-called in-up-and-out personnel policy of the Peace Corps, which restricted the length of employment in the Peace Corps so as to maintain a higher rate of innovation and what might be called "organizational youth" (Textor 1966). My own experiences in development administration involved small-scale policy formulation in response to a community development effort on an American Indian reservation.

One can not overlook the cases where anthropologists have assumed high-level administrative positions in federal and state government. Some noteworthy examples are: Philleo Nash, who served both as commissioner of Indian Affairs in the U.S. Department of the Interior, and lieutenant governor of the State of Wisconsin (Landman and Halpern 1989); Aguirre Beltran, who served as director of the National Indian Institute of Mexico; Jomo Kenyatta, who was the first prime minister of Kenya; and Nirmal Kumar Bose, who was appointed Commissioner for Scheduled Castes and Scheduled Tribes in India (Sinha 1986). In all these cases these people were intimately involved in policy formation. There are of course a number of knowledgeable applied anthropologists who have argued very eloquently against such involvement. A good example is Homer G. Barnett, who did extensive applied work in the Pacific following World War II. He argued that our effectiveness as applied anthropologists would be reduced if we took over administrative functions (1956).

In any case, most involvement of anthropologists in the policy arena is as researchers. In this framework they are said to be most effective at the local level (Chambers 1977); or, when they work at the level of national policy formation, they function best in large multidisciplinary research teams (Trend 1976). Both Chambers and Trend seem to be arguing from the same ground, which is that the traditional, holistic, participant-observation-based research methodology works best in smaller-scale contexts. While this is probably true, there are ways of escaping the effects of the constraint. One is to learn other research techniques.

Policy research is not a monolith. There are many different types. For example, each stage in the policy process is associated with different research needs. There are many different types of current policy research practice that see anthropological involvement. Anthropologists conduct evaluation research, needs assessment, social impact assessment, social soundness analysis, and cultural resource assessment, as well as various other kinds of policy research. In addition to the research carried out in support of the development, implementation, and evaluation of specific policies, there is also research that is referenced to general areas of social concern. This can be referred to as policy-relevant research.

In regard to this distinction, it is possible to speak of anthropology *in* policy, and anthropology *of* policy. This follows a contrast originally made by the medical sociologist Robert Straus (1957), who spoke of researchers serving in support of medical care, as opposed to researchers who study medical care. The first was referred to as sociology *in* medicine, the second as the sociology *of* medicine. DeWalt applied this distinction to his analysis of agricultural anthropology (1985). Both are very important. It is, however, important to recognize the distinctions between the two kinds of work. All the policy anthropology that we refer to here is of the "anthropology in policy" type.

All the different types of policy anthropology represent important kinds of research activity for anthropologists in many different employment situations. Further, if one considers all the different purposes and funding mechanisms for research by anthropologists, one finds that the contrast between applied and basic research becomes reduced. We have, on the one hand, research that is specified, bought, and paid for by clients to meet some practical need, and, on the other hand, research planned and carried out by researchers referenced only to their curiosity and sense of the direction of the discipline.

What exists between these polar types is the product of a mix of personal inclination and many different incentives. For example, many programs that fund basic research will fund that research in terms of a set of priorities that are derived from general policy questions. These specific economic incentives come to be converted to "hot topics" and short-run tendencies in research topic selection. Under certain circumstances, research produced for specific applied purposes can begin to appear in print as if it were basic research. This then influences research topic selection in yet another way. The point is that the contrast between applied and basic research is rather weak. Further, there is a great deal of flow between the two realms.

CURRENT TYPES OF POLICY RESEARCH PRACTICE

The types of policy research discussed here range from standardized research methods geared to specific policy issues, to large and generalized research orientations applicable in a wide variety of situations. The contribution of anthropologists to the development of the methods and techniques used varies from a great deal to very little. Except for a few cases, the anthropologist involved in the use of these practices needs to know general social science research methods in addition to those more traditionally associated with anthropology. As is mentioned in Chapter 12, on evaluation, one needs an integrated research methodology in which the researcher is capable of drawing on a variety of different techniques, depending on the problem at hand.

A glimpse at the various types of policy research is provided below. As suggested above, some of these types have specific technical meanings, while other categories are general and include a wide variety of research functions.

Evaluation. In evaluation, research is done with the goal of determining the worth of something, such as a project, program, or set of training materials. The process can involve a wide variety of research designs, from highly structured experiments with control groups to descriptive ethnographies. Evaluation can serve many purposes. Many evaluations are done to determine the effects of a specific project or program. Evaluation can also be done to see if some activity is working as expected, with the goal of improving it. Evaluators can use a wide variety of data collection techniques. Evaluation can be used to test the feasibility of wider application of innovations. Research can be used to evaluate alternatives in the design process. Evaluation is one of the most important types of policy research done by the applied anthropologist.

There is currently increased interest in the use of ethnography in evaluation. Using this approach, the task becomes one of finding out what is going on in a specific situation, rather than technical determination of effects. The chapter on evaluation includes case studies of evaluations that involved anthropologists. Anthropologists working in evaluation often use case study methodologies. In some cases they serve as ethnographers studying large-scale projects as part of multidisciplinary teams.

Social Impact Assessment. In social impact assessment, research is geared toward predicting the social effects of various kinds of projects. Usually the process involves the examination of unplanned effects of major construction projects on families and communities, before the project is built. In this limited sense, social impact assessment is a kind of effect study. Social impact assessment is especially important in the design process. Usually the process involves the consideration of the effects of various design alternatives. Social impact assessment often involves the use of secondary data.

This is an important kind of policy research for cultural anthropologists. An entire chapter is given to social impact assessment in this text. It is worth noting here that often the research methodologies used in social impact assessment are mandated by the contracting agency. In the United States, various kinds of impact assessment research is done in compliance with a number of different federal laws, including those concerned with protecting the environment.

Chapter 11 contains an expanded discussion of social impact assessment, with a case study of a specific assessment project. You will find that social impact assessment, in part, resembles the traditional anthropological/sociological community study, except that it places emphasis on the use of secondary data. The use of secondary data is encouraged because of the need for speed and standardization between different project assessments. While social impact assessment can be done in many different settings, it is specifically geared for use in conjunction with the planning of projects in the United States. It is used in a wide variety of settings involving the projection of the effects of everything from dam construction to fisheries management policies. This kind of research is done to evaluate design alternatives prior to implementation.

Needs Assessment. In needs assessment, research is done to determine deficiencies that can be treated through policies, projects, and programs. It is done as part of the planning process and is sometimes thought of as a kind of evaluation. Sometimes needs assessment takes the form of large-scale survey research projects that identify and rank preferences for certain developments. Such surveys usually require two waves of standardized data collection, one to identify and one to rank. Needs assessments can also be based on existing census data used as social indicators. Many factors that are targeted by policy can be measured this way, such as education and income levels, number of violent deaths, and disease rates. Working in smaller-scale contexts, the needs assessment process may involve the use of community meetings of various kinds.

Obviously, needs assessment occurs early in the policy process and can set the scene for a variety of policy research procedures. The operation of many intervention strategies may involve needs assessments of various kinds. The identified needs often are used in program monitoring and evaluation at subsequent stages.

Social Soundness Analysis. Social soundness analysis is used to determine the cultural feasibility of development projects. This generalized approach to project assessment came to be used by researchers working for the U.S. Agency for International Development, starting in the mid-1970s. The approach, in large part, was developed by the anthropologist Glynn Cochrane. Cochrane had done assessment work for various development agencies, including the World Bank and the British Ministry of Overseas Development. The term social soundness analysis comes from U.S. Agency for International Development documents.

The process is described in Cochrane's book *The Cultural Appraisal of Development Projects* (1979). An important element in social soundness analysis is the identification of the different beneficiary groups associated with the effects of a specific project. This is important because of the policy framework of American international development efforts, which, since the amendments made to the Foreign Assistance Act in 1973, have had a mandate to direct their attention to the needs of the "poorest of the poor." This required a commitment to what Cochrane called social mapping. Social mapping is basically a process of ethnography that involves the collection of data on ethnicity, social organization, belief systems, wealth forms, patterns of mobility, and access to basic human needs.

The project design process as outlined by Cochrane directs the attention of the appraiser to a number of criteria that should be considered during project design.

Criteria Used in Cultural Appraisal of Projects

Contextualism—assuring that the project ideas fit with the cultural landscape.

Incrementalism—assessing the magnitude of the social change involved.

Minimum participant profiles—analyzing the social characteristics of project participants.

Spread effects—estimating the magnitude of project impact.

Motivation—providing reasons for participation in projects.

Estimating time factors—approximating the length of time required for social change.

Benefit incidence—observing who gains and who loses during the life of a project.

Communication and learning—seeking ways of facilitating and encouraging innovation and adaptation.

Design of extension efforts—building the organization of extension work.

Using indigenous organization—maximizing the use of local management talent. (Cochrane 1979)

The cultural appraisal process outlined by Cochrane is nontechnical, in that it does not present much beyond a checklist with illustrative cases as a means of specifying the research process. In any case, the approach is currently used in the U.S. Agency for International Development project planning process, in conjunction with other research approaches.

Technology Development Research. In an effort to help assure the appropriateness of technology developed for use in less developed countries, a number of agencies have become committed to the use of social science to inform the technology development process. This is well developed in farming systems research (DeWalt 1989; McCorkle 1989; Norman and Summons 1982; Hildebrand 1976; Ruthenberg et al. 1980). Farming systems research is geared toward linking farmers with those who develop agronomic technology. Part of this linkage is the provision of comprehensive accounts of the farming system. The concept of the farming system is focused on analysis of the production and consumption decisions of farm households. In this research, attention is paid to the identification of development constraints and opportunities. One way that technology development research can operate in the agronomic context is through on-farm research. This involves the actual implementation of agronomic research on the farms rather than in the experiment stations. In this setting the social scientist can serve as a broker for the experimentation program.

Most farming systems research of the type briefly described here is done in conjunction with the international crop research centers, such as CIMMYT (Centro Internacional de Mejoramiento de Maiz y Trigo), or CIP (Centro Internacional de la Papa), or the commodity-focused Collaborative Research Support Programs (CRSP), such as INTSORMIL or Small Ruminants. Farming systems research, although developed outside of anthropology, is congruent with certain anthropological tendencies in methodology.

Cultural Resource Management. Since the early 1970s a great deal of archaeological research in the United States has been carried out in response to legislative mandates. This has led to the emergence of cultural resources management (CRM). CRM is concerned with identifying the impact of federal and other kinds of development on archaeological sites, historic buildings, and similar things, and then managing the impact in various ways. Management usually involves identification and documentation, but may include mitigation and protection. Mitigation may include thorough research and documentation of the resource. Protection may include physical stabilization and the establishment of zones of protection.

Large numbers of archaeologists, architectural historians, and other researchers have been active in CRM. Recently this assessment process has begun to be directed toward contemporary communities as cultural resources. The emphasis in this research is toward the documentation of the folk knowledge of communities that are displaced by development projects. This kind of research is not common. The research methodology is based on traditional ethnographic practice. An example of this kind of work is the Big South Fork Project, carried out by Benita Howell and the National Park Services Applied Ethnography Program.

Of course, there are other types of policy research besides those mentioned here. Nevertheless, these are important because of the numbers of anthropologists involved in them. Clearly, the most important are social impact assessment and evaluation research. Anthropologists have also been involved in the development of these research methodologies. This is especially apparent in the area of social impact assessment methodology developed for the Army Corps of Engineers. Also, anthropologists have served as evaluators of the products of social impact assessment and evaluation research. The point is that there are many different ways of participating in policy research endeavors.

INCREASING THE USE OF POLICY RESEARCH

Sometimes research just happens, but usually applied researchers have to work hard at it. The crucial question facing the applied or policy researcher after all this hard work is, "How can I get my research used?" In dealing with the question of utilization it is important to be neither naive nor cynical. It is necessary to recognize that our research, however sound, may not affect the situation. Also in many situations decision makers may be poised to act on the basis of the knowledge provided them through policy research.

The literature on the different types of policy research in all cases contain references to the problem of underuse of research results. It is clear that this is a consistent problem in the policy research realm. It is a problem that stimulates its own research. This section of the chapter, written with Barbara Rylko-Bauer and based on an earlier article (Rylko-Bauer and van Willigen, 1993), is intended to give practical advice on how knowledge utilization can be increased. You could think of it as a theory of research effectiveness. This advice is organized around a series of principles that when followed will help increase the impact of anthropological research. The advice is intended to be general enough to cut across the various research types.

Before discussing the framework some basics need to be established. First, because we can control our own actions we need to think primarily about what we do rather than what others do. I say this because often researchers blame the agency for not making use of the research. While this may be true to some extent, it is more productive to focus on what we can do to improve the potential for getting research used. Second, we need to treat knowledge use as something that needs to be planned into the design of projects. Research designs guide research projects. Applied research should include a knowledge utilization design or plan. The discussion below suggests elements that can be included in such a plan.

Third, we need to think realistically about our goals and look at utilization broadly. Researchers in this area point out that a narrow conception of utilization overlooks the complexity of policy making, and fails to recognize that reducing uncertainty, clarifying issues, and providing new understanding of how programs work are also real effects (Beyer and Trice 1982; Caplan 1977; Patton 1986; Weiss 1977, 1981). More significantly, research "can gradually cause major shifts in awareness and reorientation of basic perspectives" without seeming to be directly and immediately applied (Weiss 1981:23).

The following discussion includes factors to be considered in developing a utilization design. The context of a research situation will determine which knowledge utilization factors have more relevance.

Collaboration

The most significant factor in getting research findings used is collaboration between researcher and clients (Alkin 1985; Burry 1984; Glaser, Abelson, and Garrison 1983; Leviton and Hughes 1981; Patton 1986; Rothman 1980). Collaboration means involving decision makers and other potential stakeholders, such as community members, in the research process. Carefully working with people to identify their information needs and ways they can use the research will increase their commitment to the application of the research. It is important to foster a relationship with an individual that personally cares about the project and the information it generates. Patton refers to this as the "personal factor" (1986).

User participation presents some potential ethical dilemmas. A frequently noted concern is cooptation of the researcher, which may occur if decision makers shape the research to provide results that support preferred or already existing policies and actions, and do not challenge their role within the organization (Ballard and James 1983; Beyer and Trice 1982; Dawson and D'Amico 1985). Selecting stakeholders involves a judgment about whose questions will guide the research (Mark and Shotland 1985), creating potential for a different sort of cooptation—the preempting of criticism of the project by the inclusion of stakeholders who might have been likely to do so. Finally, if the researcher does not provide stakeholders with the necessary information for effective and knowledgeable collaboration, then user participation can become a form of "pseudo-empowerment" (Mark and Shotland 1985:143-44).

Models of collaborative research are well developed in anthropology (e.g., Stull and Schensul 1987), and evolved from a value orientation that recognizes the validity of self-determination as a major force in sociocultural change. Recently the idea of user participation has been explicitly suggested as a strategy for increasing the use of anthropological knowledge (Davidson 1987; Schensul 1987; Stern 1985; Whiteford 1987).

Communication

Communication of research findings is often limited to the writing of a final report; yet this is not a very effective way of passing on information, and often results in too much, too late. Perhaps the most important strategy is to discuss preliminary findings throughout the research process and maintain an ongoing dialogue with feedback between researcher and information users (Glaser, Abelson, and Garrison 1983; Rich 1975). This is much easier to do if decision makers are collaborating in the research process (Dawson and D'Amico 1985; Patton 1986).

Other communication strategies include using multifaceted and appropriate means of communication, such as workshops, conferences, trade magazines, journals from other disciplines, and widespread distribution of short draft reports (Ballard and James 1983; Beyer and Trice 1982; O'Reilly and Dalmat 1987; Patton 1986; Schensul 1987). Presenting findings in the language and style of users is supported by our common sense, yet all social scientists have great difficulty avoiding jargon, keeping reports brief, and presenting findings and recommendations in a manner familiar to potential users (Ballard and James 1983; Rothman 1980). It is important to communicate findings directly to relevant decision makers. Practitioners need to provide concrete, specific recommendations about what is to be done, by whom, and when (Patton 1986; Rothman 1980). Policy makers do not usually expect primary data and research reports; they want recommendations on what to do (Cernea 1991).

Client

Collaborative research is more likely to succeed if one understands the client agency, community, or group, and the political context within which the research and knowledge would be used. Do an ethnography of the research situation. Becoming informed about the ways in which communities and groups may be affected by the research, and about the client group and its decision-making process, gives the researcher some understanding of the relationships among relevant groups, who the key decision makers and community leaders are, and the potential areas of conflict and possible forums for resolving them.

In studying the nature of the client group, one can focus on questions such as who are the relevant decision makers and potential users of the information, how are decisions made within the organization, what are the usual channels of communication, and what are the constraints and/or incentives to use of the information within the agency.

Community and Politics

Always be aware of the potential impact of research findings, and try to understand the relationship that exists between the client agency and those individuals, groups, or communities that may be affected. Often, the client may be in a position of relative power vis-à-vis the community, and the agency's values and bureaucratic needs may conflict with those of community members. Recommendations perceived as threatening by those outside the agency may enable a community to mobilize public support to defeat such action. Conversely, the agency may decide not to act on recommendations perceived as going against its best interest, even if they are beneficial to the community that the agency serves. Research based in an established community institution with political clout has greater likelihood of having an impact and bringing about desired social change (Schensul 1987).

Research Process

Research should be designed, from the onset, with utilization in mind (Patton 1986). There are three features of research that increase the potential for use.

First, diversity of research methods, in particular the creative combination of quantitative and qualitative methods and analysis, can provide an insightful, valid, and convincing representation of social reality. At the same time, diversity can help meet time constraints, as well as criteria of reliability and generalizability that policy makers often expect (Beyer and Trice 1982; Fetterman 1989; Schensul 1987; Trotter 1987).

Second, use of research is directly related to the credibility of the research process (Caplan 1977; O'Reilly and Dalmat 1987; Weiss and Bucuvalas 1980; Whiteford 1987). This includes perceived accuracy, fairness, understandability, and validity of research design and methods (Patton 1986). Research quality issues become more important in situations of political debate, where the policy maker cannot afford to have the research discounted due to uncertain methodology (Weiss and Bucuvalas 1980).

Third, the potential for use also increases if the research focuses on variables that can be acted upon, that are accessible to control (Gouldner 1957). We call this applicability. Several studies suggest that decision makers are more likely to use findings if recommendations are feasible, and the results conform to users' expectations or existing knowledge (Caplan 1977; Leviton and Hughes 1981; Weiss and Bucuvalas 1980).

Time

Policy research often has a short time frame. Recognition of this has led to many new methods for anthropologists doing policy research (van Willigen and DeWalt 1985). Perhaps most notable is the development of problem-focused, short-term research techniques such as focus groups and rapid appraisal (van Willigen and Finan 1991). One example is the informal or reconnaissance survey done in farming systems research. In these efforts there is a heavy reliance on key informant interviewing, judgmental sampling, use of secondary data, and on-site observation. Another example is "rapid assessment procedures," such as those developed for evaluating and improving primary health services (Scrim-shaw and Hurtado 1987).

Advocacy

Promoting one's research findings and recommendations also can improve the prospects for use (Barber 1987; Jones 1976; Rothman 1980; Siegel and Tuckel 1985). Advocacy works best from inside the system. One way of personally ensuring that research is used is to become one of the decision makers. It is much harder to influence the policy process from the outside, and increasingly anthropologists encourage direct involvement in program management and policy making (Cernea 1991). In whatever role you choose, you have to be committed to change.

Clearly there are many variables that influence whether or not research is used. Above all, the policy researcher must include in the design of his or her research a knowledge utilization plan to increase the probability that the research will be used.

SUMMARY

Anthropologists provide a wide variety of research services in response to various needs associated with the process of policy formation, implementation, and evaluation. More detailed charting of the policy process would no doubt produce even more types of applied or policy research. While anthropologists bring certain methodological and conceptual tendencies to these research efforts, the content of these approaches is defined in reference to the policy process itself, as well as other disciplines.

The major types of applied research done in reference to the policy process are: evaluation, social impact assessment, needs assessment, social soundness analysis, technology development research, and cultural resources assessment.

Certainly other specific types will emerge in the future. The differences between these research methods are not based so much on technique and design but on purpose and intent. Further, in some settings the research technique used is really geared toward being appropriate to specific administrative requirements. It is clear that involvement in policy research calls for broad preparation in social science as well as knowledge of the traditions of ethnographic research.

FURTHER READING

Belshaw, Cyril S. 1976. *The Sorcerer's Apprentice: An Anthropology of Public Policy.* New York: Pergamon Press.

A view from the perspective of the British Commonwealth.

Chambers, Erve. 1989. "The Policy Idea," in *Applied Anthropology: A Practical Guide.* Prospect Heights, Ill.: Waveland Press.

This chapter discusses the nature of policy and the policy process.

Sanday, Peggy Reeves, ed. 1976. *Anthropology and the Public Interest: Fieldwork and Theory.* New York: Academic Press.

Useful to get a perspective on policy-relevant anthropology.

van Willigen, John, Barbara Rylko-Bauer, and Ann McElroy, eds. 1989. *Making Our Research Useful: Case Studies in the Utilization of Anthropological Knowledge.* Boulder, Colo.: Westview Press.

Presents a variety of case examples of anthropologists having an impact through their research.

11

Social Impact Assessment

Social impact assessment (SIA) is a kind of policy research frequently done by cultural anthropologists. While the term is applied to a variety of policy research activities, it usually entails the collection of sociocultural data about a community for use by planners of development projects. The data is usually intended to help project planners decide whether a particular project should be built or how it should be modified. Considered in its most narrow context, SIA is done as part of the environmental impact assessment process carried out under the mandate of the National Environmental Policy Act (NEPA) and other federal statutes.

DEFINITION OF SIA

A useful general definition of SIA is provided by the Social Impact Assessment Committee of the Society for Applied Anthropology. The committee, chaired by Michael Orbach, defined the process in the following way: "Social Impact Assessment (SIA) is the study of the potential effects of natural physical phenomena, activities of government and business, or any succession of events on specific groups of people" (Orbach 1979). This definition covers a range from the highly structured research mandated by federal statute and regulation, to generalized futures research. In this book our concern is more with the various types of structured research carried out to comply with law than generalized futures research.

SIA can be done in reference to a variety of potential events. Some of these are natural disasters; establishment of new federal, state, or local regulations; closure of governmental agencies, such as military bases; changes in industrial production practices; and the construction of large-scale projects like power lines, dams, and highways. SIA can serve many different purposes. The most appropriate to our interests here is the use of SIA in conjunction with the planning of major governmental projects.

In this setting, the social impact assessor is called upon to provide projections about future effects to inform all the parties involved in the project, including planners, designers, political leaders, and the public. Often this involves assessing a number of different project options. For example, an interstate highway could be routed in a variety of ways, have interchanges in various locations, and vary in other features of design. Usually one design alternative considered is ''no project.'' This type of SIA will often require a number of determinations of impact as the project is redefined. In addition to the data collection effort, the social impact assessor may also be involved in the process of informing the public about the project and the findings of the research.

Work in SIA can take other forms. Some of these are research and development leading to new SIA methods. These may be expressed in the form of agency regulations and guidelines as well as in general field research manuals. Another type of research that is similar to agency-sponsored SIA work is research done on behalf of a community that is engaged in resistance to a planned project. This type of job, of course, is less frequent, and may be done on a voluntary basis. In the United States, resisted projects end up in court, and this can involve the presentation of a number of different views of a specific project.

NATIONAL ENVIRONMENTAL POLICY ACT

The most practical component of NEPA for anthroplogists and other social scientists is paragraph (c) of section 102. This paragraph enjoins all agencies of the federal government to

include in every recommendation or report on proposals for legislation and other major federal actions significantly affecting the quality of the human environment, a detailed statement by the responsible official on—(I) the environmental impact of the proposed action, (II) any adverse environmental effects which cannot be avoided should the proposal be implemented, (III). alternatives to the proposed action, (IV) the relationship beween local short-term uses of man's environment and maintenance and enhancement of long-term productivity, and (V) any reversible and irretrievable commitments of resources which would be involved in the proposed action should it be implemented. (U.S. Congress 1971:853).

This portion of NEPA has led to the emergence of environmental impact assessment (EIA) practice and a new form in the literature of science, the environmental impact statement, or EIS (Burchell and Listokin 1975:1). SIA is often an aspect of environmental impact assessment.

As is typical with federal laws of this significance, NEPA stimulated a tremendous quantity of interpretive literature. This included general federal administrative guidelines, case law, specific agency guidelines, and various commentaries from the academic community, as well as the EIS's themselves. In addition, the law served as a progenitor for substantial parallel legislation at the state and county level. The ''Progeny of NEPA'' present interpretive problems of their own (Burchell and Listokin 1974). Following the development of this practice in the United States, EIA has become important in domestic policy of other countries (Carley and Bustelo 1984:2), and in international development work (Derman and Whiteford 1985).

Although it is clear that section 102(2) (c) of NEPA requires an EIS on "major federal actions significantly affecting the quality of the human environment" (U.S. Congress 1971:853), it is not always possible to determine where an EIS is required. In addition, it is not apparent from NEPA what constitutes an appropriate method for determining impact, nor does the law indicate the relative importance of social impact as opposed to environmental impact. Further, there is a great deal of variation in methodologies used in social impact analysis. The extent to which the social dimension is considered is often limited, although social impact assessment would seem to be part of the requirement of an adequate environmental impact assessment.

Environmental Impact Statement

According to federal regulation, agencies of the federal government are subject to the EIS provisions of section 102 (2) (c) of NEPA. Each agency is to view the act as supplementary to its own authorization. A wide range of actions are included in the purview of the act. These include all "new or continuing projects and program activities: directly undertaken by federal agencies; or supported in whole or in part through federal contracts, grants, subsidies, loans, or other forms of funding assistance . . . or involving a federal lease, permit, license certificate or other entitlement for use" (Council on Environmental Quality 1973:20551).

In order to be reviewed, projects of the types indicated above must be "major" and be capable of "significantly affecting the quality of the human environment." The responsibility for making this determination is in the hands of the specific agency that must consider the "overall, cumulative impact." A number of related small-scale projects may be subjected to this analysis if the projects taken as a whole have significant impact. The significance of a project may relate as much to location as to project design. That is, "the significance of a proposed action may also vary with the setting, with the result that an action that would have little impact in an urban area may be significant in a rural setting or vice versa" (Council on Environmental Quality 1973:20551). The agencies were instructed to determine guidelines that would in some way define significance.

Each EIS is to cover the following points:

I. A. Description of the proposed action.

B. Description of the environment affected.

II. Relationship of the proposed action to land use plans, policies, and controls for the affected area.

III. Probable impact of the proposed action on the environment.

    A. Positive and negative effects.

    B. Secondary or indirect, and primary or direct effects.

IV. Alternatives to the proposed action.

V. Any probable adverse environmental effects that cannot be avoided.

VI. Relationship between local short-term uses of the environment and the maintenance and enhancement of long-term productivity.

VII. Any irreversible and irretrievable commitments of resources that would be involved in the proposed action should it be implemented.

NEPA and its related regulations require that individual agencies develop their own guidelines for carrying out their charge. This means that EIS's done for individual federal agencies should follow specific defined sets of practice, many of which are derived from the more general NEPA expectations. In addition, certain agencies, such as the Army Corps of Engineers, are subject to the requirements of their own versions of NEPA.

In the case of the corps, there is section 122 of the River and Harbor and Flood Control Act of 1970 (Public Law 91-611), which provides for economic, environmental, and social assessments. This law states that "the Chief of Engineers . . . shall . . . promulgate guidelines designed to insure that possible adverse economic, social and environmental effects relating to any proposed project have been fully considered in developing such projects" (U.S. Congress 1972:1823). Section 122 of the law goes on to specify a number of adverse effects that must be assessed. These include: (1) air, noise, and water pollution; (2) destruction or disruption of man-made and natural resources, esthetic values, community cohesion, and the availability of public facilities and services; (3) adverse employment effects, and tax and property value losses; (4) injurious displacement of people, business, and farms; and (5) disruption of desirable community and regional growth. Similarly, the Housing and Community Development Act of 1974 also provided for its own type of impact analysis. The River and Harbor and Flood Control Act is especially noteworthy, however, because of its explicit treatment of social variables.

It must be made clear that environmental impact assessment and social impact assessment are not the same thing. The original CEQ guidelines that respond to NEPA do not single out and stress the social component of the total impact of a project. The orientation, although at times vague, is more holistic. Social impacts are seen as part of the total "package" of effects to be reviewed. In this context we might think of SIA as a term that is applicable to a portion of the entire EIA process.

Even a cursory reading of the CEQ guidelines indicates the importance of the social component in total impact determination. This orientation is made even more explicit in many of the developed agency guidelines. For example, the Army Corps of Engineers has funded a number of projects that have led to the publication of various guidance documents for preparing and contracting for what are explicitly labeled as social impact assessments. Thus in certain agencies SIA is an official concept.

Although the EIA procedure originally seemed to be oriented toward bio-physical data, it is quite apparent that the role of the social scientist in the EIA process has developed in a significant way.

CASE STUDY: EL LLANO PROJECT

El Llano project is described in *Social Impact Assessment: Experiences in Evaluation Research, Applied Anthropology and Human Ethics,* by Sue-Ellen Jacobs (1977). The value of this particular volume is enhanced by Jacobs's thoughtful inclusion of a "Field Guide for Conducting Social Impact Assessment," although she stresses that it "presents one person's purview" (Jacobs 1977:i). In this rapidly changing area of inquiry, various alternative approaches should be reviewed and considered.

The proposed El Llano project would entail the construction of a diversion dam, canal, and lateral system to be built two miles upstream from Velarde, New Mexico, on the Rio Grande. The $13 million project was designed primarily for irrigation rather than flood control or recreation. The official name of the project was El Llano Unit of the San Juan-Chama Project. Its principal social impact zone encompassed an area nineteen miles long and three miles wide, within which there were twenty-two communities. Jacobs's impact assessment activities focused upon the communities in one of the two counties affected.

Community Characteristics

Using 1970 census data, Jacobs determined that there were 11,888 people living in the impact zone studied. The majority of the population was Spanish-American, with about 9,930 or 83.5 percent reported. The other large segment of the population was from two Indian pueblos: 1,255 persons from San Juan, and 916 persons from Santa Clara.

The population for the impact zone was increasing, in that the county within which it was located increased its population 4 percent per year between 1960 and 1970. The anticipated growth would be urban in nature. Jacobs notes some of the planners' projections:

Land use is expected to shift from "vacant-agriculture" acreage (which makes up 96 percent of existing acreage) to developed acreage which would provide increased housing, industrial development, school sites and other neighborhood developments in order to accommodate this increased trend to urbanism. Simultaneously, it has been recommended that because of the Llano Unit potential to irrigate new lands, concerted efforts should be made to increase high yield agricultural endeavors. (Jacobs 1977:4)

The economic activities of the region reflected a mixture of subsistence agriculture and wage labor supplemented by agriculture. The unemployment rate in the county was very high, often over 19 percent (Jacobs 1977:4). This rate, which is of course extraordinarily high, may not have adequately accounted for gainful traditional agricultural pursuits. The community manifested a pattern of increasing rates of employment and unemployment, which is not an unusual pattern in communities of this type. Data from the 1970 census indicated that over 14 percent of the impacted families received public assistance. The percentage of the population receiving public assistance was substantially lower than the percentage eligible. Jacobs also suggests that there was a great deal of mutual aid, trading, and bartering in rural areas of the impact zone, which helped assure that a person's basic needs were met. Community members traded craftwork, labor, and surplus produce. Some persons sold garden and orchard produce at a local farmers' market in order to obtain money to reinvest in farm improvements. Among the important crops were apples, peaches, apricots, and plums.

The farming system was difficult to characterize because it seemed to manifest features of both traditional and modern systems. That is, the farms produced both for the market and for household consumption. Most farms were small because of the land inheritance patterns of the predominantly Hispanic and Indian population. It was unclear whether these patterns were traditional or a more recent development.

One of the most interesting features of the region was the system of community-controlled irrigation ditches and the traditional organization that maintained them. The system, which was established under provisions of the Treaty of Guadalupe Hidalgo, was maintained by an elected supervisor, or *mayordomo*. The *mayordomo* role was best performed by a fair-minded person who could allocate water equitably in periods of shortage. He needed to know the requirements of the land and crops, the water laws, and practical ditch management skills. The role, defined largely by tradition, possessed substantial power. Through the *mayordomo*'s power, he could prevent and resolve conflict in the realm of water and land use, as well as aspects of community life beyond the ditches. In addition to the water allocation responsibilities, the *mayordomo* had also to organize annual ditch-cleaning activities.

Parts of the irrigation system extant in the impact zone antedated the system established by the treaties with the Spanish. To the south of the region were the Indian pueblos of San Juan and Santa Clara. This irrigation system was maintained in a somewhat different way.

Because the water development project was threatening the land, in her report Jacobs discusses the land in terms of its role in the religious belief system of the various communities. She stresses the sacred nature of the land both in the Hispanic and Indian portions of the zone of impact. Her discussion of the religious life of the region accentuates the parallels between the Hispanic and the Indian communities. For example, certain parallels also exist in the social organization of the Hispanic and Indian populations. Jacobs emphasizes the importance of family relations during various stages of life among virtually all the people in the area. The Hispanic and Indian groups have been linked through marriage from the late seventeenth century. Jacobs suggests that this pattern has continued until the present day.

One of the most interesting components of the area's traditional social organization was the system of ritual godparenthood, called *compadrazgo*. This institution provided a means for extending parenthood beyond the consanguineal parents for the purpose of "sponsorship" and support in conjunction with life crises and events such as baptism and confirmation. The roles of *comadres* (godmothers) and *compadres* (godfathers) were quite important in both the Indian and Spanish communities.

METHODS AND TECHNIQUES

The following discussion of SIA methods and techniques is based on Jacobs's "Field Guide for Conducting Social Impact Assessment" (1977). It is very important to note that SIA methodology is highly variable. The social component review of any project will vary in importance because of the lack of uniform criteria for evaluating SIAs. That is, in Jacobs's work we have examples of assessment directly focused on the social component of impact. In many other projects, the social component is an afterthought, given limited focus. The factors that may influence the nature of the social component are indicated in Table 11.1. It is very important to emphasize that the research standards for SIA are improving through time.

Let us have Jacobs define the framework for her discussion of methodology.

In social impact assessment, there are some specific goals to be reached. We want to know how and upon whom a project will have impact in a region or community. It is certain that any project will have some social effects, but we cannot know with absolute certainty just what the full impact will be, nor can we know whether the impact will be positive or negative because it is not possible accurately to predict the full range of human responses that are likely to occur as a result of intrusions into existing sociocultural systems. However, we can make some good speculations about what *might* happen. So, we also want to know what impacts are likely to occur, how to judge potentially adverse impacts, how to mitigate against adverse effects, and how people in a community are likely to change as a result of a project. (Jacobs 1977:1)

Unfortunately much of the methodology that we learn as anthropologists that focuses on culture change is retrospective in nature. Yet in SIA we must predict the future. Even standard trend analysis is difficult to apply because the treatment that we are trying to assess has not yet happened. The most basic studies of culture change attempt to identify baseline data with which to compare post-change data so as to determine the extent of change.

The primary task of the preliminary phases of SIA is the identification of the relevant populations and the assimilation of as much information as possible

Table 11.1
Factors Influencing the Nature of the Social Component of SIA

Project Factors

   Project types (dams, channelization, canals, reservoirs, irrigation systems, etc.)

   Project scale

   Project use (flood control, domestic water, irrigation, water quality improvement, recreation, etc.)

Community Factors

   Population density

   Culture and cultural diversity

   Residential stability and community cohesion

   Uniformity of impact

   Community knowledge of project

Administrative Factors

   Lead agency

   Existence and nature of guidelines

   Case law

Researcher Factors

   Knowledge of laws and SIA practices

   Availability of time and personnel

   Quality of secondary data and its availability

Political Factors

   Level of community value consensus on the project, for or against

   Openness of planning process

   Level of organization of resistance or advocacy

Methodological Factors

   State of the art

concerning the group. Details as to the scope of the area of impact can often be determined from an analysis of the technical specifications of the project.

Once the social scientist has been told that a proposed project is expected to be located at a given site, the first attempts are made to locate the people who will be affected. These attempts will include the reading of maps, aerial photographs, [satellite] images, and other locational sources in order to identify human clusters (such as towns, villages, farmsteads, and in the case of cities, neighborhoods). At this point, we also begin collecting preliminary secondary data (books, reports, newspaper articles, letters, vital statistics, and other written materials) that will tell us about people in the area. (Jacobs 1977:3)

Following an initial assessment of the project and project area, the researcher must develop some notion of who he or she will be attempting to draw into the research activities. In certain kinds of projects it is necessary to supplement the research team with special expertise. Special experts may include other social scientists, community members, and "lead" agency personnel who might have special knowledge of the design of the project. Some agencies require multidisciplinary teams. As understanding of the project develops, it is necessary to comprehend how the particular project is justified in legislation. For the social scientist the important factors are the specific laws and regulations that govern social impact assessment. This knowledge will strongly affect the methodology selected.

It is beyond the scope of this text to delineate the complexities of the methodology selection process, but it is necessary to assert that there is not one "right" methodology for this type of analysis. As indicated above, the process is influenced by many factors.

The selected research design may be continually refined. This recognizes the impact of the research on the researcher, who will redefine approaches as understanding emerges. This indeterminate discovery process is important because it will increase the chances of understanding the diversity of the project and its potentially changing nature.

In the case of El Llano Project, Sue-Ellen Jacobs used a generalized and flexible assessment technique. Initially, she spent time developing a sense of the place. This involved "windshield" surveys and consultations with maps. This was followed by intensive analysis of secondary data sources. Jacobs emphasizes that in SIA, even the most trivial personal maintenance activities, such as renting an apartment, buying groceries, and setting up later interviews, are all important sources of data. As the investigator becomes more involved in the assessment process, more and more time is invested in direct purposive interviewing.

Because of the diffuse nature of the research process in its early stages, data recording must be done very carefully. Certainly the data storage system should reflect various areas of potential impact, conditioned by the relevant regulations. Jacobs notes:

Some social scientists function on the premise that to have categories established prior to data collection introduces a bias which causes data to be forced into artificial categories. Those social scientists argue that data will fall into "natural" categories if the researcher enters the field without a preconceived notion of how data should aggregate. (1975:5)

The anthropologist must contact individuals who reflect a variety of life experiences. Besides the usual categories of concern such as sex, socioeconomic strata, age, and occupation, there must be an attempt to identify and interview those who are supporters or opponents of a specific project, as well as those who are neutral. Additional stratification can be made based on levels of knowledgeability of the project. One way to monitor this issue is to create a representation grid in which persons in the various significant categories of representation are tallied as compared to the appropriately proportioned ideal. It is assumed that given time constraints and the difficulties in establishing an adequate sampling frame, the number of individuals in various categories will be somewhat disproportionate, and selected judgmentally or opportunistically.

The collection of diverse data allows the researcher to "profile" the community. Profiling is the process of organizing and displaying data for later interpretation. Profiling is common to virtually all SIA situations, for example, it is explicitly referred to in the laws that affect SIA for the Army Corps of Engineers. Stated simply, a profile consists of characterization of the "ambient conditions of the human environment" (Vlachos 1975:20). Or alternately, "profiling is the development of complete baseline data in order to provide a basis for projection and planning" (Van Tassell and Michaelson 1977:14). The data included in the baseline inventory or profile can vary significantly. Vlachos and colleagues state: "No study can include all the variables since a selectivity always operates as to which ones are considered as important in any given project or any given time" (Vlachos et al. 1975:21).

A Community Profile Outline

(after Vlachos 1975)

Section One: Structural Variables
I. Human Ecology
   A. Demographic Characteristics
      1. Population Size
         a) Composition/ethnic mix
         b) Rate of growth/urbanization
      2. Population Density
      3. Population Mobility
   B. Spatial Distribution
      1. Land use
      2. Housing
      3. Land ownership
      4. Rural-urban
      5. Core-suburban
      6. Neighborhoods
      7. Transportation patterns
II. Characteristic Institutions
   A. Family
   B. Education

    C. Religion

    D. Political

        1. Interest groups

        2. Community Services

        3. Citizen participation

        4. Governmental administration

    E. Economic

        1. Occupation

        2. Wage structure

        3. Income levels

    F. Health

    G. Leisure and Recreation

III. Social Collectivities

    A. Formal associations

    B. Informal associations

        1. Power groups

        2. Ethnic groups

        3. Class

Section Two: Cultural Tracts

 I. Life-styles

    A. Subsistence

    B. Communications

        1. Language

        2. Other expressive media

        3. Transportation

        4. Proxemics

    C. Religion

        1. Beliefs

        2. Practices

        3. Sacred places, events, and objects

        4. Places of worship

    D. Housing

        1. Styles of shelter

        2. Clusterings

        3. Relationships to kin-networks and work

    E. Geographic location of people, businesses, farms, and other physical features of the community

    F. Institutional characteristics and relationships

G. Health
  1. Culture-specific definitions of health
  2. Local health practices
  3. Local health facilities
  4. Health practitioners
H. Education
  1. Formal
  2. Informal
I. Leisure, cultural, and recreational activities
J. Politics (at various levels)
  1. Formal
  2. Informal
II. Historical Features
  A. Artifacts
    1. Contemporary
    2. Archaeological
  B. Physical Representations
    1. Contemporary physical structures
    2. Structures of antiquity
III. Worldviews, Beliefs, Perceptions, and Definitions of Reality
  A. Cognitive and Religious Systems
  B. Value Systems
    1. Historic values
    2. Aesthetic values
  C. Belief systems
  D. Perceptions of own group and others
IV. Intercultural Perceptions

The Vlachos profile checklist also includes reference to interrelationships, although it does not include any specific content. In addition, each element should be conceived as being in process. This condition is implicit in a conception of impact assessment.

A review of this list and other similar ones reminds one of other checklists such as the *Outline of Cultural Materials*, which was published by the Human Relations Area Files to serve as a means of coding world cultures, or the checklists associated with characterizations of the community study method (Arensberg and Kimball 1965). It is quite clear that cultural anthropology is a scientific discipline that is highly appropriate to the goals of profiling.

The next step in "standard" SIA practice is projection (Vlachos 1975; Van

Tassell and Michaelson 1976; Jacobs 1977). One source notes that "projection involves the selection of a broad range of alternative courses of action, and elaborating their consequences for the present profiled situation over a specified period of time" (Van Tassell and Michaelson 1976:24). The first step in projection is the specification of alternative "treatments" or projects. Obvious alternatives would include locational choices, alternative designs, scheduling, and, of course, the "no project" alternative (Van Tassell and Michaelson 1976:24). The alternatives should reflect those considered in technical studies and public discussions.

The second component of the projection process is "forecasting," that is, actually to predict the future. It is essential in the SIA process to make predictions concerning the future. However, because of the state of the art, this tends to be a "black box" affair. That is, specific data is collected in explicit ways and somehow forecasts are made. There are many ways of doing this, but most of the techniques are largely intuitive.

SOME FORECASTING TECHNIQUES

Flow Chart and Diagram Construction. Some techniques cited are simply means for displaying the relevant data. Flow charts and other graphic displays of this type can be used to depict the directions of change and, more important, the interaction between various components of the project and the "human community." These approaches can vary significantly in terms of sophistication.

Metaphors, Analogies, and Comparison. Project effects can be determined by comparing the unimplemented project with those that are similar. The applicability of this approach is limited by the shortage of comparative data and the lack of bibliographic control and access to relevant case studies. The diversity of each completed project makes it difficult to carry out controlled comparisons.

Delphi Technique. Delphi technique was developed at the Rand Corporation in the late 1940s.

Delphi is an attempt to elicit expert opinion in a systematic manner for useful results. It usually involves iterative questionnaires administered to individual experts in a manner protecting the anonymity of their responses. Feedback of results accompanies each iteration of the questionnaire, which continues until convergence of opinion, or a point of diminishing returns, is reached. The end product is the consensus of experts, including their commentary, on each of the questionnaire items, usually organized as a written report by the Delphi investigator. (Sackman 1975:xi)

Trend Extrapolation. This technique assumes some constancy in existing processes of directional change. That is, trends determined between the present and the past will relate to conditions at some future point. There are various types of trend extrapolation.

Scenarios. Scenarios are "future histories" or "narrative descriptions of potential courses of developments'' (Vlachos et al. 1975:63). Scenario writing draws, in an intuitive way, on the profile narrative. Scenarios are very useful for presenting the nature of the project and its effects to a lay audience. The scenario should reflect various alternative courses of the project.

Cross-impact Matrices. Emerging out of environmental impact assessment practice, matrix analysis explicitly depicts the interaction of various project features. In the absence of a scheme of analysis standards, matrix analysis is merely a way to logically present intuitive judgments. It is defined as

an experimental approach by which the probability of each item in a forecasted set can be adjusted in view of judgments relating to potential interactions of the forecasted items. Such an approach analyzes cross effects through an elaboration of potential interrelationships in the direction of the interaction, strength of the interaction and time delay of the effect of one effect or another. (Vlachos et al. 1975:65)

ASSESSMENT

Formally, the next step in the SIA process as defined here is the assessment of impact. Clearly, the distinction between impact projection and assessment is difficult to demonstrate. Assessment involves summarization and comparison of the various projections. The type of assessment used relates very closely to the kinds of projections. Assessments can deal with the following characteristics of the project/context situation:

Affected groups

How they are affected

The likelihood of effects

The timing of effects

The magnitude of effects

The duration of the impact

The breadth and depth of impact, or the diffusion of effects

The source of impact, or the organization

The controllability of the impact generated by given technologies

(Vlachos et al. 1975:62)

Without discussing the details of the assessment process, let us simply emphasize that it is possible to overestimate its power and utility. Social costs are in particular very difficult to determine prospectively. Needless to say, the realm of social indicator analysis is potentially the most productive. One area where productive assessment is more possible is the determination of who is affected.

This was an important consideration in Jacobs's assessment of El Llano project, to which we now return.

POTENTIAL IMPACTS OF EL LLANO PROJECT

Jacobs's research revealed that the residents of the impact zone were highly concerned about the project. These concerns were for the most part negative. Earlier in the predevelopment period, a community group was formed to resist the dam project and the related irrigation system. The group was named Association of Communities United to Protect the Rio Grande (ACUPRG). It carried out an active public education and resistance program.

The perceptions of the project and its impact were colored by the nature of the planning procedure used by the Bureau of Reclamation, the lead agency, and the cooperating agency, the Bureau of Indian Affairs. A thorough reading of Jacobs's account, which includes a fair number of basic documents from the project, suggests that the agencies' planning style was a significant causal factor in generating community resistance to the project. The intent of the various agencies involved was not fully disclosed.

One of the major objections to the construction of the project was that it would result in the obliteration of the three-hundred-year-old irrigation system structures. Project planners did not seem to recognize the antiquity and cultural significance of the traditional irrigation system. The ditches were referred to as "temporary diversion structures." The fact that the old dams associated with the ditches were attached to local descent groups was simply not recognized by the official documents.

The local community was also concerned that the new dam would result in reduced water flow, an issue that was not made clear in the earlier documentation of the project. The people feared and objected to this because of the potential problem it would cause the orchards, and the aesthetic cost of a dry river and the associated dam.

The loss of the traditional irrigation system and the initiation of control of the irrigation water by the irrigation district would result in the loss of control of the water by the *mayordomos* and the governor of San Juan Pueblo. In her report Jacobs suggests the "grave concern" of the *mayordomos* for the "future equitable distribution of water" and the future expression of their responsibilities. Jacobs notes: "If this authority and power is, in fact, taken from the *mayordomos* then one of the strongest measures of local government in the Spanish American communities will be lost" (1977:30).

Jacobs's report to the Bureau of Reclamation in Amarillo, Texas contained references to other kinds of "potential social impacts." These include the negative aesthetic effects of construction noise, the problems associated with the population growth stimulated by the project, as well as the associated relocation problems. Jacobs suggested that the area would lose some of its ethnic diversity because of the increased influx of Anglos. The community members were very

concerned about the project's effect on the appearance of the river. They were
worried about the river going dry and the disappearance of the *bosques*, or
groves, along the banks of the stream.

The project would have an adverse effect on historic and archaeological resources. A number of houses perhaps as old as two hundred years would potentially be harmed by the project. Various archaeological sites were similarly
threatened.

Community members were concerned that the construction process would
disrupt classroom instruction in local schools as well as cause threats to the well-
being of the students. Related to this were fears that the physical transformation
of the communities' life space would result in changes in the informal processes
of socialization within the community.

The communities had made use of the existing recreation potential of the river
by swimming and fishing. Residents felt that the marginal improvements in
recreation potential would not adequately compensate for the negative impacts.

The report also makes the case that the project, during construction and after
completion, would result in various health hazards. These would include increased threat of drowning, breeding of insects, and airborne dust. There was
also some concern about the possibility of an earthquake that would cause the
dam to break.

EVALUATION—THE LAST STEP

Social impact assessment in the final analysis is not a scientific practice as
much as a political one. Which is to say, SIA produces documents that assist
the process of decision making. This decision making is based on the evaluations
presented in the report and the politicians' interpretation of them. The decision
takes the form of a selection from among the alternatives. The analyst does not
evaluate in the final accounting. That is the task of the politicans and/or the
public. This step of the process is often made more public than earlier stages.

Because evaluation is a political process, it is difficult and unpredictable. Its
difficulty is caused by the confrontation of local community and development
agency values. The focal point may in fact be the impact statement itself. The
stress generated by the confrontation can be mitigated by openness in executing
the impact assessment. The amount of stress relates to the amount of controversy
concerning the project. More controversial projects should be more public, and
the openness should occur right from the very beginning.

El Llano Project became controversial. The planning process became more
public. Finally, the project was killed in Congress because it was apparent that
the positive benefits of the project would not outweigh its negative effects (Jacobs
1978). In this way the anthropologist's policy research efforts served as a means
of protecting community values.

SUMMARY

Social impact assessment is a type of policy research frequently done by anthropologists. In many ways it is very similar to the community study method used by both anthropologists and sociologists for many years. The process of social impact assessment can be highly structured by agency requirements. As this field has developed, the number of regulations and guidelines that structure the work has increased dramatically. A person engaged in SIA must carefully keep up with agency procedures. Just as agency guidelines change and develop, so does the market for such services. An important factor in shaping the market is the amount of federal spending in construction. Decreases in spending on such construction, recently coupled with changes in federal policy toward the whole environmental impact assessment process, has decreased the amount of this kind of work.

An interesting quality of social impact assessment is that learning its techniques can be very useful for most cultural anthropologists. There is great utility in learning how to acquire secondary data and how to treat it in the context of change. An emerging adjunct to the social impact assessment process is the field of public participation coordination.

Further Reading

Derman, William, and Scott Whiteford, eds. 1985. *Social Impact Analysis and Development Planning in the Third World.* Boulder, Colo.: Westview Press.

Contains good case material and overview discussions.

Jacobs, Sue-Ellen. 1978 " 'Top-down Planning': Analysis of Obstacles to Community Development in an Economically Poor Region of the Southwestern United States." *Human Organization* 37(3):246-256.

Contains an account of the author's involvement in the social impact assessment process in El Llano project.

Millsap, William, ed. 1984. *Applied Social Science for Environmental Planning.* Boulder, Colo: Westview Press.

Good collection of materials on a number of issues that relate to social impact assessment.

Preister, Kevin. 1987. "Issue-Centered Social Impact Assessment." In *Anthropological Praxis: Translating Knowledge into Action*, Robert M. Wulff and Shirley J. Fiske, eds. Boulder, Colo: Westview Press.

Documents anticipated impacts of the development of a skiing area in Colorado.

12

Evaluation

Evaluation is a kind of policy research. It shares some fundamental features with social impact assessment. First, both are concerned with the impact or effects of different actions on people. Second, both can make use of the same kinds of research methods and techniques. But the two kinds of research are different in certain important ways. SIA is primarily concerned with discovering *before* the fact any costly unintended effects of an activity. For example, governments build dams to impound water so that floods are reduced, agricultural production is increased, or recreational opportunities can be developed. In this situation an SIA might be done to predict whether this would have adverse effects on nearby communities. The purpose of dams is not to displace communities, so it is important to planners to identify all the effects.

Evaluation is most often concerned with determining *after* the fact whether the intended benefits of an activity occurred, or alternatively discovering whether a project with intended benefits is working. For example, an agency might establish a program to increase employment of high school dropouts, and then do research to determine whether the dropouts became employed. In addition, evaluation can be used to examine program operations as well as program effects.

INTEGRATED RESEARCH METHODOLOGY

Our treatment of evaluation will focus primarily on research design. The discussion will start with consideration of classical experimental design. From this base we will consider a number of research design alternatives. Our perspective will be that of general social science as much as anthropology. The specific uses of ethnography in evaluation will be considered. It is important to note that contemporary evaluation research makes use of many different research strategies and that these methods and techniques are used by evaluators regardless of the discipline they were trained in. One is likely to pick up an ethnographically oriented evaluation research report, based on participant-observation, and find that no anthropologists were involved in the study. And, of course, the reverse is true: it is possible to find anthropologists involved in executing pre-test, post-test, control group experimental designs. Ethnographic practice is one tool, a very useful tool, but only one tool. The implications are clear—evaluation researchers need to know a number of different designs whether they are anthropologists, sociologists, psychologists, political scientists, economists, or other kinds of researchers.

This statement on evaluation takes an integrated research methodology approach, which may combine qualitative and quantitative research (Cook and Reichardt 1979). The integrated research methodology approach requires that we control a variety of research designs and data collection techniques. This implies the possession of the necessary technical skill to process and analyze the data derived through a variety of techniques. The integrated research methodology approach means carefully identifying which research data collection technique is required to solve a research problem. What works? What carries us the furthest in understanding? What is efficient? What research technique is the most credible? These questions represent some of the dimensions that can be considered when we make a judgment about the research approach that will be used.

The criteria that we use to judge which design and technique we will use are quite broad. Of course, basic notions of validity and reliability are among the most important. Another important consideration is cost, both in money and time. The best design in the world is worthless if one can not afford to implement it. Ethnographic practice sometimes involves a great deal of time spent in research. Yet, a good ethnographer can learn a lot about what is going on in a situation by interviewing one person. In any case, there is a large range of legitimate concerns in terms of research design and technique selection. A final, important question is, Does the researcher have the skill to do the task?

Anthropologists can be involved in evaluation in two different ways. First, and most important, is as a broadly trained social scientist who is prepared to do a variety of evaluation research tasks as needed. The second is as a specialized evaluation ethnographer, who contributes to evaluation through nonexperimental, unobtrusive, qualitative, and participatory research techniques as these skills are needed. In this second role, the anthropologist may also be valued because he or she has knowledge of the group within which the evaluation is taking place, in addition to knowledge of technique. While ethnographic skills are very useful in the evaluation process, as we will discuss later, the most promising approach is the first. There are opportunities for professional, ethnographically oriented evaluators, it is just that pathways for career development are more open to people with somewhat broader technical training in research design and data analysis. M. G. Trend speaks of ethnographic evaluators being stuck at the lower levels of large evaluation programs, being relegated to a "go-fer" role with lower pay and less job security (1976). For more discussion of these issues see Chapter 14, "Making a Living."

One implication of the view expressed above is that there is not an anthropological way of evaluating. It is more useful to think of a multifaceted and loosely structured social science of evaluation in which individual problems in evaluation are addressed using a variety of techniques. Anthropologists can do their job better if they have control of a variety of techniques. The task is not to mimic sociology or psychology, but to participate in a larger contemporary tradition in social or behavioral science. The effect of this on anthropology will be positive.

This chapter will have three parts: (1) a discussion of the evaluation process, with description of alternatives for evaluation design; (2) a discussion of differing perspectives on the role of evaluation; and (3) case studies in evaluation done by anthropologists. The cases used are evaluations of the Administrative Agency Experiment of the Department of Housing and Urban Development, the Tumaco (Colombia) Health Project of Foster Parents Plan International, the Job Shop/ Job Club Program of the Community Education Center of West Philadelphia, and a needs assessment done for the United Way of Saskatoon.

EVALUATION PROCESS

Because this single-chapter treatment of evaluation is necessarily brief, our presentation of evaluation may make the field seem much more orderly than it really is. Evaluation encompasses all the disarray that you would expect in a relatively young field in which persons of many disciplines participate. This situation has been exacerbated by the fact that important segments of the field, most notably educational evaluation, have undergone rapid growth forced by huge federal subsidies. For example, the Elementary and Secondary Education Act of 1965 carried a provision that educators receiving grants in support of education programs had to submit evaluation reports that identified the effects of the program. Basically, a lot happened quickly, and there has been little synthesis. There are a number of competing viewpoints and substantial semantic difficulties. Now then, what is evaluation?

At its very core evaluation is what the dictionary says it is, that is, "the determination of the worth of something. While all of us are constantly evaluating things, activities, and ideas, evaluation in a technical sense requires much more than the casually subjective, and largely private, assessments of worth that we produce everyday. Let us consider evaluation as a process.

First, a general technical definition: "Evaluation is the determination of the worth of a thing. It includes obtaining information for use in judging the worth of a program, product, procedure, or objective, or the potential utility of alternative approaches designed to attain specified objectives" (Worthen and Sanders 1973:19). When evaluation is done, it is almost always done in reference to activity that is intended to affect people in one way or another. Evaluation can be used to determine worth in both negative and positive aspects. While many research designs used in evaluation stress the determination of whether planned objectives were accomplished, evaluation can also be used to discover unintended consequences of programs and projects. The activities evaluated are always motivated by some desired end state.

The evaluation process is a process by which values are rationalized. The idea of treatment borrowed from the literature on experimental design is useful as a label for the actions, projects, programs, and so forth that are carried out to achieve goals. Other dimensions to the evaluation process are the nature and characteristics of both the agency providing the service and the individuals and groups that are the focus of the agency.

At a general level there are three types of evaluations:

I. Effects studies—The basic task here is the determination of whether a program (or other entity) is achieving its goals. This is the classic evaluation task. It has also been referred to as product evaluation (Stufflebeam 1973) or outcome evaluation. Effects studies done during the life of a program that are intended to inform program managers or sponsors about program operations can be thought of as process evaluations (Stufflebeam 1973). Effects studies can be directed at the dissemination of practices to other settings to help guide decisions about continuance, enhancement, curtailment, and modification.

II. Process studies—The basic task here is to determine how a program is operating. This is a managerial task. This type of evaluation is also called operations analysis (Riecken 1972). Both process and effects studies may be designed in the same way. Process evaluations may consist of long-term program monitoring.

III. Needs assessment—The basic task here is to determine the needs of a potentially served population (McKillip 1987; Neuber 1980; Scriven and Roth 1978). One could include needs assessment in a discussion of planning. Needs assessment can also occur during the life of a program so as to allow program redefining. That is, it can be part of program planning and management. Needs assessment can be ongoing.

This general typology implies a number of dimensions. These include: the purpose or role of the evaluation, the timing of the research, and to some indirect extent, the research design. There are a number of very useful discussions in the evaluation literature that address these dimensions. Let us focus on design.

Research design is what is unique about evaluation research when compared to other types of research. Measurement and data analysis techniques are quite comparable in evaluation and basic research. Let us start our discussion of design by considering the classical design pattern and then expanding from that base.

Carol H. Weiss depicts the "traditional formulation" of evaluation research in the following way (1972:6):

1. Finding out the goals of the program;
2. Translating the goals into measurable indicators of goal achievement;

3. Collecting data on the indicators for those who have been exposed to the program;

4. Collecting similar data on an equivalent group that has not been exposed to the program (control group);

5. Comparing the data on program participants and controls in terms of goal criteria.

This is, of course, a generalized version of experimental design used in behavioral science. An understanding of this basic pattern can be supplemented by reading *Experimental and Quasi-experimental Designs for Research* by Donald T. Campbell and J. C. Stanley (1965); *Research Design in Anthropology: Paradigms and Paradigmatics in the Testing of Hypotheses* by John A. Brim and David H. Spain (1974); or *Quasi-experimentation: Design and Analysis Issues for Field Settings*, by Thomas D. Cook and Donald T. Campbell (1979). These volumes very clearly lay out research design alternatives.

Campbell and Stanley (1965) define five different research designs. The list starts with the least rigorous, the one-shot case study. In a one-shot case study of a program one would measure the effects of the program only once, after the research subjects had participated in the program. What is absent from this method is a baseline measurement, called a pre-test, to determine the "before condition." One has to assume a great deal about the program participants' prior state. Some researchers attempt to strengthen the one-shot case study design by using documentary evidence or reconstructions based on self-reports. At worst, one-shot case studies take the form of program-serving testimonials. Fortunately, there are many circumstances where the one-shot case study can be valuable, because the design is very common. Much ethnographic evaluation takes the form of a one-shot case study. All the examples discussed later in this chapter are of this type.

An enhancement of the one-shot case study is the one-group, pre-test, post-test design. The addition of the pre-test allows one to measure change more objectively. The pre-test, however, does not allow one conclusively to attribute the change to the program. Change can occur because of other events, such as normal change through time, the pre-test's effects, ineffective measurement, and participant fatigue, as well as other factors.

A third type of research design is the static group comparison, which adds a control group to the one-shot case study. In this method, a group that has experienced the program is compared with a group that has not experienced it. The weakness is that the design does not allow certainty about the differences between the groups before the treatment. It is possible to strengthen this design through matching of participants and the use of retrospective measures.

The fourth type is the pre-test, post-test, control group design, which involves setting up two groups before the program. In terms of research design quality, the best way of doing this is by random assignment. There is a before and after measurement to determine effects of the program. This design, although very good, does not control for the effects of the research procedure. This can be controlled for through the use of the final research design, the Solomon four-

231group design, in which the effects of the research are examined along with the effects of the program.

These design alternatives do not address issues relating to needs assessment, but are applicable to many contexts in both effect and process studies. The problems with needs assessment mostly revolve around having the research sample be consistent with the group that actually receives the service after program implementation.

While these are standard designs, and each represents an incremental increase in the capacity to specify cause, there are costs associated with increases in experimental control. This is one reason why much evaluation is carried out using the one-shot case study design. The more complex, error-reducing designs are used quite extensively in education to evaluate curricula in anticipation of wider use. It is clear why; the treatments are usually more readily definable and control groups are easier to find and match. Treatments will consist of a set of test materials administered in an adequately standardized way, and, if you need a control group, other classes of student "subjects" are available. Similar patterns occur in the evaluation of drug treatment programs, in which the participants have diminished control because they are in the program by order of the courts.

Outside of certain specialized areas, it may be very difficult to apply the more complex research designs. While there are many statements in the literature on evaluation that present the more complex designs as ideals, it is very important to view these designs as alternatives to be selected for application as appropriate. Selection should always be based on the most appropriate design, not the most elegant one.

A very large array of factors needs to be considered in evaluation planning, in addition to basic research design. Perhaps most important is the intended purpose of the evaluation. Some researchers may place too high a value on the elegance of their design, and too low a value on assisting the program to serve its clients better. Anthropologists in evaluation seem to be more committed to clients' needs than others. Other factors to consider are cost, available time, and the nature of the service population.

Soft Designs

As we know, in many circumstances soft and fuzzy is good. Much of the research methodology literature is geared toward an idealization of hard and definite. This is changing somewhat as researchers become disenchanted with operationalism. Yet one still finds defensiveness on the part of soft methodologists. Hard versus soft is not the same as good versus bad. Both approaches are subject to their own problems of quality. By soft designs we mean, among other things, research that stresses qualitative methods, naturalistic observation, discovery, induction, and holism. By hard designs we mean, among other things, quantitative methods, structured observation, verification, deduction, and particularism (Cook and Reichardt 1979:10). For example, ethnography, with its emphasis on key informants and participant-observation, tends toward softness; survey research, with its emphasis on randomly selected subjects and instrumented observation (i.e., questionnaires) tends toward hardness. Again, we are not arguing for anything other than the selection of appropriate methods. When are soft methods appropriate?

Soft methods are useful because they are often less of a burden for the program staff. The more structured the research design is, the greater the chance of the evaluation interfering with program functioning. It is very difficult to burden useful programs with certain kinds of highly structured research. The selection of softer designs is called for where obtrusiveness is an issue. Soft methods are useful where program goals are less well-defined, or are especially complex and diverse. Soft approaches are really useful for discovery. Ethnographers seem to do research more to raise questions than to answer them. Soft methods are often the only way to realistically handle complex situations. The more structured the research design, the fewer variables it can consider. Program goals are often not very well defined. Soft techniques can be fit into ongoing program development better than hard approaches. The before and after measures specified in the experimental designs can be replaced with during-during-during measures, which are more workable with softer techniques.

Softer methods often prepare the way for implementation of results better than hard methods because the researchers often end up with an excellent understanding of the persons managing programs and the constraints under which they must operate. In fact, it may be best to have the evaluation include continual feedback to the program with correction. This kind of arrangement is unworkable with hard designs because it interferes with the outcome of the research. Further, hard research designs assume too much about the stability of programs while they are being evaluated. Mid-study change in program administration disrupts the hard studies, but for the soft designs this kind of activity simply represents more data relevant to the program. We might say that soft techniques are useful in rapidly changing circumstances.

Hard Designs

Hard research designs are especially appropriate if the program has clear-cut, measurable objectives that are identified within the program. Hard designs are appropriate where program staff are familiar with, and value, research along with their commitment to service. This orientation is appropriate to situations where control groups are readily available. The idea of the control group is sometimes antithetical to the service orientation of program administrators. In some circumstances, establishing control groups requires one to deny access. Hard approaches work well where there is relative program stability and a lower expectation or need for mid-course feedback. A useful application of hard approaches is in the production of the final evaluation of demonstration projects, with the goal being to inform potential adopters of the program.

Both hard or soft techniques must be executed in a way that allows their results to be applied to real-world decision making. The inflexibility of the hard techniques can relate to less timeliness—that is, the research has to run its prescribed course. Soft techniques, on the other hand, can be so unfocused that the researcher meanders through a program without attending to the needed research issues. It is important to remember that the primary use of evaluation is to provide information for decision making. Late research is bad research.

PERSPECTIVES ON THE ROLE OF EVALUATION

Evaluation has a number of different roles, both legitimate and illegitimate. A useful understanding of the roles of evaluation can be derived from the ideas of Michael Scriven and Daniel L. Stufflebeam. Both have developed concepts of evaluation that can serve to direct it toward greater utility.

In a very important and frequently reprinted article entitled "The Methodology of Evaluation" (1973), Michael Scriven provides a number of concepts useful for thinking about the role of evaluation. Although his discussion is focused on evaluation in education, with emphasis on the evaluation of new teaching methods and curricula, his ideas are very widely applicable. As he notes, the roles of evaluation can be quite variable. All these roles relate to the primary goal of evaluation: to determine worth. The role of evaluation in some ways structures the evaluation itself.

Scriven conceives of two types of evaluation research: formative evaluation and summative evaluation. Formative evaluation is carried out in the course of a project, with the goal of improving project functions or products. The evaluation may be done by an outside consultant, but the information produced by the evaluation is for the use of the agency. As Scriven notes, "the evaluation feedback loop stays *within* the developmental agency (its consultants), and serves to improve the product" (1973:62). Formative evaluation is conceptualized as a mid-term outcome study of the product or effects of the program, rather than a more general kind of process study, which might answer the question, What is going on here?

Summative evaluation serves to determine worth at the end of the process and is intended to go outside the agency whose work is being evaluated. The evaluation serves to increase utilization and recognition of the project. According to Scriven, program monitoring is a hybrid type of summative evaluation in that it is intended to go outside the agency being evaluated, but at an intermediate time.

Both formative and summative evaluation can make use of the same research designs. However, because of their different roles they require different communication strategies. The essence of the formative-summative contrast rests in the direction and purpose of the communication of evaluation results. Scriven also contrasts what he calls *intrinsic* and *pay-off* evaluation. Intrinsic evaluation evaluates the content of the project's product or treatment, whereas pay-off evaluation is focused on effects. These four concepts—formative versus summative, intrinsic versus pay-off—are useful because they focus the evaluation on a specific purpose.

Scriven's ideas make us sensitive to the various roles of evaluation; Stufflebeam's work models an entire process of evaluation. His work, also developed in the context of educational evaluation, rests on the assumption that evaluation is done to aid decision making. The information that it provides should be useful to decision makers. Evaluation is a continuing process and is best organized in coordination with implementation. Data collection needs to be consciously targeted on decision-making needs. The total evaluation process ultimately involves collaboration between evaluator and decision maker.

This view of evaluation is integrated by Stufflebeam into a comprehensive process referred to as the CIPP evaluation model. The model specifies different kinds of evaluation, which serve various purposes and inform various types of decisions. These decision types are: (1) *"planning decisions* to determine objectives"; (2) *"structuring decisions* to design procedures"; (3) *"recycling decisions* to judge and react to attainments"; and (4) *"implementing decisions* to utilize, control and refine procedures" (Stufflebeam 1973:133). The four types of decisions are served by four types of evaluation. These are *context evaluation, input evaluation, product evaluation,* and *process evaluation.*

Context evaluation supports planning decisions. This category would include what is called needs assessment by others, but would also identify resources that are not being used, and constraints that affect needs. Products of context evaluation include identification of the client population, and of general goals and objectives. Input evaluation supports structuring decisions. The important task here is the identification of resources that relate to project objectives. Part of the process involves the determination of current agency capability. Also included is the identification of alternate strategies for accomplishing objectives. Input evaluation also involves costing out alternatives. Process evaluation supports implementing decisions. This type of evaluation is used to find defects in procedures and implementation, to inform ongoing decisions, and to document activities of the program. Product evaluation informs recycling decisions. The task here is to evaluate project accomplishments at various points in the life of the project. Product evaluation requires operational definition of objectives, development of a measurement strategy, and standards against which measurements are compared.

CASE STUDIES: FOUR EVALUATIONS

These four projects were selected to illustrate evaluation in different settings, all executed by anthropologists. The fact that all four evaluations are case studies is not an accident. Evaluation anthropologists rarely use control groups. While the evaluations are all case studies, they are quite different. They differ in terms of how they structure analytical comparisons. This is especially apparent in the first case, on housing and the third case, on employment. The second case, on health care, is primarily concerned with documenting project completion. The fourth case is a needs assessment for a community service agency.

Evaluating Housing Policy Innovations

The Administrative Agency Experiment (AAE) was one of three social experiments initiated by the U.S. Department of Housing and Urban Development (HUD) in the early 1970s to test the use of direct-cash housing allowance payments to assist low-income families improve the quality of their housing through the open market (Trend 1978a). Housing vouchers had been considered as an alternative to subsidized public housing by politicians and policy makers for a considerable amount of time. This program attempted to test the workability of this approach and to develop effective management practices. Most other programs for improving housing for the poor presented beneficiaries with limited choice. The AAE payments were made directly to the families, with the stipulation that they had to spend the money on housing.

The three experiments tested different issues. In addition to the AAE, experiments were designed that tested the effect of direct payments on housing supply and demand. The AAE tested various approaches for management of such a social policy. The AAE was implemented by eight public agencies in different localities throughout the country. The agencies were given substantial control over administrative procedures and implementation at their site. Each local project was allowed to enroll up to nine hundred families for the two-year period of the experiment. The sites were in Springfield, Massachusetts; Jacksonville, Florida; Durham, North Carolina; Tulsa, Oklahoma; San Bernardino, California; Portland, Oregon; Peoria, Illinois; and Bismarck, North Dakota.

The evaluation was carried out by Abt Associates, Incorporated, a large research consulting firm located in Cambridge, Massachusetts. The project made extensive use of anthropologists, especially for on-site observation, but also in subsequent analysis. Most of those employed were fresh out of graduate school.

The AAE was intended to provide information on different methods for administering a housing allowance program. The evaluation task was complex and included documenting both effects and administrative procedures. The AAE was implemented by four different types of organizations: local housing authorities, metropolitan government agencies, state community development agencies, and welfare agencies. HUD provided fewer administrative requirements for implementation than normal. They included certain eligibility rules, payment formulas, a locally defined housing standard requirement, restriction to rental property, a lease requirement, a standard payment plan, and certain reporting procedures. Beyond this, variation was encouraged. Agencies had flexibility in various administrative functions. These included outreach methods, enrollment procedures, certification procedures, payment practices, inspection standards, community relations activities, and overall program management. Variation in the form and effectiveness of these different functions was an important focus of the evaluation task. The local agencies generated the program features that were to be evaluated.

The AAE was a naturalistic experiment and therefore did not test hypotheses. The evaluation involved after-the-fact determination of success, with emphasis on documenting and evaluating the various solutions to the problems of implementation. Thus the evaluation questions were determined by the design decisions that were made as the programs developed in the eight sites.

The evaluation was based on data from a variety of sources; most important were the on-site observers. These observers spent a year documenting administrative agency activities. While these observations focused on the agency as a whole, the observations and field notes they produced were referenced to fourteen functions, such as outreach, certification, and inspection, as mentioned above. This allowed cross-project comparison. When variations between agencies were apparent, these variations were examined to determine relative effectiveness and impact. These assessments were addressed in reports that compared projects across functions. The reports provided information that facilitated knowledge transfer to other similar projects. This is the summative evaluation function at work.

The evaluation design required that work be done toward two kinds of research objectives. These included data collection that focused on operational measures, such as numbers of enrollees and payment levels, as well as qualitative assessments of hard-to-measure features, such as fairness and dignity of treatment of participants.

Some measures of function were defined early in the experiment and collected through the use of program documents. Background data on participants and the local community was collected throughout the project. In addition to the information on cross-agency differences, information on common features was also collected. In this frame, outcome data was compared. In addition, the evaluation process also produced separate case studies in reference to specific functions and agency programs that were problematic. Many of these case studies were based on observational data.

Six types of data were collected and used: direct observation of agency activities; surveys of participating households; data from administrative agency forms on participants; agency management reports; site environmental data; and samplings of administrative records. The full-time, on-site observers produced field notes that were formatted to allow comparison between programs categorized by the previously mentioned functions. These materials were used for various purposes, but were especially useful for interpretation. The survey component collected information on income, household composition, and attitudes toward the program on the part of participants. In addition, the time of project employees was charged to the various function areas. All in all, the amount of data collected was immense. For example, over twenty-five thousand pages of field notes were accumulated.

The analysis attempted to assess the overall utility of the direct payment approach to meeting housing needs, while making recommendations as to how direct payment might best be done. The variation-focused evaluation helped identify what were thought to be more effective administrative practices. For example, the Bismarck agency found that they obtained reliable certification results with simpler income determination procedures than the other agencies. The Jacksonville agency evaluation addressed the problems of making the approach work in a tight housing market.

Perhaps most important, the experiment demonstrated that poor people could effectively operate in the open housing market in terms of their own choice. The project also showed that the allowance program did not raise housing costs in these markets. On the negative side, the AAE did not reduce housing segregation significantly. The evaluators concluded that AAE was a useful tool in dealing with the housing problems of poor people from a policy perspective. Ultimately, many of the approaches demonstrated in the AAE came to be implemented in federal housing law.

Evaluating a Health Project Sponsored by a Private Voluntary Organization

Foster Parents Plan International (PLAN) is a private organization that sponsors community development projects in twenty-two developing countries. As a private voluntary organization, or PVO, it is not funded as a government agency, nor is it a profit-making firm (Buzzard 1982). Most of the funding for the Foster Parents Plan program comes from individual sponsors (called foster parents) in Australia, Canada, the United Kingdom, the Netherlands, and the United States. These individuals are matched with individual needy foster children. This arrangement is the best-known component of the program. PLAN provides these foster children with various services depending on local resources. A portion of the foster parents' contribution may go directly to the family, often to pay school expenses. In addition, these funds can be aggregated and used for community projects. Community projects may start with a request from the local community. Local PLAN offices are budgeted to fund these projects. In addition, some funds are available from the international headquarters in Rhode Island for special projects. Also PLAN may solicit money from government agencies to fund projects.

The project evaluation considered here was part of the PLAN program funded by the U.S. Agency for International Development (AID) to train community health workers in four field locations—two in Colombia, plus Ecuador and Indonesia. The project discussed here was located in Tumaco, a densely populated seaport town in the Pacific lowlands of Colombia.

Tumaco was faced with a very difficult public health situation. There was limited clean water and no means of sanitary human waste and garbage disposal. Houses were typically built on piles driven into the tidal flats of river estuaries and beaches. Wastes were disposed of in the water, garbage accumulated near the simple houses, and people defecated on the beaches or in the fields. Although there was a water system, it was old and dilapidated, providing ineffective treatment. In any case, the transport and storage of the water from the tap to its use resulted in more contamination. The effect of this was endemic parasite infestation and high incidence of gastroenteritis, with its debilitating diarrheal disease. Hand washing was infrequent and probably ineffective given the nature of the water. The boiling of water was rare and difficult to get done.

The health problems related to these conditions were exacerbated by poor nutritional status and bad economic conditions. The local diet was based largely on bananas, rice, and cassava. Although the economy was based on littoral fishing and shrimping, many families could not afford these protein-rich foods. As a result, severe protein deficiency could be observed in some children. The generally poor nutritional status of the population tended to increase the effects of the gastrointestinal problems. In this population, diarrheal disease killed children. Other significant health problems were tetanus (especially among newborns), malaria, measles, as well as accidents among the fishermen. Health care facilities were limited.

It was in this context that PLAN initiated the Tumaco Health Project. The project was funded through an agreement with AID. The primary objectives were the improvement of the health and nutritional status of PLAN families, with emphasis on the needs of mothers and children under six years of age. The specific objectives of the five-site project included: (1) decrease the mortality and morbidity from diseases that could be controlled through vaccination; (2) improve sanitation in the family setting to an adequate level; (3) achieve an adequate nutritional level (monitored by age for weight), with special attention to children under six years of age; (4) improve the level of health care and nutrition of mothers during pregnancy and lactation; (5) provide to families health education concerning prevention and treatment of disease; and (6) improve knowledge and access to effective family planning practices.

The Tumaco Health Project sought to achieve these objectives in a number of ways. The core activity was the recruitment, training, and placement of fourteen health promoters from the local community. This required the establishment of an administrative infrastructure and a training program. The functioning of the health promoters and related programs was to be monitored through a record-keeping and evaluation system that would improve quality of management. Program objectives showed a concern for integration of the Tumaco Health Project with the regional system through referral to existing clinics and collaboration with the Ministry of Health. The project was also to result in the construction and staffing of four health posts, installation of public water systems, and the construction of public latrines. All these activities were to be carried out with maximal community participation.

PLAN sought to evaluate the project mid-term, following the training and placement of the health promoters and the establishment of the health posts.

Unlike many other PVOs, PLAN has an ongoing program of evaluation. The evaluation of the Tumaco Health Project reflected the experiences of the PLAN evaluation organization and the reporting requirements associated with the use of AID funds. The evaluation had two primary purposes: the monitoring of the project by PLAN headquarters, and the documentation of the project's functioning for the instruction of others doing similar projects.

The project evaluation was conceived as a case study. Presumably because the evaluation was intended for both internal and external use, there was much reporting of background information on health conditions and the local community. The design of the evaluation was not structured as an experiment to determine program effects. The primary emphasis was the identification of project plan attainments rather than project effects.

The data upon which the evaluation was based was collected using a number of techniques. Participant-observation was used to gain a general familiarity with project functions. The participant-observation data included information gathered by accompanying health promoters on their rounds and the observation of daily activities in the health posts. More data was gathered by interviewing various participants in the program and its planning. This included Ministry of Health administrators as well as health service providers and users. Given the basic task of documenting what went on during the implementation portion of the project, the review of project internal correspondence was quite important. This aspect of the data collection process allowed the evaluator to chronicle the changes in the program. This data was supplemented with reviews of hospital records, health post records, and the data collected through the baseline survey carried out by the health promoters themselves.

The evaluation was more concerned with whether program treatments were implemented than with the actual effects of the treatments, as is often called for in an experimental design. The researcher found that the program was sound. This focus was consistent with the holistic case-study approach used. It shows the importance of the ability to use relatively unstructured inquiry and existing program documents in the evaluation process. The evaluation report shows the utility of an ethnographic approach to evaluation. This particular evaluation was carried out by anthropologist Shirley Buzzard.

Evaluating a Jobs Program in Philadelphia

One of the most significant problems facing inner-city America is unemployment. Programs designed to solve this problem are widespread. The Job Shop Program of the Community Education Center of West Philadelphia is one such program. Awarded a contract from the Pennsylvania Department of Community Affairs, the center was to provide services to unemployed persons in three Philadelphia neighborhoods (Simon and Curtis 1983).

The program was to offer job search assistance, employability training, and job development services to help unemployed clients. These services were offered as an integrated package of services. The program had four objectives. First, the training of 100 to 120 workers in job readiness, job-seeking skills, and job retention skills, and second, placement of at least 60 percent of these workers in unsubsidized employment or training programs. Third, the program was to assess the employment needs of local employers and to identify potential sources of employees. Fourth, the center was to help program participants retain their jobs by means of counseling and support services.

The center recruited participants through local media, community groups, advertisements, social service organizations, and local churches. The program was intended to serve people in the local neighborhoods. Program participants took classes in getting and keeping jobs. Instructional activities included writing resumes, dealing with applications, reading want ads, the interview experience, and good work habits. Following completion of class work, the participants were to actually search for work using their new skills with the help of project staff. Throughout the project, the staff was to work with local employers to identify possible jobs.

The contract that brought the funds to the center for the project required that the program be evaluated. The evaluation was carried out by Elaine Simon and Karen Curtis, who used a variety of data sources. Program activities were observed and compared with those specified in the proposal. In this way, the "treatment" that the participants received was described.

The proposal presented a rather generalized view of planned program activities. This pattern is very common in evaluation research. It is often the case that programs do not have clearly defined goals. In that goals are frequently the reference point for evaluation, it is not surprising that evaluators often have to spend time identifying goals or using goal-free evaluation techniques.

The evaluation made use of data on individual participants that included referral source, ethnicity, age, education, and previous work history. This was coupled with information on outcomes in employment, referral to other services, and program completion. This data was derived primarily from program records. An interesting component of the evaluation was extensive description of the content of training. The evaluation was further contextualized through the use of a number of participant histories in which their experiences in the program were documented. The individuals selected for profiling in this way were all successful cases. The profiles showed the interrelationship between aspects of the training and preparation and the program's overall success.

The design did not make use of control groups. Moreover, there was no explicit measure of effects of the training on the participants other than the important one, whether they were employed. There was no assessment of levels of new knowledge or changes in attitude. The core of the evaluation consisted of assessing whether the program achieved the numbers of planned participants and whether the predicted placement rates were achieved. These dimensions were compared in a generalized way with the experiences of other such programs. The quality of the employment that these persons obtained was also considered by examining employment in terms of classification by job type.

The evaluation revealed a program that had largely accomplished its originally stated goals. Coupled with this conclusion were a series of recommendations about the effects of certain participant referral sources. The study showed that participants referred to the program from welfare agencies were less likely to finish the program or to be employed if they did finish.

Assessing Community Needs in Saskatoon

The Saskatoon Needs Assessment Project was carried out by a team from the Department of Anthropology and Archaeology of the University of Saskatchewan, led by Alexander M. Ervin (Ervin et al. 1991). The idea for the project came from the board of the United Way. The executive director of the agency approached Ervin about doing the research. The project was funded in 1990 by a community foundation, the university, and the United Way. Saskatoon's population was about 200,000 at this time. The economy of this prairie city includes agriculture, mining, and forestry, as well a growing manufacturing segment. Unemployment was over 10 percent. There were increases in the use of food banks and soup kitchens.

The project was to provide baseline information for the agency to support their decision making in a number of areas. These included "identifying needs and public perceptions to assist agencies in meeting those needs; allocating funds by working with agencies to target programs in identified needs; evaluating new agencies which have applied to join United Way [and] fundraising by focusing marketing efforts on identified needs which the United Way serve" (Ervin et al. 1991:1).

The research design was developed by the project leader in consultation with an advisory committee, United Way's staff and board, and the research staff. Designs of other Canadian United Way needs assessments were consulted. The assessment process called for six data collection activities. The team reviewed available reports relevant to Saskatoon's needs. These reports, including those from the city government, nongovernment organizations, and academic programs, were abstracted for the final report. The team attempted to review social and economic indicators with the assistance of Statistics Canada. These indicators included census data, household structure, birth rates, labor force, employment, income, disability, and other data. The research team organized three public forums that were highly publicized. They conducted 135 interviews with key informants from community agencies. Five focus groups were held with client groups and one was held with representatives of self-help groups (Greenbaum 1988; Merton, Fiske, and Kendall 1990). Data was also collected using a three-stage Delphi procedure with an expert panel consisting of 28 United Way agency executive directors. Overall the needs assessment had remarkable breadth of contact with community groups. Over 140 agencies or organizations participated in the interviews and forums, or submitted written briefs.

Delphi procedure was developed as a means of collating the opinions of a panel of experts in a way that allows them to be aware of each others' opinions during the process without them being able to influence each other through their personalities. This technique is also discussed in the chapter on social impact assessment. In this case the process started with a single exercise: "Please list what you consider to be the most important social or human needs that should be addressed in Saskatoon, regardless of what agencies or levels of government are responsible for them." The experts were to type in their answers in ten boxes of equal size. The expert panel never spoke with each other directly, yet they communicated to each other through the research team.

The research team analyzed the responses and put them into standardized phrasing and related clusters. This produced a list of 108 needs. In the second round the experts were asked to choose the top twelve needs in rank order, and then to make comments. This produced another list of 86 needs, ranked in terms of their raw scores. The experts were then asked for any adjustments. The need that was ranked highest was the need "to eliminate hunger and therefore the necessity of food banks." Other highly ranked needs were: "need for more emphasis on preventive services," "need for accessible, affordable, quality accommodation; perhaps based on income (i.e. not low-income ghettos)," and the "need to increase core funding for non-government agencies to enable long term planning and development."

The Delphi panel data was used, along with data from all other sources, to produce an abstract of community needs on "the widespread social problems that are confronting Saskatoon" (Ervin et al. 1991:20). Also reported were the needs of organizations, referred to here as metaneeds. The more than two hundred needs identified were organized into seventeen sectors, including general health, mental health, seniors, native issues, racism and discrimination, immigrant and refugee resettlement, and rehabilitation, among others. The sectors were derived from a directory of community information published by the public library. The research team produced a series of recommendations for the United Way.

SUMMARY

Evaluation research is a rapidly growing area in applied anthropology. Preparation for careers in evaluation should include training in both experimental and case study design, as well as the appropriate data collection techniques. Research methods traditionally associated with anthropology are useful for a number of important evaluation tasks, but these need to be supplemented to meet the entire array of evaluation problems. The utility of ethnographic evaluation methods is directly related to the purpose of the evaluation. Ethnographic evaluation techniques are especially useful when one of the purposes of the evaluation is the documentation of program operations, or the discovery of what went wrong with a program. Ethnographic techniques serve as a good foundation for providing recommendations for program improvement.

Anthropologists in evaluation do not make extensive use of experimental designs. Usually they rely on various kinds of case study approaches. These approaches are quite variable and represent a significant array of research tools in their own right. The utility of the case study approach can be seen in the interest in these approaches shown by nonanthropologists. The literature on evaluation methodology places an emphasis on the use of experimental designs other than the case study. It is important to recognize that in spite of this, much evaluation is done using the case study approach. The reasons for this are largely practical. In many settings, it is expensive and politically awkward to use the more complex experimental designs. In addition, there are many problems in evaluation where the best and perhaps only approach is the case study method. In spite of the continued importance of the case study method there is relatively little discussion in the literature of refinements to the case study methodology.

FURTHER READING

Cook, Thomas D., and Charles S. Reichardt, eds. 1979. *Qualitative and Quantitative Methods in Evaluation Research*. Sage Research Progress Series in Evaluation, vol. 1. Beverly Hills, Calif.: Sage Publications.

Contains a number of good articles dealing with the qualitative–quantitative contrast. See especially the article by M. G. Trend on the Administrative Agency Experiment.

Fetterman, David M., and M. Pitman, eds. 1986. *Educational Evaluation: Ethnography in Theory, Practice, and Politics*. Beverly Hills, Calif.: Sage Publications.

Fetterman, David M. 1988. *Qualitative Approaches to Evaluation in Education: The Silent Revolution*. New York: Praeger.

David Fetterman has provided leadership in the use of ethnography in evaluation.

13

Technology Development Research

Technology development research is a type of policy or applied research that places the research anthropologist as a communication link between producers and users of new technology. The communication may range from relatively informal interaction to highly organized research and extension projects. The research itself may include elements of needs assessment, evaluation, baseline description, social soundness analysis, as well as extension. This type of policy research requires that the researcher have good understanding of the technology being developed and the occupational culture of the technology developers.

What is called technology development research for the purposes of this chapter includes all those research enterprises that serve the goal of the creation of culturally appropriate technology. These functions are carried out in many contexts, including architecture (Clement 1976), landscape design (Low and Simon 1984), medical treatment (Kendall 1989; Coreil 1989), energy source development (Practical Concepts, Inc. 1980; Roberts 1981), mariculture (Stoffle 1986), reforestation (Murray 1987; Smucker 1981), waste disposal (Elmendorf and Buckles 1978), and housing (Esber 1987; Mason 1979; Wulff 1972). This general type of research is most common in agricultural development (McCorkle 1989; Rhoades 1984).

The achievement of cultural appropriateness is an important goal of most of the intervention and research techniques that are discussed in this book. This value is emphasized in technology development research and cultural brokerage. Cultural appropriateness is, of course, conceptually related to the idea of appropriate technology or intermediate technology, developed by E. F. Schumacher (Schumacher 1973; Dunn 1979; McRobie 1981; Stewart 1977). Developers working within the framework of appropriate technology emphasize the design and manufacture of "small, simple, capital-saving, nonviolent technologies and their supporting institutions" (McRobie 1981: 13).

FARMING SYSTEMS RESEARCH

Technology development research is best represented by what is called farming systems research (FSR). This policy research tradition has emerged since the late 1970s as an important approach to rural development. It is the product of the work of agricultural economists, sociologists, and anthropologists. The work of Michael Collinson and David W. Norman is often cited in discussions of the development of the approach. According to Deborah Sands, for example, their work in Tanzania and Nigeria, respectively, demonstrated the complexity of small farmer resource allocation decisions (1985:3). This implied "that farmers' management strategies and decisions could only be understood within the context of the whole farm system," and "that ideal management in any specific enterprise is not feasible in the small farm situation" (Sands 1985:3). Yet this agricultural research was usually based on the assumption of ideal procedures, and was usually achieved at an experiment station, under conditions very different from a real farm.

A useful definition of FSR is provided by Shaner, Philipp, and Schmehl:

[FSR is] an approach to agricultural research and development that views the whole farm as a system and focuses on (1) the interdependencies between the components under the control of members of the farm household and (2) how these components interact with the physical, biological and socioeconomic factors not under the household's control. Farming systems are defined by their physical, biological, and socioeconomic setting and by the farm families's goals and other attributes, access to resources, choices of productive activities (enterprises), and management practices. (1982:13)

The definition shows FSR's emphasis on sociocultural factors as salient features of farming systems. In this framework sociocultural factors are not viewed as extraneous to the development process, but as essential components that must be understood if the development process is to work.

The perspective represented in this definition is consistent with some fundamental attributes of anthropological theory and method. Two important consistencies are the commitment to holism and the understanding of ecological relationships. Perhaps it is because of these consistencies that anthropologists seem comfortable working in this framework.

Historic Antecedents

Farming systems research has a number of historical antecedents. Perhaps most important is that agricultural research virtually requires, in the opinion of some, the assumption of a systems perspective (Dillon and Anderson 1984). Others argue that the approach was influenced by American farm management economics as it developed earlier in the twentieth century. The point is well taken because this type of economic analysis was focused on the efficient use of technology to increase farm income. As part of the farm management perspective, analysts studied the total farm in order to understand the relationship between economic activities. The holism characteristic of the farm management economics came to be largely lost in agricultural research, which became strongly reductionist after World War II (Gilbert, Norman, and Finch 1980). Research became more bounded by disciplines and focused on specific commodities. The research tradition became more geared to an agribusiness perspective while it grew in experimental rigor. In an effort to control variables experimentally, plant breeding and agronomic research became less appropriate to the needs of poor farmers.

Narrow commodity-focused research did have tremendous impacts on international agricultural development processes. It was the commodity research tradition that produced the hybrid rice and corn seeds that served as the foundation for the Green Revolution. In spite of the ongoing critique of these developments, all would agree that this represents technical success (Ruttan 1977; Wellhausen 1976; Dalrymple 1974). However, the technical success produced substantial social costs, ranging from displacement of rural populations to loss of genetic diversity of native plant stocks.

The commodity focus in international agricultural development was expressed organizationally through the network of International Agricultural Research Centers (IARCs), such as the International Rice Research Institute (IRRI), the Centro Internacional de la Papa (CIP), the International Crops Research Institute for the Semi-Arid Tropics (ICRISAT), the Centro Internacional Mejoramiento de Maiz y Trigo (CIMMYT), and others. These efforts were sponsored by the Rockefeller Foundation as well as other donors.

While the IARC-produced revolutions are remarkable, the development of agriculture in the Third World will in all likelihood be more gradual than in the past. Unfortunately, the need for increased production is more urgent now than when the first of the revolutionary seeds were introduced to tropical farmers. Simmonds notes:

The IARCs have done much good work and, either directly or indirectly, have had diverse local impacts on agricultural production. But there have been no more Green Revolutions; in retrospect none was to have been expected. The Green Revolution succeeded where wheat and rice were already grown under irrigation and were susceptible to the application of new technology. (1984:5-6)

Limits of the Top-down Approaches

For a number of reasons, the socially uncontextualized, high-technology agricultural innovations developed at the international centers came to be questioned, as did many "top-down" approaches to development. New agricultural technology that was developed without reference to local conditions did not work well. Often the new seed required the use of complex, poorly understood and expensive "packages" of "inputs" that were beyond the reach of small farmers. Local researchers lacked the techniques and facilities to adapt the technology to local needs and conditions. The effect was that the new technologies were not attractive to local small farmers. These innovations were resisted by so-called traditional agriculturalists because they were too risky, unprofitable, and unsuitable to local conditions. As has been demonstrated, these farmers were not simply conservative or traditional in their orientation, but were effective, rational scrutinizers of a largely unsuitable technology, and hence, they rejected the offered innovations (DeWalt 1979; Schultz 1964). The innovations did not make sense within the framework of the constraints faced by the farmers. The innovation-producing researchers did not adequately understand or account for the conditions under which these local, small farmers operated. For this reason much of the investment in agricultural research was fruitless.

FSR grew out of the need to deal with this failure by creating a flow of reliable information to researchers about farmers' needs and frustrations to increase the probability that the new technology can be used and will meet a need. This perspective can be applied to a wide variety of problems outside the realm of agriculture.

FSR PROCESS

As with many innovative approaches to problem solving, there is some disagreement about exactly what is entailed in doing FSR. There are even different names for the activity, and inappropriate use of the terms associated with FSR to dress up traditional approaches. Nevertheless, there are a number of important features that are part of the perspective.

FSR takes a generalized systems perspective with the goal of understanding the complex relations between the physical, biological, and socioeconomic conditions under which farmers operate. The focus on so many linkages and interactions forces a multidisciplinary approach to the development of technology that links plant breeders, agronomists, animal scientists, agricultural engineers, social scientists, and agriculturalists. Of most significance to us is that FSR "places relatively more importance, than in the past, on integrating the social sciences into the research and development process" (Shaner, Philipp, and Schmehl 1982:15). The FSR anthropologist is an integral part of the team, not an isolated critic.

FSR is farmer-oriented. The farming systems researcher looks "at the interactions taking place within the whole farm setting and measures the results in terms of farmers' and society's goals" (Shaner, Philipp, and Schmehl 1982:14). The farmer orientation is expressed in many ways, including the fact that basic research on the farming system is carried out before innovations are developed, and farmers participate directly in aspects of the research process (Matlon et al.

1984). FSR practice calls for substantial on-farm research that includes breeding trials, engineering prototype testing, and farming practice evaluation. This results in continual iteration between researcher and farmer, and reduction in the distinction between extension and research. In large part, FSR is a bottom-up strategy. In this way FSR contrasts with typical disciplinary commodity research. In spite of this contrast it is important not to think of FSR as a substitute for or alternative to orthodox commodity-focused disciplinary research, but as a complement to it.

FSR is a problem-solving process. Farmer constraints are a continual focus of the research and technology development process. Growth of knowledge is a secondary consideration. The problems that are solved tend to be farmer problems.

FSR programs can be thought of as having four stages (Gilbert, Norman, and Finch 1980). These are the diagnostic or descriptive stage, design stage, testing stage, and extension stage. The primary product of the diagnostic or descriptive stage is baseline documentation of the farming system, with special reference to constraints and potentials. The design stage produces strategies for dealing with the constraints enumerated during the diagnostic stage. These strategies are evaluated under farm conditions during the testing stage. Developed strategies that are shown to be effective through testing become recommendations for dissemination during the extension stage.

Anthropologists seem to be most involved in FSR at the diagnostic stage, while some have been involved in the testing stage (Rhoades 1984). Certainly, the diagnostic phase draws heavily on anthropological research skills. FSR diagnostics vary in scale from elaborate in-depth research to short-term informal surveys.

The short-term informal surveys used in the diagnostic stage, often called *sondeo* (Hildebrand 1981), informal agricultural surveys (Rhoades 1982), or rapid rural reconnaissance (Honadle 1982; van Willigen et al. 1985), are especially interesting methodologically. They are useful when it is necessary to scope out an unfamiliar situation quickly. While these practices do vary considerably, it is possible to identify some attributes that appear consistently. This type of survey is always done by the researchers themselves rather than enumerators. There is always direct observation involved. While the time allotted to these surveys is limited (one week to a month or two), observer-days are increased through use of a team. The team is always multidisciplinary.

Data is collected through key-informant interviews, sometimes done by the team as a group, and direct observation. Interviews are often carried out in the fields to facilitate researcher understanding of the farmer's situation. The process is iterative, that is, the research team continually meets and discusses their current understanding and data needs. Research questions are continually reformulated, often on a daily basis. Purposive rather than random sampling is used. Researchers are focused on learning from the research subjects rather than testing a series of hypotheses.

Rapid Research Techniques

The diagnostic phase may be based on a rapid survey technique, an in-depth sample survey, or a staged combination of rapid reconnaissance and an in-depth survey. Investment of resources in diagnostic research varies with the length of time of the development commitment, level of regional documentation, and amount of regional variation. There seems to be an awareness of the importance of timely and parsimonious research efforts in FSR. These qualities need to be kept in mind in all policy research settings.

Some anthropologists are too quick to call attempts at parsimony or efficiency "quick and dirty." The criticism is often inappropriate. There is a very strong case against the use of elaborate survey methods. Robert Chambers, for example, develops an argument in reference to research done in support of rural development:

The costs and inefficiencies of rural surveys are often high: human costs for the researchers; opportunity costs for research capacity that might have been better used; and inefficiencies in misleading "findings." . . . Preparing, conducting, analyzing and writing up a rural survey are heavily committing activities, the demands of which are habitually ignored or underestimated, and the duration of which almost always exceeds that planned. (Chambers 1983:51)

DIAGNOSIS AND DESCRIPTION

The diagnostic or descriptive stage includes a number of elements. The first step is the determination of the target area (Sands 1985). This is usually based on either policy or geographic criteria. Subsequent to defining the area for the FSR activity, it is necessary to identify the types of farming systems to be focused upon. As in much policy research, there is a heavy emphasis on the use of secondary data. It is especially important in the establishment of the baseline. The diagnostic baseline, derived from secondary sources, may include "physical factors such as climate, land, soil, and water resources; as well as socio-economic factors such as input-output markets, infrastructure, population density, land tenure systems, and organization of farm production/consumption units" (Sands 1985:14).

During this phase the FSR team establishes recommendation domains based on the accumulated data (including both secondary and survey data). A recommendation domain is "a group of roughly homogeneous farmers with similar circumstances for whom we can make more or less the same recommendation. [These domains] may be defined in terms of both natural factors—e.g., rainfall— and economic factors—e.g., farm size" (Byerlee et al. 1980). This concept is very important in FSR. Recommendation domains can be defined on the basis of a number of different variables. This quality of recommendation domains is communicated well by the following statement from a CIMMYT field manual:

Recommendation domains can be defined on the basis of various farmer circumstances. They may be determined by variations in the natural circumstances of the farmer such as rainfall, soils or diseases. A given region may contain many *agro-climatic environments*. These are areas where a crop exhibits roughly the same biological expression so that we would obtain, for example, similar varietal or fertilizer responses, *everything else being equal*. These agro-climatic environments are, however, often modified by socio-economic circumstances that produce different recommendation domains. For example, close to a large town maize may be grown largely for sale as fresh ears while further away it is a subsistence grain. Such differences may impose modifications on varietal selection and planting date. More commonly, even if all locations are in the same agro-climatic environment, the resource endowments of farmers may lead to different technological needs. For example, small farmers with scarce capital relative to labor and who place more emphasis on food security may follow quite different cropping patterns and practices from large farmers in the same agro-climatic environment. (Byerlee et al. 1980:10)

Once the general nature of the recommendation domains is described researchers may return for more focused verification.

The idea of recommendation domains can be transferred to a variety of other contexts outside of FSR. The concept is useful in situations where information or advice is being provided that is specific to a particular type of client. This approach requires that the research accurately deal with internal variation within the community being studied, and a subsequent adjustment of the data collection and analysis procedures. The theoretical significance of documenting variation is great, and goes far beyond the need to make focused recommendations in policy research. For a useful discussion of these issues read "Intra-cultural Diversity: Some Theoretical Issues," by Pertti J. Pelto and Gretel H. Pelto (1975).

The coordinated use of qualitative and quantitative research techniques makes FSR diagnostics a very comfortable setting for the contemporary research anthropologist. The contribution of anthropologists to the FSR diagnosis process is substantial. Some examples are the work of Robert Rhoades, Robert Werge, and colleagues at CIP (Rhoades et al. 1982), Billie R. DeWalt and Kathleen M. DeWalt for the International Sorghum/Millet Project (INTSORMIL) in Honduras (1982), Edward B. Reeves and Timothy Frankenberger for INTSORMIL in Sudan (1981), Jeffrey Jones for Centro Agronomico Tropical de Investigacion y Ensenanza (CATIE) in Costa Rica (1982), Constance M. McCorkle for the Small Ruminants Coordinated Research Support Program (1989), and Robert Tripp for CIMMYT (1982).

Following the initial diagnostic phase and the subsequent design stage, the FSR process usually involves on-farm experiments (Rhoades 1984). These activities are based upon the diagnostic research. In this phase technical solutions to farmer production constraints are tested under actual farm conditions. Tests include new varieties of plants and animals, and new equipment and facilities. The degree of researcher and farmer involvement can be quite variable. Early in the process the tests are researcher-managed, with the cooperation of the farmers. Later, the experimental program is managed by farmers.

The on-farm experiment stage improves the researchers' understanding of the farming system and increases the integration of the farmer into the research process. This also has the effect of blurring the distinction between research and extension. The testing phase emphasizes the evaluation of technical improvements in an area under farmer control. The testing program is referenced to a range of potential users and is geared toward fine-tuning the technology in response to farmer needs, constraints, and management practices. Much is learned from the observation of the farming system's response to the experimental program. The continual interaction and mutual support of the on-farm and experiment station research programs is an important characteristic of FSR.

Anthropologists can be involved in the on-farm experiment activities in a substantial way (Tripp 1985). They are often the staff members with the most extensive relations with farmers, and thus are in a good position to manage this aspect of the program. Tripp notes: "Anthropological experience on how to elicit opinions from farmers, make and record observations informally, utilize different types of data, and explore a wide range of topics of interest to particular research goals is all directly applicable to field management of on-farm experimentation" (1985:117).

The last stage of FSR is extension and evaluation. Tested technology is made available to farmers of a specific recommendation domain through extension programs. As noted, the different stages tend to merge into each other in FSR. This is viewed as a positive outcome. Often, descriptions of early reconnaissance data collection methods will advise that extension workers be included in research teams.

Evaluation is developing in importance. As FSR takes a broader perspective, so too should evaluation considerations. The commodity-focused research tradition tended to focus on yields, productivity, and profit. Anthropologists are making progress in the use of nutrition and health as factors for evaluation (DeWalt and Fordham 1983; Tripp 1982; Fleuret and Fleuret 1983). While the development of nutritional and health criteria for evaluation appears promising, it is important to use evaluation criteria that are as direct as possible. More research is necessary in this area to develop suitable evaluation criteria.

CASE STUDY: NORTH KORDOFAN (SUDAN) SORGHUM AND MILLET STUDY

The FSR project that is presented as a case example here was done from 1981 to 1982 as part of the socioeconomic component of the International Sorghum and Millet Collaborative Research Support Program, that is, the INTSORMIL CRSP. There are a number of CRSPs, all funded as part of the research and development program of the U.S. Agency for International Development. The CRSPs represent an innovative way of organizing research at United States universities in response to the need for developing agriculture in the Third World. Social scientists participate in a number of these programs, including those on small ruminants, beans and cowpeas, peanuts, and nutrition, as well as sorghum and millet. The research investment is primarily in agronomy, but all programs have social science components.

Research Methods

It was the goal of the North Kordofan diagnostic to "identify the socioeconomic constraints that impede agricultural production in the el-Obeid area [of western Sudan]," with emphasis on the relationship between sorghum and millet and the cash crops (Reeves and Frankenberger 1982:1). In addition, the project attempted to contribute to the improvement of understanding of sorghum and millet in the agricultural research community through INTSORMIL. The el-Obeid FSR team worked in collaboration with the Western Sudan Agricultural Research Project (WSARP) in order to provide extensive baseline data on the farming systems to the staff of this newly developing research center. WSARP was investing in a research station at el-Obeid as part of their total program.

In addition to the WSARP collaboration, the team also established relations with Khartoum University; the regional Ministry of Agriculture, Kordofan Province; the Sudan Agricultural Bank, el-Obeid; the International Crops Research Institute for the Semi-Arid Tropics (ICRISAT), Sorghum and Millet Breeding Program; the CARE Renewable Energy Project, Desertification and Control Coordination and Monitoring Unit; and the U.S. Agency for International Development Mission—Sudan.

The research focused on both agricultural production and marketing. These major components were supplemented with research into food preparation and consumption. Each of the research components varied somewhat in their approach, although each topically focused research activity was based on a reconnaissance survey of eighteen villages, and an initial ethnographic study of three villages in the area. The information generated from these activities was used to "design a survey instrument of farming operations" to be used in an area-wide sample of fifteen villages (Reeves and Frankenberger 1982:5).

Initial data collection was broad and included coverage of "farmers access to land, labor, and capital, how they manage these resources, as well as how these resources are channeled into cropping patterns, animal husbandry and off-farm economic activities" (Reeves and Frankenberger 1982:5). The initial data collection relied heavily on key-informant interviewing. There was an emphasis on collecting local terminology for farming operations, crops, tools, and stages in the growth cycle of millet.

Following this initial exploratory stage a report was issued to potential users before the research went on. This report focused on the farming system per se. The key informant data was expanded upon with an intensive study of three villages. This included a nearly 100 percent sample household survey dealing with household size, total landholding size and area cultivated in sorghum, millet, sesame, and peanuts. Following this, a sample of forty farmers from the three villages was drawn and stratified in terms of landholding and household size. The preliminary survey allowed the refinement of the data collection approach when it was applied to the survey of fifteen villages.

Throughout the study the researchers consulted with various agricultural scientists. These included agronomists, plant breeders, and entomologists. These specialists provided technical information that served to guide portions of the study. As part of these collaborations, the researchers collected local seed for inclusion in germ plasm banks.

The marketing study made use of documentary evidence in the form of government tax receipts and key-informant interviews. This data was supplemented with direct observations, time series grain price data, and price comparison of a market basket of goods. Data was also collected from farmers on marketing in reference to all fifteen villages. Four market centers were selected for their hetereogeneity and examined more closely. Because of the nature of commerce in the el-Obeid area, it took substantial time to develop rapport with merchants—many of them were also smugglers. Four data collection forms or interview schedules were used in the marketing centers. These were directed at inventorying marketing services, interviewing village merchants (career history, capital assets, and farming activities, as well as other attributes); interviewing periodic vendors (stock-in-trade, residence, and market visiting patterns, as well as other attributes); and interviewing market visitors (occupation, sales and purchase, market visitation patterns).

Farming System

The North Kordofan diagnostic revealed the following farming system. The farms of the region are poor, combining both subsistence and cash crops. Farmers raise sorghum and millet primarily as subsistence crops. These are supplemented with cash crops, including sesame, peanuts, watermelon, and roselle (a flavoring for drinks). Production is diversified through livestock, including cattle, sheep, goats, camels, donkeys, and horses, and poultry, including chickens and pigeons. Gum arabic is collected from acacia trees and sold. Most families engage in some nonfarm economic enterprises. These include charcoal making, water hauling, and retailing. Poorer families sell labor to better-off families during the rainy season. Others migrate to urban areas or large mechanized farms. Some families' incomes are supplemented by remittances from family members that are working in cities and abroad in places like Saudi Arabia.

The rural population is settled in villages that range from five or six to over a thousand households. Village population expands during the rainy season, when most of the crop-related farming activities take place. The households average between seven and eight members. Nuclear family residence is most typical, although extended families, matrifocal families, and other arrangements are common alternatives. While the household is an important unit of cooperation in both production and consumption, household members may have different decision-making interests. Husbands and wives may manage separate farms; unmarried sons and daughters of sufficient age may also manage farms. Most households have members who work off-farm, usually seasonal.

Just over half the land available for cultivation in a given year is being farmed. This indicates that there is insufficient land available for the fallowing cycle to be effective. Ideally under this regime one would need about 80 percent of the land in fallow (Reeves and Frankenberger 1982:9). One-third of the total cultivated land is being rented. Most of this is poor farmers renting from the better-off. Land rents are low; the economic motive to rent land to another person is closely related to the shortage of labor. Poor farmers can not afford to hire labor, which would allow them to expand their production.

The most common crops are millet, sorghum, sesame, and peanuts. Millet and sorghum are mostly consumed at home, although some surpluses are sold. Millet is an important staple of the rural diet. The millet stalks are used universally as building material. Fully 95 percent of the households grow millet; it represents 38 percent of the sown land. While sorghum is less common, it too is widely planted.

Sesame is an important cash crop; almost half the land is sown to it. Often intercropped, over 90 percent of the farmers plant it. Sesame is sold at regional markets for the urban cooking oil trade. Sesame market prices are stable. Peanuts are also planted, but suffer from wide price fluctuations due to the fact that this crop goes to the world market. About 10 percent of the crop land was sown to peanuts during the year of the study.

In addition to the crops discussed here, some less important crops are grown. These include roselle, cowpeas, okra, and watermelon. Watermelon is sometimes used as fodder for livestock because of its water content.

Land clearing starts the crop cycle in January to April. From April to August the major crops are planted. The long-maturing local variety of millet is planted first. If adequate soil moisture is present and germination occurs early, the farmer avoids the depredations of insects and birds that attack later-maturing plants. If the early plantings do not germinate, the farmer may replant or choose a crop with a shorter maturity. Plantings of sorgum, sesame, and peanut occur in June and early July.

Farmers prefer that all crops be weeded twice. Poor farmers are often forced to sell their labor during peak work seasons, and thus are not able to work their own fields. Wealthy farmers may have three or four weedings. Harvest takes place from late August to January, with the bulk of the activity occurring in October and November.

While weather represents a major constraint, labor supply also presents problems in the production cycle. For many farmers the largest production input cost is labor. It was determined that the greatest return on labor was with millet. However millet is subject to pests. Sesame, a popular crop, offered a lower return on labor inputs. Despite this, sesame cultivation was attractive because it represented risk-aversion. Peanuts were more risky and also required substantial labor inputs.

Animals are important in this farming system. Over 90 percent of the households own animals, although there are wide differences in number from household to household. The ownership of cattle and sheep is especially concentrated. Goat ownership is diffuse, on the other hand, because of the relative low cost of goats and their utility as dairy and meat animals. Animals represent a good means of storing resources from a good crop year through bad years. Unfortunately, the animals have a deleterious effect on the environment and seem to contribute to desertification. While some crop residues and crops are used to feed working animals (donkeys and camels), most graze on lands beyond the cultivated zone of the village.

The other important component of the farming system is the activities that occur off-farm. Most every household supplements its income with off-farm activities of various kinds. Some farmers migrate during the dry season for wage labor or other activities such as water hauling, tailoring, carpentry, charcoal manufacturing, or itinerant marketing. Others derive income from village shops, bakeries, flour mills, oil presses, cisterns, and trucks. About a fourth of the families receive remittances from members who have gone elsewhere to work.

Based on their analysis, Reeves and Frankenberger concluded that "farming in this region is *not* subsistence-oriented" (1982: iii). There is continual trading and selling of crops to local merchants to obtain needed commodities. The researchers were able to demonstrate that the farming systems of the el-Obeid area were well adapted to the uncertainties of the environment through diversification of the basic farm enterprise.

Constraints

Perhaps the most important research goal was the identification of constraints in the farming system. The identified constraints serve as foci for the subsequent research and extension that closes the FSR circle. Reeves and Frankenberger divide constraints into three broad categories: crop production constraints, input constraints, and other constraints. These are presented with the farmer's compensating strategies for dealing with the constraint and a set of recommendations for both research and extension. The researchers identified constraints related to wind erosion, pests and diseases, loss of soil fertility, availability of rainfall, access to labor, access to seeds, chemical inputs, availability of drinking water, credit, crop auction procedures, gum arabic price policy, limited farming knowledge, and transport and storage.

To learn more about constraint identification, let us examine one set of constraints, compensating strategies, and recommendations—that of wind erosion. Reeves and Frankenberger describe the wind erosion constraint in the following way:

High winds in this area often blow away freshly planted seeds or newly germinated crop seedlings in farmer's fields. Millet and sesame are particularly susceptible to such wind erosion. This often forces farmers to bear the time and labor cost of replanting. In addition, such wind erosion removes top soil from farmer's fields which adversely effects crop output. (1982:90)

The researchers excerpted information from their ethnographic data base that was related to this particular problem. The compensating strategies identified in the research are:

1. Farmers plant sorghum in the same hole with sesame. The firm root structure and sturdy stalks of sorghum make the sesame plant less susceptible to wind erosion.

2. In addition to sorghum, farmers plant a number of other crops with sesame in the same hole. The other crops prevent winds from uprooting the sesame.

3. Farmers often leave trees and bushes in their fields until after the first weeding to protect the soil and newly planted seeds from wind erosion.

4. Farmers plant excessively large amounts of seeds per hole so that the crop germinates as a bush. By increasing the density of plants per hole wind is less likely to blow them away.

5. When farmers clear their fields prior to planting, they sometimes leave cut-up bushes, grasses and crop residue lying on the field to protect the soil from wind erosion. When planting begins, some farmers remove this debris while others plant around it. (Reeves and Frankenberger 1982:90)

In the framework of this particular constraint, the researchers recommended both research and extension activities. Researchers were encouraged to examine the relationships between intercropped commodities so that the most appropriate crop combinations could be identified. This was seen as a way of encouraging intercropping. Soil scientists were requested to research the effects of early land clearing and planting in this area. These farming activities may be implicated in the desert encroachment that occurs throughout the Sahel. Field clearing is done to synchronize with labor availability rather than the optimum time for the curtailing of wind erosion. Because of this, fields may sit cleared for a long period of time. The researchers pointed out that suggestions to delay land clearing would be followed with reluctance because of the labor "bottleneck" that it would cause.

The extension workers were encouraged to recommend to farmers that the cut weeds and crop residue be left on the fields altogether so as to reduce wind erosion and increase soil moisture retention. Crops could be planted through this debris using a minimal tillage technique. The researchers also suggested that tree shelter belts be planted around farmers' fields. They also requested that certain potential shelter belt trees be evaluated by researchers.

The recommendations themselves were derived from a number of sources. An important source was the farmers themselves. They, like farmers everywhere, were able to discuss solutions to their problems. In addition, recommendations were developed in conjunction with the collaborating researchers.

SUMMARY

The North Kordofan FSR study illustrates one approach to doing farming systems research. FSR is the most elaborately developed type of what we are calling technology development research. While it may be difficult to estimate the future growth and demand for these kinds of services, the field is developing very rapidly and is associated with the development of academic interest in agricultural research. Practice within FSR may prove instructive for all policy research anthropologists. Some elements that may be useful in other subfields are the idea of recommendation domains, the rapid reconnaissance survey, and the very close level of cooperation between the anthropological producers of research and the agricultural scientist consumers of it.

FURTHER READING

DeWalt, Billie R. 1985. "Anthropology, Sociology, and Farming Systems Research." *Human Organization* 44(2):106-114.

This review essay serves as an introduction to a series of articles on aspects of farming systems research to be published in *Human Organization*. The introduction of this chapter is based on this treatment of the topic.

Byerlee, Derek, Michael Collinson, et al. 1980. *Planning Technologies Appropriate to Farmers: Concepts and Procedures*. Mexico: CIMMYT.

A useful how-to manual produced by the economics program of CIMMYT. Contains a good treatment of the idea of recommendation domains.

McCorkle, Constance M. 1989. *The Social Sciences in International Agricultural Research: Lessons from the CRSPs*. Boulder, Colo.: Lynne Reiner Publishers.

Documents the participation of anthropologists in the development of agricultural technology.

Rhoades, Robert E. 1984. *Breaking New Ground: Agricultural Anthropology*. Lima, Peru: International Potato Center.

Highly instructive case study of the use of anthropology in the development of new potato technology.

Schultz, T. W. 1964. *Transforming Traditional Agriculture*. New Haven: Yale University Press.

While not an example of FSR, this book, by the Nobel laureate Theodore Schultz, provides a clear statement about the essential economic rationality of the traditional agriculturalists.

Part IV

Being a Professional

14

Making a Living

Here we discuss various aspects of professional life after training. Most important is the process of finding a job. The job market for anthropologists is based for the most part on demand for persons with skills in social science research methodology. The market is not very much aware of anthropologists as such, there being a limited market for anthropology graduates *as* anthropology graduates. And, while there are many opportunities for professional work, very few are designed strictly for anthropologists. This circumstance is not limited to anthropology; it is typical of many of the social sciences and humanities. Still, it is possible to be meaningfully employed doing things that are consistent with your training in anthropology.

The anthropologist seeking work must be ready to deal with employers who are unfamiliar with the true capabilities of well-trained, contemporary anthropologists, or even employers who hold grossly inaccurate stereotypes of the anthropologist's capabilities. The most adaptive response to these conditions includes a commitment on the part of the anthropologist to educating the employer, and a strategy of self-presentation that is based on experience and capabilities rather than diploma and transcript. This does not represent a problem because these days, except for a very few occupations, it works this way for most everyone.

LOOKING FOR WORK

Success in the job hunt requires special preparation and tactics. The key to success is continual self-assessment in terms of your employment goals, and the continual investment of a substantial amount of creative energy. One might start the process by reading one of the useful guides to the creative job search. The best of these are *What Color Is Your Parachute? A Practical Manual for Job Hunters and Career Changers*, by Richard N. Bolles (1991); *Who's Hiring Who:*

How to Find That Job Fast, by Richard Lathrop (1989); and *Stalking Employment in the Nation's Capital: A Guide for Anthropologists* (Koons, Hackett, and Mason 1989).

The Bolles and Lathrop volumes taken together provide an excellent general approach to the job search. While neither author makes specific reference to the problems of anthropologists, their advice on finding employment is excellent. Bolles stresses an overall approach based on detailed self-assessment, including the specification of individual career goals and research into the characteristics of the potential employing organizations. This is complemented by the idea that the job hunter must assume control of his or her occupational destiny. The Lathrop volume provides good advice on individual career goal assessment, resume writing, letter writing, and employment interviews. The "stalking" volume was prepared by members of the Washington Association of Professional Anthropologists, and provides advice on strategy and information on numerous employment settings and roles. While this volume is designed for persons looking for work in the Washington scene, it provides useful ideas for the job search anywhere by expanding our conception of appropriate anthropology careers.

The first step toward meaningful work is a complex of difficult decisions concerning what you are to do and where you want to do it. These decisions should not be made haphazardly or by default. *Who's Hiring Who* provides useful career analysis guidelines that serve the job hunter well at this phase. Lathrop's scheme leads you through a number of steps that result in an assessment of your abilities as these relate to job functions. The process results in specification of an ideal job from a number of different standpoints, including location, work relationships, job flexibility, work environment, pay goals, and fields of work that have a high potential for you.

No matter what technique for assessment you use, you should document what you learn about yourself, the job hunt, and employers. Therefore, early in the process of job hunting, start a job hunt field notebook in which you record your observations about the process in much the same way as you would in a fieldwork situation. You might find it useful to list in your notes some possible jobs that represent meaningful careers to you. This is really just an extension of your study of the domain of application.

Career ideas may be obtained by regular reading of classified ads in local or out-of-town newspapers and professional newsletters. You might simply clip ads and paste them in your notebook so as to record as much information as possible about work opportunities. Other sources of information about jobs include the *Anthropology Newsletter* of American Anthropological Association, which usually lists a small number of nonacademic jobs. The Society for Applied Anthropology and the National Association for the Practice of Anthropology jointly sponsor an electronic communication network for its members, which includes job information. One might also consult newsletters and other publications in the domain of application, such as urban affairs, education, planning, health care delivery, and evaluation. College placement bureaus can also be useful sources, although these organizations vary in quality. Look also at the bulletin boards of academic departments who are training the competition. Do not overlook state and local government employment offices. The federal government has a rather complex system of disseminating employment information. What are some other sources? Share them with your network.

Very early in the process you should begin thoroughly to document existing jobs within actual organizations for which you would like to work. This should happen months or even years before the actual search. You can begin to eliminate organizations that are less attractive to you and concentrate your efforts on the best prospects. This screening will allow you to begin to research each organization with sufficient comprehensiveness to allow you to identify specific jobs and their requirements and needs.

Relatively few employers have a clear conception of what anthropologists can do. This relates to three basic conditions that you will face on the job market:

1. You will be competing with persons who are not trained in anthropology, such as social workers, sociologists, urban planners, and so on.

2. You will be hired on the basis of what you can do, not who you are. This requires that you be able to communicate to people what you can do.

3. You will have to work to overcome stereotypes potential employers will have toward anthropologists. This will require that you focus on your skills in your self-presentation. In your training you will need to focus continually on the acquisition of skills. You must be able to *do* things.

You must acquire a range of skills that are appropriate to the goals the potential employing organizations possess. This is why training and the job hunt coincide. Decisions about the training you will seek are decisions about seeking employment.

You must identify all your skills. In this case, "all" means skills you acquired both within and outside anthropology. Skills should be stated in terms of *functions* rather than experiences, although you should also be able to provide evidence of where you used these skills. These skills should be listed in your job-hunting field notebook. The Richard Bolles volume referred to above provides a number of exercises that can lead to better self-assessment in this area. Bolles provides a set of activities that will produce a good self-assessment. In the 1991 edition there is an appendix entitled "The Quick Job-Hunting (and Career-Changing) Map," which will serve you well if you do the suggested activities.

ANTHROPOLOGISTS AND THE JOB MARKET

The job market for anthropologists is difficult to characterize. First of all, we anthropologists must be aware of a large number of different job markets, and that these markets exist at a number of different organizational levels. That is, we must be aware of jobs at the local, state, national, and international levels.

We can also think in terms of various sectors of the economy, such as education, health care, business, planning, government, and so on. In addition, we might also think in terms of the public job market and the hidden job market.

Many persons writing about job-hunting strategies stress the importance of a focused approach to the job market. It is argued that without focus you will expend your energies ineffectively. Focus is necessary if one is going to be in the position to carry out the research required for the successful job hunt. The requirement to know the market, which is generally important, is absolutely crucial in anthropology, since so few employers are aware of the potentials and nature of anthropology. It will be necessary to "sell" anthropology by showing the usefulness of the skills you have learned. It is your responsibility to do this— attempts by the relevant associations and departments to tout the potentials of anthropology simply will not be of sufficient scale to have any meaningful effect upon you and your efforts. *You* must do it. Do not be resigned and fatalistic, remember you are in a better position because of your acquired anthropological perspective in problem solving. They need you—they just don't know it yet.

The truly creative job-hunting anthropologist should select potential employing organizations and do sufficient research so as to identify the organization's problems. Then you can show them how you can help them, and convince them to hire you. You must know enough about the organization to be able to identify their problems and to associate your skills with solutions to their problems. Moreover, as Bolles asserts, you must identify "the person who has the power to hire you for the job that you want" (1991:152).

The matching of skills with problems occurs at the individual level. It is necessary to make direct contact with the person who needs you. If you are isolated from the person by a personnel department, you will not have the opportunity to tell your story where it counts. This means that even when you are applying for a civil service position, you must contact the person directly prior to the decision to hire. Remember, you will not be hired on the basis of your being the best anthropologist; they must see you as a problem solver whose skills relate to the organization's need to be more efficient, more sensitive, more effective, more responsive, or more profitable.

To review, the effective job search is based on:

1. Early synthesis of job-hunting strategies and anthropology training.

2. Continual research into potential work roles, potential employers, and needed skills.

3. Continual self-assessment of values and skills.

4. Research into specific potential employers and their needs and problems.

5. Self-presentation as a skilled problem solver.

Another aspect of the job search is the research market. Obtaining research support through grants and contracts is both a highly marketable skill and the most important means of job development. If you can earn your keep from outside monies, many organizations will hire you. Further, it is possible, as some anthropologists have done, to create your own research firm based on grants and contracts, which would then "hire" you. Another employment situation to consider is that of the consultant.

BEING A CONSULTANT

Before launching into this role it would be useful to read a volume like Herman Holtz's *How to Succeed as an Independent Consultant* (1983). Also useful is Nancy Yaw Davis's "Cultural Dynamics: A Case History of a Research and Consulting Business" (1987), which is a personal narrative of her experiences establishing a consulting firm as an anthropologist.

There are many reasons why consultants are hired. One might suggest that the client's need for information the consultant can provide is a less frequent motivation than one would imagine. In any case, let us consider the reasons for the establishment of the client–consultant relationship. The reasons relate to the special skills of the consultant, the special needs of the client organization, and the limitations of the client organization. Although consultant-like roles can develop internal to an organization, we are going to regard consultancy as essentially an outsider's role. The consultant may have a substantially reduced stake in the organization. In some cases the fact that the consultant is an outsider is essential to his or her contribution. In other words, he or she may be hired as an outsider, and less as an expert. In addition to these factors, consultants may be hired on the basis of requirements of law.

Reasons for Using Consultants

1. The consultant's knowledge of a specific region or aspect of culture may not be available within the organization.
2. The consultant's special research skills may not be available within the organization. These skills may be derived from the generalized pool of social science techniques (e.g., questionnaires and survey techniques) as well as techniques specific to anthropology (e.g., excavation, ethnosemantic techniques, and participant-observation).
3. The consultant's special problem-solving skills are not available within the organization. This may relate to the goal of improving the organizational functioning of the client's group.
4. The consultant may possess skills which, although available in the client organization, are required to meet temporary shortfalls in manpower.
5. The consultant may be "certified" to have the skills necessary to meet certain legal requirements that the client must satisfy.
6. The consultant's status as a credible outsider may allow him or her to provide a noninvolved, and therefore objective, evaluation of the client group's functioning.
7. The consultant's status as a credible outsider may be used by the client to reduce the

social cost of certain organizational or policy changes. That is, the interventions for change may be designed by the client for application by the consultant.

8. The consultant's teaching skills, coupled with her knowledge, may allow her to contribute to the development of the client organization's knowledge and skill levels.

9. The consultant may provide the client a mechanism for increasing organizational prestige, or may serve as a "headliner" attraction for a conference or other meeting.

Consulting Process

Useful sources on the consulting process include Edgar Schein's *Process Consultation: Its Role in Organizational Development* (1969) and Peter Block's *Flawless Consulting* (1981). The consulting process is very effectively addressed from the anthropologist's perspective by Maureen J. Giovannini and Lynne M. H. Rosansky in *Anthropology and Management Consulting: Forging a New Alliance* (1990).

The consultant and the client must develop mutual understandings and expectations concerning the desired outcome of the consultant process. The problem definition stage may result in a formal written statement, perhaps in the form of a contract, or the understanding may be more informal. The most important area of negotiation and specification is client needs. There may be major discrepancies between the client's perceptions of needs and the anthropologist's ultimate assessment of the situation. Needs assessment is a complex process that should ultimately focus on the total situation. This process can be particularly difficult when the client is a service-providing agency whose links to the target population may be poorly developed. The anthropologist may soon discover in such cases that the needs perceived by the client are different from and perhaps contradictory to the needs discovered in the community at large. As is consistent with the holism of anthropology, the anthropologist may identify a significantly larger range of needs within the total community served by the agency. A key question is whether or not the needs are attributed to the community or the agency.

The negotiation concerning needs also has to consider the needs of the anthropologist as a professional. A number of issues must be considered. It is important for the client to have a clear understanding of the resources needed for the work to be completed. The anthropologist's need for information access has to be clearly explained and understood by the client. During planning the anthropologist may discover that effective consulting is not possible in a setting, and may "walk away" from it (Giovannini and Rosansky 1990: 11-12). Giovannini and Rosansky cite "lack of organizational readiness," "lack of fit between consultant capability and client needs," "inability to accept client's goals or policies," and "lack of client commitment" as reasons for not proceeding (1990:12).

The client must understand the professional ethics of the anthropologist. Presenting a copy of the ethics statement of the Society for Applied Anthropology or the National Association for the Practice of Anthropology may be called for. One of the products of the negotiation process will usually be an improved understanding of the nature of anthropology as an applied discipline. Although the potential ''consumers'' of applied anthropology services represent a rather substantial group, it would seem reasonable to say that applied anthropology does not have a large informed constituency among policy makers, community leaders, and other potential consumers. It is important that the anthropologist clearly discusses the nature of anthropology as a research discipline so the client is made into an informed consumer.

It is surprising how immutable is the image of the anthropologist as a researcher of the exotic, remote, or preindustrial. For example, an M.A. graduate of the University of Kentucky's applied anthropology program was hired by the Kentucky State Police as a program coordinator in the planning department. As soon as his co-workers found out that he was an anthropologist, they started to bring in cigar boxes full of arrowheads for him to identify. These conceptions are not difficult to deal with once an encounter has developed, but these views tend to limit the number of encounters that might lead to consulting relationships. Many potential consumers may never see the need for hiring the bush-jacketed, pith-helmeted comic stereotype of the anthropologist.

While one of the results of the negotiation process should be an improvement of the client's understanding of anthropology, the criterion for engaging a problem or complex of problems should not be whether or not it is an anthropological problem. We might strongly assert here that there are no such things as anthropological problems—there are only client problems or community problems. This is not to say that anything is fair game or that there are no criteria for engaging a problem. But we cannot practically limit ourselves to the common understanding of what anthropology is. As applied anthropologists we cannot afford compulsively maintained boundaries. Attempts to define rigidly what is or is not anthropology are unproductive. Further, in certain contexts it can be irresponsible. Our focus of concern as applied anthropologists is not our discipline, but reality, a reality that we perceive through what we have learned as anthropologists (van Willigen 1976:90).

It is assumed that the anthropologist, like any other consultant, will not necessarily engage in a formal research project in every consultancy situation. In many situations it is simply not necessary to engage in research at all. It is possible to ''just know it.'' In fact, the importance of old-fashioned scholarly expertise is consistently underemphasized in much of the material written about applied anthropology. Much of this material stresses the nature of the applied role, ethical problems and concerns, and special research contexts and strategies. But when one reviews the history of the field it is apparent that applied anthropologists with sustained involvement as consultants are often recruited as area experts rather than social scientists. This reality is rarely recognized in applied training programs. It is important to note that the so-called new applied anthropology is not based on area knowledge but on knowledge of research techniques, either as part of social science or specific to anthropology (such as participatory fieldwork).

Clearly, consultancy serves a large number of purposes. As purposes vary so do the consumers of the consultants' products. Consultants may produce materials that are directly used by the client. Although this would seem to be the most typical scenario, consultants very frequently produce material for third parties. Such is the case when the consultant is hired to provide legally required documentation or evaluation of aspects of a specific program. Such consultation may be specified in the conditions of funding support.

Client organizations may use consultants to produce an impact on third parties. The consultant may be hired to "tell the client's story" or to improve or enhance the client's image in the community. Presumably the client needs the special expertise of the anthropologist in these cases, but frequently it would seem that clients hire consultants for cosmetic reasons, thereby increasing the credibility of the message. This statement is not intended to represent a cynical criticism of certain types of consultancy situations; clients have many legitimate needs that can best be met by consultants.

When one engages in consultancy one very quickly discovers the political implications of information. Information can be used as the substance from which power is formed. Clients may use the anthropologist as a means of solidifying, protecting, or enhancing their political position. Because of the centrality of the anthropologist in the information acquisition process, he or she can be buffeted by various political forces. As a corollary, the anthropologist can use his or her position of centrality to increase control and access to information. This may be done through selective control of the release of information. Information management has very important ethical implications.

Consultants rarely have a well-developed political constituency. Yet such a constituency may be very important for an anthropologist working in a community setting. An applied anthropologist working on an evaluation of a social service agency may find that if he or she wants to maximize his impact on the agency, it may be necessary to build an auxiliary clientele in the service population of the agency. This will have two potential effects. First, it will help provide the anthropologist with useful information about the community being served, and second, it will serve to buffer the anthropologist's position politically.

COMMUNICATION WITH CLIENTS

The process of communication is of course very important and often associated with difficulty. The source of difficulty is the contrast in language and concepts of the anthropologist and his or her client. This source of difficulty is inevitably present to varying degrees. When the anthropologist engages a client's problem, he or she must to some extent conceptualize the problem in anthropological terms. This allows the anthropologist to deal with the problem, but it also creates the need for translation of the results into terms that are significant to the client. A translation process must always occur for effective communication, because anthropologists, like any other scientists, communicate using their own special code.

It should be apparent that client–anthropologist communication can be difficult. Not only must knowledge be transferred, but there must be a certain number of conceptual shifts. That is, the knowledge conveyed will probably have to be reconceptualized by the client. To the extent that it is possible, the anthropologist should attempt to avoid much of the reconceptualization by communicating in the client's cognitive framework. The standard wisdom is, "Don't use jargon." Clearly, the purging of complex terminology from technical reports is an important first step, but it is not sufficient to insure effective communication. It is also important to control the complexity of the message in order to maintain a higher level of comprehensibility. The consulting anthropologist must use facts parsimoniously and decisively, limiting communication to essentials so as not to confound the message.

The style of communication can vary with the length of time spent in the consultancy, and the urgency and concern communicated by the client concerning the issues. When one thinks of the communication process, one often thinks of a technical report submitted at the conclusion of the consultancy period. It is very clear that the one-shot, written, end-of-term report can be limited in its effectiveness. Assuming that the anthropologist and client have sufficient time to develop rapport, communication of useful knowledge should start early and proceed continually. This may allow the client to participate in the discovery process, perhaps to better understand and assimilate the results. This process can result in increasingly effective use of the anthropologist's skills, and therefore, a potential for improving the efficiency of meeting client needs. Such interaction can obviate the need for the "big report," because all the relevant data may have been communicated less formally. In such cases the report may merely serve as historic documentation or a means of meeting a contractual obligation.

DOING RESEARCH FOR THE GOVERNMENT

The major source of funding for both grants and contracts is the federal government. The U.S. government's commitment to research support started long ago. As early as 1803 the government provided funds for the Lewis and Clark expedition. The first research project funded by congressional action was in 1842, when Samuel F. B. Morse was awarded $20,000 to test the commercial feasibility of the electromagnetic telegraph. Since these beginnings, expansion has been dramatic, with most growth in federal research spending occurring after World War II. Prior to the war most research was done in-house. Funding is made available for various types of research activities. These include basic research, applied research, and development programs that have a research component. These distinctions are important to our discussion in that each is a discrete category with an appropriate funding mechanism unto itself (Scurlock 1975:ix).

Opportunities for the academic and nonacademic applied anthropologist occur in all these categories. Each funding program is subject to compliance with certain statutes, regulations, and administrative policies. It is beyond the scope of this chapter to account for the complexities of the procedures. We will, however, consider in general terms some of the important issues in federal research funding. The need to know procedures and policies is greatest for the small-scale consulting firm. Academic applied anthropologists at larger universities usually have access to an office of sponsored research and a support staff. Anthropologists hired by larger-scale consulting firms also have the benefit of such specialists. In order to be consistently successful, it is often necessary to have the support of specialists who continually search for research opportunities, provide preliminary support, assist in proposal preparation, and negotiate contracts properly. It must be made clear that all these processes are highly competitive, and that success is based upon competence in both the research and the funding process.

An anthropologist may do federally sponsored research in a number of ways. First, an anthropologist may be engaged on a direct-hire or consultant basis to do in-house research for a federal agency. One might also be hired as a staff member of an organization that has agreed to carry out a project on the basis of a grant or contract. In this section, however, we will deal with the opportunities afforded by applying for contracts rather than the direct-hire means.

Basically, five types of entities vie for the federal applied research dollar. These are universities, profit-making firms, not-for-profit research organizations, individual consultants, and the government agencies themselves (Trend 1977:212). Each of these organizations has specific characteristics that influence their competitiveness. In some ways the academic department is in the worst position to compete because of inherent lack of flexibility in scheduling and staffing. Further, departments are usually staffed by persons of a single discipline, which can cause conceptual and methodological narrowness. The problems associated with this bias have led to the establishment of alternative kinds of organizations on university campuses to help applicants compete for grants and contracts.

It has been noted that the profit-making consulting firm has certain advantages in the competition for grants and contracts. Their staffing is much more flexible and diverse than academic departments. Further, ''they are willing to work on problems that have been partially defined beforehand by a government agency, and work closely with the client to narrow or change the focus of the research. Senior staff members are skilled in translating policy questions into research questions'' (Trend 1977:212). The not-for-profit organizations are perhaps somewhat less flexible; further, they probably are poorly capitalized for the most part and therefore can afford less ''internal seed-money.''

Some sense of the relative importance of these organizations can be obtained by looking at the expenditures of federal agencies "buying" social science. For instance, during the fiscal year 1970, the Department of Health, Education and Welfare "bought" 45 percent of their program evaluation projects from profit-making firms; 29 percent came from not-for-profit organizations, while universities accounted for 21 percent (Trend 1977:212). The remaining projects were done by individuals and government agencies. Applied social science research has received more than twice as much federal funds as has basic research, every year for the last twenty (Trend 1977:212). Trend notes that "contrary to popular wisdom, there has been no 'sudden shift' from basic social science research underwritten by grants, toward applied policy-oriented research that is funded by contracts" (1977:212).

Contracts and Grants

Here we are concerned with the source of the basic ideas that when expanded and elaborated can serve as the basis for an applied research proposal. We are less concerned with the so-called unsolicited proposal, which is more typical in the basic research areas, although it is clear that this too can result in significant opportunities for the applied anthropologist. Here our concern is with research done in response to specifications provided by entities other than an individual researcher. Design criteria may vary extensively in terms of level of specificity. It should also be recognized that the researcher may arrange to have a research contract procurement procedure set up so as to allow bidding on a research idea generated by the researcher. In these cases it usually involves the researcher submitting an unsolicited proposal and the agency responding by putting out a request for proposals in response to the idea. In subsequent deliberations the original submitter of the idea is in a good position competitively.

Research support can be obtained through either grants or contracts. Both are subject to their own special kind of procedures and regulation. Although at times it is difficult to distinguish between grants and contracts, it is possible to point out certain differences. Contracts provide a means of paying for an activity that meets a specific need identified by an agency. In most cases the agency has clearly determined the actual format of the desired service, including expected outcomes, schedule, and cost. The agency selects the contractor on the basis of proximity to the research site, budget bids, professional qualifications, and previous performance. Contracts are more strictly managed than grants. Grants tend to be more frequently used where researcher-initiated experiment and development is involved. Grantees are not subject to such rigorous reporting requirements. Although the term grant connotes some type of gift, it is subject to many of the same controls as a contract. For the purposes of fostering untrammeled scientific inquiry, the conception of the grant as a gift is a useful fiction; however, one must remember that for legal and administrative reasons, it is best to think of it as what it is, a kind of contract. The consistent principle in case law is that the acceptance of a grant establishes a contractual relationship between grantor and grantee (Scurlock 1975:4).

There are a number of important concepts concerning grant budgeting that will be noted in passing here. Fundamental to the budgeting process is the notion of "allowable costs," which includes those expenses that "are related to the conduct of the research" (Scurlock 1975:4). Allowable costs are of two types, direct and indirect. Direct costs are expended solely on the activities of the research project, whereas indirect costs are for the support and maintenance of research personnel and equipment. Indirect costs are rarely budgeted directly. Usually a research group calculates the portion of their total enterprise that is involved in the supported research. Facts relating to these costs are presented in negotiations with the relevant federal agencies. These negotiations result in an indirect cost rate that would apply in all grants to the research group. The rate is often expressed as a percentage of salaries and wages. There often is a lower rate for projects carried out at a remote site. The indirect cost rate, often labeled "overhead," varies from agency to agency. Further, the various types of research groups, that is, universities, consulting firms, and so on, charge different rates. I have heard of ranges from about 25 percent of salaries and rates to over 100 percent. Large-scale consulting firms tend to have the highest overhead rate. A corollary to indirect costs is the concept of cost sharing. This is based on the recognition that research grants significantly benefit the group receiving the money. In some cases this means that the group receiving the grant will contribute to the cost of the research. This seems to be quite common for university grants.

Government procurement is dominated by certain themes. The most important is the goal of receiving "acceptable goods or services at the lowest practical price in order to avoid waste in the use of public monies" (Scurlock 1975:11). In addition, procedures are established so as to avoid favoritism and corruption. Originally, the preferred method of procurement was based on formal advertising and the submission of a firm bid by the potential contractor. As time passed and the scale of government expenditures increased, this single procedure proved inadequate and was supplemented by the so-called negotiated contract. This system allows the federal government to use a wider range of criteria than just price, and more closely resembles the procedures used in the private sector.

Agencies may formulate a problem in a number of ways. The idea for the research may be developed within the agency and then put out for competition. Sometimes an unsolicited proposal can serve as the basis for a government-sponsored competitive solicitation or negotiated contract. The decisions concerning form are usually up to the agency. Normally the agency will use the competitive bidding process, in which it is possible to specify the required research procedure, involve sufficient qualified bidders for adequate competition, and have enough time for adequate bidding. Two-step formal advertising is used in cases where the problem to be researched may have a range of possible solutions, thus making it somewhat more difficult for the agency to specify procedures and outcomes. At times, an agency may use this procedure to support research that will result in a research plan, which in turn would be put out to bids for final implementation. In a manner similar to standard practice, a researcher may submit a so-called technical proposal. This proposal does not have a cost component. The agency may consult with the researcher in order to improve the proposal. All persons who submit a qualified technical proposal will then be issued an invitation for bid. If only one bid is submitted, it may be contracted, in which case it would be a so-called sole source contract.

In certain cases the research goals and procedures may be very difficult to specify, as is typical in basic research projects. In addition, the range of necessary proposal evaluation criteria may be more complex than price and design. As Scurlock notes, "the skills, interest and availability of research personnel and the resources at their disposal are all factors to be considered in selecting the research contractor" (1975:14). There may still be competition, but it goes beyond the narrow range of criteria characteristic of the more formal procedures. The negotiated contracts process starts in very much the same way as the more formal types.

The most important source of information on contracts and other federal research opportunities is the *Commerce Business Daily* (*CBD*). This daily publication of the U.S. Department of Commerce lists government procurement invitations, contract awards, subcontracting leads, sales of surplus property, and foreign business opportunities. In *CBD*, one will find notices concerning ongoing negotiations as well as notifications of new opportunities. In addition to *CBD*, some agencies have their own publications for announcing contract opportunities. An example is the *NIH Guide for Grants and Contracts*.

Qualified individuals may ask for and receive the so-called request for proposals (RFP). The important component of the RFP is the scope of work, which is rather like a proposal in reverse. The work scope specifies what needs to be done. Evaluation criteria may also be stated. Proposals submitted in this way are subject to substantial modification in the review and funding process. The proposal review is usually carried out by a specialized review board consisting of scientists from the specific area of inquiry. Contact between the researcher and the agency is maintained through a contracting officer, who solicits answers to questions raised in the analysis process. The negotiation process produces a final research design that is hoped to be the most efficient and appropriate and least costly. After a defined period of time the negotiations are closed, review is complete, and the contract is awarded.

One way of facilitating the obtaining of research funds is to create one's own not-for-profit research organization. Information on establishing such an organization may be obtained by writing to the Internal Revenue Service for publication 557, entitled *Tax-Exempt Status for Your Organization*. This booklet outlines the procedure for being exempt from the income tax. Incorporation may also be recommended so as to limit liability. The federal tax code allows such organizations to be established if the research is in the public interest. The definition of public interest seems quite broad. Research is considered to be in the public interest if the results are made available to the public "on a nondiscriminating basis" (U.S. Department of the Treasury, Internal Revenue Service 1988). Research carried out for federal, state, and local government can also justify exemption. Various other activities are included. There are anthropologists who have established such organizations.

TIES TO THE ACADEMIC WORLD

The nonacademically employed anthropologist usually will not have other anthropologists as work associates. This situation is different for anthropologists. This raises some questions about how the anthropologist can maintain theoretical and methodological currency as well as obtain the emotional sustenance so necessary for work satisfaction. As noted earlier, nonacademically employed anthropologists may have some of their needs met by joining national general-purpose organizations, such as the American Anthropological Association, or the national and international specialized groups, such as the Society for Applied Anthropology, National Association for the Practice of Anthropology, Society for Medical Anthropology, and the Council on Anthropology and Education. Another alternative is joining the many regional general-purpose organizations, such as the Southern Anthropological Society, Central States Anthropological Society, Northeastern Anthropological Association, Alaska Anthropological Association, or the Anthropological Society of Washington. Other relevant organizations include the American Ethnological Society, American Folklore Society, American Society for Ethnohistory, Association for Political and Legal Anthropology, Association for Social Anthropology in Oceania, and the Society for Cross-Cultural Research.

Most of the organizations listed above have memberships that are virtually all academic. Being of and for academics, their programs and organizational structures are clearly addressed to the needs of this constituency. The most important need of academics is addressed by providing a medium for publishing research output. The competition for publication slots is substantial, and it would appear that the academic anthropologist will continue to dominate the pages of journals such as the *American Anthropologist*, *American Ethnologist*, and *Human Organization*. Annual programs of these associations will probably continue to be dominated by academics in spite of many positive accommodations to the needs of nonacademic applied anthropologists.

The Society for Applied Anthropology has been committed to the advancement of applied anthropology for a longer time than the older American Anthropological Association. Both of these associations have an important complementary role to play at the national level. The Society for Applied Anthropology was founded in 1941 (Foster 1969). According to Spicer, "the [SfAA] was not enthusiastically welcomed into the world of anthropology. The newborn was regarded as something of a monstrosity and as a consequence it began its first growth in the limbo of illegitimacy" (1976:335).

Spicer divides the history of the SfAA into four phases. These coincide more or less with the 1940s, the 1950s, the 1960s, and the 1970s. During the first phase there was a great deal of debate concerning the nature of applied anthropology. This seemed to relate to the general quest for legitimacy for applied anthropologists. Often expressed in the pages of the journal of the society was the notion that there was an inadequate body of anthropological theory and knowledge. Publication policy stressed the case study based on direct observation. A large segment of both the members of the society and the authors of the journal articles were not anthropologists.

During the 1950s the SfAA made its "most important contribution to anthropology as a whole" (Spicer 1976:336). The society was the first anthropology organization to deal actively with the issue of professional ethics. This resulted in the issuance of an ethical code (Mead, Chapple and Brown 1949:20-21). The society developed a succession of schemes before other organizations dealt with this serious issue. During this period, Spicer notes, there was a somewhat greater identification with academic careers. This was the trend during the next two decades.

Today the SfAA is a mature and successful association with a robust annual meeting and publication program. Although the society has been dominated by academics, it is making a number of accommodations to its nonacademic members. Currently its executive, nominations, and elections committees are elected from both academic and nonacademic slates. In addition, its annual meeting includes "skills sessions" on topics such as social impact assessment.

The leadership of the SfAA is strongly committed to maintaining lower student membership fees. Student membership includes a quarterly journal, *Human Organization*, the career-oriented publication, *Practicing Anthropology*, and a newsletter. For more information, write to the Society for Applied Anthropology, P.O. Box 24083, Oklahoma City, OK 73124.

In 1984, the National Association for the Practice of Anthropology was formed as a unit within the American Anthropological Association. This association is made up of members of the American Anthropological Association who opt for participation in this unit. NAPA has provided the ideas and energy that have made the AAA annual meetings more useful for practicing anthropologists. NAPA Bulletins, the organization's monograph series, provide an alternative publishing format for practitioners. Recent numbers have dealt with a variety of useful topics, including ethnicity (Keefe 1989), government employment (Hanson et al. 1988), and various aspects of consulting (Davis, McConochie, and Stevenson 1987; Giovannini and Rosansky 1990). NAPA publishes a directory, sponsors a student award, and runs a mentoring program for young professionals. To belong to NAPA you must first join the American Anthropological Association. NAPA student membership fees are charged in addition to the American Anthropological Association costs. For details, write to the American Anthropological Association, 1703 New Hampshire Avenue NW, Washington, D.C. 20009.

Probably the best organizations for "keeping in touch" are the local practitioner organizations, often referred to as LPOs. These vary considerably in size and the complexity of their programs. The LPOs offering the most comprehensive programs are the Washington Association of Professional Anthropologists (WAPA) and the High Plains Society for Applied Anthropology (HPSFAA). WAPA has a largely local membership and is concerned with the practical needs of nonacademically employed anthropologists. WAPA fosters such activities as job-hunting skills workshops, "theoretical up-date sessions," a job network to assist members, and a newsletter publication. HPSFAA includes members from Arizona to Montana. Their program is geared to the low density of the distribution of anthropologists in the Rocky Mountain West. They offer a journal and a lively annual meeting.

The active list of LPOs changes from time to time. Linda A. Bennett wrote a descriptive account of these worthwhile organizations that was published by NAPA (1988). She listed active organizations in Memphis, New York City, southern California, Phoenix, Detroit, Tampa, New Jersey, the San Francisco Bay Area, Tallahassee, and Ann Arbor, in addition to the Washington, D.C. and High Plains groups. It is very important to support and make use of these organizations.

SUMMARY

As you complete your course of study in anticipation of a career in applied anthropology, it is very important to assess who you are and what you want to accomplish in the future. This requires continual self-assessment. Self-assessment makes sense only if it is the foundation for the strategic acquisition of new skills and experience in their use. An excellent way to learn about yourself is the process of putting together a resume geared to a specific job. This forces you to think about who you are and what you are capable of doing to help meet societal needs.

The number of work opportunities for anthropologists *as* anthropologists is quite small. But there are many opportunities for people who know and do what anthropologists know and do. The basis for employment is what you can do, not what the market believes about anthropology. Except for a few cases, you will compete with people with many different types of training. Therefore you have to be aware of other disciplines and their relationship with the job market.

The job search starts as soon as training begins. As students, we have to work for the skills needed on the job market. Success is not based on indifferently following a course of study with individual curiosity the only guide. Success requires clear specification of goals as these relate to the needs of potential employers. The end point is not a cynical market orientation, but a careful assessment of what society needs and then action in terms of those needs.

Applied anthropologists often have to master special knowledge about doing business as an anthropologist. Which is to say, they need to be able to assume the responsibilities of being a consultant if that is the employment framework within which they are working. This includes special attention to working with clients to solve their problems, and overcoming the problems of communication.

FURTHER READING

Bennett, Linda A. 1988. *Bridges for Changing Times: Local Practitioner Organizations in American Anthropology*. NAPA Bulletin no. 6. Washington, D.C.: National Association for the Practice of Anthropology.

Provides contact points and historical background for fourteen LPOs.

Bolles, Richard N. 1991. *What Color is Your Parachute? A Practical Manual for Job Hunters and Career Changers*, 20th anniversary ed. Berkeley, Calif.: Ten Speed Press.

This book must be read cover to cover if you are serious about the job search. Read it as soon as possible because it will help you think more clearly about your training needs. Get a copy and do the exercises in it.

Koons, Adam, Beatrice Hackett, and John P. Mason, eds. 1989. *Stalking Employment in the Nation's Capital: A Guide for Anthropologists*. Washington, D.C.: Washington Association of Professional Anthropologists.

This volume must be read even if you are not trying to work in Washington. This is a rich source of useful information. Contains thirty-six chapters on getting work in various content areas and organizations.

Lathrop, Richard. 1989. *Who's Hiring Who: How to Find That Job Fast*. 12th ed. Berkeley, Calif.: Ten Speed Press.

This book has a superior section on the preparation of resumes. Try it now. Spend some time telling yourself who you are.

Bibliography

Aberle, David F. 1950. "Introducing Preventative Psychiatry into a Community." *Human Organization* 9(3):5-9.

Academy for Educational Development. 1987. *Public Health Communication Model.* Washington, D.C.: Academy for Educational Development.

Agar, Michael, and J. Hobbs. 1985. "Growing Schemas out of Interviews." In *Directions in Cognitive Anthropology*, J. Dougherty, ed. Urbana: University of Illinois Press.

Aiyappan, A. 1948. *Report on the Socio-Economic Condition of Aboriginal Tribes of Madras.* Madras: Government of Madras.

Alers, J. Oscar. 1971. "Well-being." In *Peasants, Power and Applied Social Change, Vicos as a Model*, Henry F. Dobyns, Paul L. Doughty, and Harold D. Lasswell, eds. Beverly Hills, Calif.: Sage Publications.

Alexander, Jack, and William Chapman. 1982. *Initial Security Classification Guideline for Young Males Classification Improvement Project.* Working Paper 11, State of New York, Department of Correction Services.

Alinsky, Saul D. 1946. *Reveille for Radicals.* Chicago: University of Chicago Press.

Alkin, Marvin. 1985. *A Guide for Evaluation Decision Makers.* Beverly Hills, Calif: Sage Publications.

Allen, W., Max Gluckman, D. U. Peters, and C. G. Trapnell. 1948. *Land Holding and Land Use Among the Plateau Tonga of Mazabuka District.* Rhodes-Livingston Papers no. 14. Livingstone: Rhodes-Livingstone Institute.

Almy, Susan W. 1977. "Anthropologists and the Development Agencies." *American Anthropologist* 79(2):280-292.

Altman, D. G., J. A. Flora, S. P. Fortman, and J. W. Farquhar. 1987. "The Cost-Effectiveness of Three Smoking Cessation Programs." *American Journal of Public Health* 77:162-165.

American Anthropological Association. 1942. "Resolution." *American Anthropologist* 44:289.

———. 1991. "1990 Ph.D. Survey Results." *Anthropology Newsletter* 32(5):1, 44.

Angrosino, Michael V., ed. 1976. *Do Applied Anthropologists Apply Anthropology?* SAS Proceedings no. 10. Athens: University of Georgia Press.

Angrosino, Michael V., and Gilbert Kushner. 1978. "Internship and Practicum Experience as Modalities for the Training of the Applied Anthropologist." In *Social Science Education for Development*, William T. Vickers and Glenn R. Howze, eds. Tuskegee Institute, Ala.: Center for Rural Development.

Arensberg, Conrad M. 1942. "Report on a Developing Community, Poston, Arizona." *Applied Anthropology* 2(1):2-21.

Arensberg, Conrad M., and Solon T. Kimball. 1965. *Culture and Community*. New York: Harcourt, Brace and World.

Asad, Talal, ed. 1973. *Anthropology and the Colonial Encounter*. London: Ithaca Press.

Bainton, Barry R. 1975. "Society of Professional Anthropologists Formed in Tucson." *Anthropology Newsletter* 16(8):4-6.

Balderston, F. E., and Roy Radner. 1971. *Academic Demand for New Ph.D.'s 1970–90: Its Sensitivity to Alternate Policies*. Paper P-26. Berkeley, Calif.: Ford Foundation Program in University Administration, University of California, Berkeley.

Ballard, Steven C., and Thomas E. James. 1983. "Participatory Research and Utilization in the Technology Assessment Process." *Knowledge* 4(3):409-427.

Barber, Bernard. 1987. *Effective Social Science*. New York: Russell Sage Foundation.

Barnett, H. G. 1942. "Applied Anthropology in 1860." *Applied Anthropology* 1:19-32.

———. 1956. *Anthropology in Administration*. New York: Harper and Row.

Bascom, William R. 1947. *Economic and Human Resources—Ponape*. Ponape, Eastern Carolines: U.S. Commercial Company.

Bateson, Gregory, and Margaret Mead. 1941. "Principles of Morale Building." *Journal of Educational Sociology* 15:206-220.

Beaglehole, E., and P. Beaglehole. 1946. *Some Modern Maoris*. Wellington: New Zealand Council for Education Research.

Beals, Ralph L. 1969. *Politics of Social Research: An Inquiry into the Ethics and Responsibilities of Social Scientists*. Chicago: Aldine Publishing.

BEBASHI. 1990. *Focus Groups: Process for Developing HIV Education Materials*. HIV Education Case Studies no. 2. U.S. Conference of Mayors.

Belshaw, Cyril S. 1976. *The Sorcerer's Apprentice: An Anthropology of Public Policy*. New York: Pergamon Press.

Benedict, Ruth. 1946. *The Chrysanthemum and the Sword*. Boston: Houghton Mifflin.

Bennett, John W. 1951. "Community Research in the Japan Occupation." *Clearing House Bulletin of Research, Human Organization* 1(3):1-2.

———. 1974. "Anthropological Contributions to the Cultural Ecology and Management of Water Resources." In *Man and Water: The Social Sciences in the Management of Water Resources*. Lexington: University Press of Kentucky.

Bennett, John W., Harvey L. Smith, and Herbert Passin. 1942. "Food and Culture in Southern Illinois: A Preliminary Report." *American Sociological Review* 7:645-660.

———. 1943a. "Dietary Patterns and Food Habits." *Journal of the American Dietetics Association* 19:1-5.

———. 1943b. "The Problem of Changing Food Habits: With Suggestions for Psychoanalytic Contributions." *Bulletin of the Menninger Clinic* 7:57-61.

———. ed. 1943c. "The Problem of Changing Food Habits." In *The Problem of Changing Food Habits*. Washington, D.C.: National Research Council.

Bennett, Linda A. 1988. *Bridges for Changing Times: Local Practitioner Organizations in American Anthropology.* NAPA Bulletin no. 6. Washington, D.C.: American Anthropological Association.

Bernard, H. Russell, and Willis E. Sibley. 1975. *Anthropology and Jobs: A Guide for Undergraduates.* Washington, D.C.: American Anthropological Association.

Berreman, Gerald. 1969. "Academic Colonialism: Not So Innocent Abroad." *Nation,* November 10, pp. 505-508.

Beyer, Janice M., and Harrison M. Trice. 1982. "The Utilization Process: A Conceptual Framework and Synthesis of Empirical Findings." *Administrative Science Quarterly* 27:591-622.

Biddle, William W., and Loureide J. Biddle. 1965. *The Community Development Process: The Rediscovery of Local Initiative.* New York: Holt, Rinehart and Winston.

Block, Peter. 1981. *Flawless Consulting.* Austin, Tex.: Learning Concepts.

Blustain, Harvey. 1982. *Resource Management and Agricultural Development in Jamaica: Lessons for a Participatory Approach.* Ithaca, N.Y.: Cornell University Rural Development Committee.

Boas, Franz. 1919. "Correspondence: Scientists as Spies." *Nation,* December 20, p. 797.

Bolles, Richard N. 1977. *What Color Is Your Parachute? A Practical Manual for Job Hunters and Career Changers.* Berkeley, Calif.: Ten Speed Press.

———. 1991. *What Color Is Your Parachute? A Practical Manual for Job Hunters and Career Changers.* 20th anniversary ed. Berkeley, Calif.: Ten Speed Press.

Brim, John A., and David H. Spain. 1974. *Research Design in Anthropology: Paradigms and Pragmatics in the Testing of Hypotheses.* New York: Holt, Rinehart and Winston.

Briody, Elizabeth K. 1988. Profiles of Practice: Anthropological Careers in Business, Government, and Private Sector Associations. In *Anthropology for Tomorrow: Creating Practitioner-Oriented Applied Anthropology Programs,* Robert T. Trotter II, ed. Washington, D.C.: American Anthropological Association.

Britan, Gerald M. 1980. *An Assessment of AID's Project Evaluation System.* Office of Evaluation Working Paper no. 34. Evanston, Ill.: Office of Evaluation, Northwestern University.

Brokensha, David, and Peter Hodge. 1969. *Community Development: An Interpretation.* San Francisco: Chandler Publishing.

Brokensha, David F., Michael M. Horowitz, and Thayer Scudder. 1977. *The Anthropology of Rural Development in the Sahel.* Binghamton, N.Y.: Institute for Development Anthropology.

Brown, G. Gordon. 1945. "War Relocation Authority, Gila River Project, Rivers, Arizona, Community Analysis Section, May 12 to July 7, 1945, Final Report." *Applied Anthropology* 4(4):1-49.

Brown, Judith, et al. 1980. *Identifying the Reasons for Low Immunization Coverage: A Case Study of Yaounde.* United Republic of Cameroon: World Health Organization, EPI/GEN/80/4.

Brownrigg, Leslie Ann, 1986. *Al Futuro Desde la Experiencia: Los Pueblos Indigenas y El Manejo del Medio Ambiente.* Quito: Ediciones Abya-Yula.

Bryant, Carol A. 1975. "The Puerto Rican Mental Health Unit." *Psychiatric Annals* 5(8):333-338.

———. "Counseling Guide." In *Breastfeeding for Healthy Mothers, Healthy Babies: Training Manual for Motivation and Training Tapes.* Tampa, Fla.: BEST START.

Bryant, Carol A., and Doraine F. C. Bailey. 1991. "The Use of Focus Group Research in Program Development." In *Soundings: Rapid and Reliable Research Methods for Practicing Anthropologists*. NAPA Bulletin no. 10, John van Willigen and Timothy J. Finan, eds. Washington, D.C.: American Anthropological Association.

Bryant, Carol A., Minda Lazarov, Richard Light, Doraine Bailey, Jeannine Coreil, and Sandra L. D'Angelo. 1989. "Best Start: Breastfeeding for Healthy Mothers, Healthy Babies—A New Model for Breastfeeding Promotion." *Journal of the Tennessee Medical Association* (December):642-643.

Bryant, Carol A., and James H. Lindenberger. 1992. "Social Marketing: Realizing Its Potential as a Social Change Strategy." Typescript.

Buehler, Karen L. 1981. *Perceptions of Hispanic Employment*. China Lake, Calif.: Management Division, Office of Finance and Management, Naval Weapons Center.

Burchell, Robert W., and David Listokin. 1975. *The Environmental Impact Handbook*. New Brunswick, N.J.: Center for Urban Policy Research, Rutgers, the State University.

Burns, Allan. 1975. "An Anthropologist at Work: Field Perspectives on Applied Ethnography." *Council on Anthropology and Education Quarterly* 6(4):28-33.

Burry, James. 1984. *Synthesis of the Evaluation Use Literature*. NIE Grant Report. Los Angeles: UCLA Center for the Study of Evaluation.

Buzzard, Shirley. 1982. *The PLAN Primary Health Care Project, Tumaco, Colombia: A Case Study*. Warwick, R.I.: Foster Parents Plan International.

Byerlee, Derek, Michael Collinson, et al. 1980. *Planning Technologies Appropriate to Farmers: Concepts and Procedures*. Mexico: CIMMYT.

Cain, Stephen R. 1968. "A Selective Description of a Knox County Mountain Neighborhood Unit 3." In *An Appraisal of the "War on Poverty" in a Rural Setting of Southeastern Kentucky*. Lexington: Center for Developmental Change, University of Kentucky.

Callaway, Donald G., Jerrold E. Levy, and Eric Henderson. 1976. The *Effects of Power Production and Strip Mining on Local Navajo Populations*. Lake Powell Research Bulletin no. 22. Los Angeles: Institute of Geophysics and Planetary Physics, University of California, Los Angeles.

Campbell, Donald T., and J. C. Stanley. 1965. *Experimental and Quasi-experimental Designs for Research*. Chicago: Rand-McNally.

Caplan, Nathan. 1977. "A Minimal Set of Conditions Necessary for the Utilization of Social Science Knowledge in Policy Formulation at the National Level." In *Using Social Research in Public Policy Making*, Carol H. Weiss, ed. Lexington, Mass: D.C. Heath.

Caplan, Nathan, Andrea Morrison, and Russell J. Stambaugh. 1975. *The Use of Social Science Knowledge in Policy Decisions at the National Level*. Ann Arbor: Institute for Social Research, University of Michigan.

Carley, Michael J., and Eduardo S. Bustelo. 1984. *Social Impact Assessment and Monitoring: A Guide to the Literature*. Boulder, Colo.: Westview Press.

Carroo, Agatha E. 1975. "A Black Community in Limbo." *Psychiatric Annals* 5(8):320-323.

Cartter, Alan M. 1974. "The Academic Labor Market." In *Higher Education and the Labor Market*, M. S. Gordon, ed. New York: McGraw-Hill.

Casagrande, Joseph B. 1960. *In the Company of Man: Twenty Portraits by Anthropologists*. New York: Harper.

Cernea, Michael M. 1991. "What Policy-Makers Require of Anthropologists." Paper presented at annual meetings of Society for Applied Anthropology, 1991.

Chambers, Erve. 1977. "Anthropologists in Nonacademic Employment." *Anthropology Newsletter* 18(6):14-17.

————. 1989. *Applied Anthropology: A Practical Guide*. Prospect Heights, Ill.: Waveland Press.

Chambers, Robert. 1983. *Rural Development: Putting the Last First*. London: Longman.

Chapple, Eliot D. 1953. "Applied Anthropology in Industry." In *Anthropology Today: An Encyclopedic Inventory*, Sol Tax, ed. Chicago: University of Chicago Press.

Chatelain, Agnes B., and Louis F. Cimino. 1981. *Directory of Practicing Anthropologists*. Washington, D.C.: American Anthropological Association.

Clark, Barton M., and John van Willigen. 1981. "Documentation and Data Management in Applied Anthropology." *Journal of Cultural and Educational Futures* 2(2-3):23-27.

Clement, Dorothy C. 1976. Cognitive Anthropology and Applied Problems in Education. In *Do Applied Anthropologists Apply Anthropology?* M. Angrosino, ed. Athens: University of Georgia Press.

Clemmer, Richard O. 1969. "Resistance and the Revitalization of Anthropologists: A New Perspective on Culture Change and Resistance." In *Reinventing Anthropology*, Dell Hymes, ed. Chicago: University of Chicago Press.

Clift, Elayne. 1989. "Social Marketing and Communication: Changing Health Behavior in the Third World." *American Journal of Health Promotion* 3(4):17-23.

Clifton, James A. 1970. *Applied Anthropology: Readings in the Uses of the Sciences of Man*. New York: Houghton, Mifflin.

Clinton, Charles A. 1975. "The Anthropologist as Hired Hand." *Human Organization* 34(2):197-204.

Clinton, Charles A., ed. 1978. *Social Impact Assessment in Context: The Tensas Documents*. Occasional Papers in Anthropology, Mississippi State University. Mississippi State: Mississippi State University.

Cochrane, Glynn. 1971. *Development Anthropology*. New York: Oxford University Press.

————. 1976. *What We Can Do For Each Other: An Interdisciplinary Approach to Development Anthropology*. Amsterdam: B. R. Gruener.

————. 1979. *The Cultural Appraisal of Development Projects*. New York: Praeger.

Collier, John. 1936. *Instruction to Field Workers, Applied Anthropology Unit*. Washington, D.C.: Office of Indian Affairs, Applied Anthropology Unit.

Collins, Jane L., and Michael Painter. 1986. *Settlement and Deforestation in Central America: A Discussion of Development Issues*. Binghamton, N.Y.: Institute for Development Anthropology.

Committee on Ethics, Society for Applied Anthropology. 1983. *Statement on Professional and Ethical Responsibilities*. Washington, D.C.: Society for Applied Anthropology.

Cook, Thomas D., and Donald T. Campbell. 1979. *Quasi-experimentation: Design and Analysis Issues for Field Settings*. Chicago: Rand-McNally.

Cook, Thomas D., and Charles S. Reichardt, eds. 1979. *Qualitative and Quantitative Methods in Evaluation Research*. Sage Research Progress Series in Evaluation, vol. 1. Beverly Hills, Calif.: Sage Publications.

Coreil, Jeannine. 1989. "Lessons from a Community Study of Oral Rehydration Therapy in Haiti.'' In *Making Our Research Useful*, John van Willigen et al., eds. Boulder, Colo.: Westview Press.

Council on Environmental Quality. 1973. *Preparation of Environmental Impact Statements, Guidelines 38(147)Pt II*. Washington, D.C.: Council on Environmental Quality.

Cushman, Frances, and Gordon MacGregor. 1949. *Harnessing the Big Muddy*. Lawrence, Kan.: Indian Service.

Dalrymple, D. G. 1974. *Development and Spread of High Yielding Varieties of Rice and Wheat in Less Developed Countries*. Foreign Agriculture Economics Report 95. Washington, D.C.: U.S. Department of Agriculture.

D'Andrade, R. G., E. A. Hammel, D. L. Adkins, and C. K. McDaniel. 1975. "Academic Opportunity in Anthropology 1974-90." *American Anthropologist* 77(4):753-773.

Davidson, Judith R. 1987. "The Delivery of Rural Reproductive Medicine." In *Anthropological Praxis*, Robert M. Wulff and Shirley J. Fiske, eds. Boulder, Colo.: Westview Press.

Davis, Nancy Yaw. 1987. "Cultural Dynamics: A Case History of a Research and Consulting Business." In *Research and Consulting as a Business*. NAPA Bulletin no. 4, Nancy Yaw Davis, Roger P. McConochie, and David R. Stevenson, eds. Washington, D.C.: American Anthropological Association.

Davis, Nancy Yaw, Roger P. McConochie, and David R. Stevenson, eds. 1987. *Research and Consulting as a Business*. NAPA Bulletin no. 4. Washington, D.C.: American Anthropological Association.

Dawson, Judith A., and Joseph J. D'Amico. 1985. "Involving Program Staff in Evaluation Studies: A Strategy for Increasing Information Use and Enriching the Data Base." *Evaluation Review* 9(2): 173-188.

Derman, William, and Scott Whiteford, eds. 1985. *Social Impact Analysis and Development Planning in the Third World*. Boulder, Colo.: Westview Press.

DeWalt, Billie R. 1979. *Modernization in a Mexican Ejido: A Study in Economic Adaptation*. New York: Cambridge University Press.

———. 1985. "Anthropology, Sociology, and Farming Systems Research." *Human Organization* 44(2): 106-114.

———. 1989. "Halfway There: Social Science in Agricultural Development and the Social Science of Agricultural Development." In *The Social Sciences in International Agricultural Research: Lessons from the CRSPs*. Boulder, Colo.: Lynne Reinner Publishers.

DeWalt, Billie R., and Kathleen M. DeWalt. 1982. *Farming Systems Research in Southern Honduras: Report No. 1*. Lexington: Department of Sociology, Department of Anthropology, Agricultural Experiment Station, University of Kentucky.

DeWalt, Kathleen M., and Miriam Fordham. 1983. "Regional Variation in the Role of Women in Agriculture in Southern Honduras." Paper presented at meeting of the Association for Women in Development, Washington, D.C.

Diesing, Paul. 1960. "A Method of Social Problem Solving." In *Documentary History of the Fox Project*, F. Gearing et al., eds. Chicago: University of Chicago, Department of Anthropology.

Dillon, J. L., and J. R. Anderson. 1984. "Concept and Practice in Farming Systems Research." In *Proceedings of ACIAR Consultation in Agricultural Research in East Africa*, J. V. Martin, ed. Canberra: ACIAR.

Dixon, Mim. 1978. *What Happened to Fairbanks? The Effects of the Trans-Alaska Oil*

Pipeline on the Community of Fairbanks, Alaska. Social Impact Assessment Series, no. 1. Boulder, Colo.: Westview Press.

Dobyns, Henry F. 1971. "Enlightenment and Skill Foundations of Power." In *Peasants, Power and Applied Social Change: Vicos as a Model.* Henry F. Dobyns, Paul L. Doughty, and Harold D. Lasswell, eds. Beverly Hills, Calif.: Sage Publications.

———. 1978. "Taking the Witness Stand." In *Applied Anthropology in America*, E. M. Eddy and W. L. Partridge, eds. New York: Columbia University Press.

Dobyns, Henry F., Paul L. Doughty, and Harold D. Lasswell, eds. 1971. *Peasants, Power and Applied Social Change: Vicos as a Model.* Beverly Hills, Calif.: Sage Publications.

Doughty, Paul L. 1986. "Vicos: Success, Rejection and Rediscovery of a Classic Program." In *Applied Anthropology in America*, 2d ed., E. M. Eddy and W. L. Partridge, eds. New York: Columbia University Press.

———. 1987. "Against the Odds: Collaboration and Development at Vicos." In *Collaborative Research and Social Change: Applied Anthropology in Action*, Donald D. Stull and Jean J. Schensul, eds. Boulder, Colo.: Westview Press.

Du Bois, Cora. 1944. *People of Alor: A Social-Psychological Study of an East Indian Island.* Cambridge, Mass.: Harvard University Press.

Dunn, P. D. 1979. *Appropriate Technology: Technology with a Human Face.* New York: Schocken Books.

Dupree, Louis. 1956a. *The Jungle Survival Field Test.* Maxwell AFB, Alabama: ADTIC.

———. 1956b. *The Desert Survival Field Test.* Maxwell AFB, Alabama: ADTIC.

———. 1958. *The Water Survival Field Test.* Maxwell AFB, Alabama: ADTIC.

Eddy, Elizabeth M., and William L. Partridge. 1978a. "Training for Applied Anthropology." In *Applied Anthropology in America*, Elizabeth M. Eddy and William L. Partridge, eds. New York: Columbia University Press.

Eddy, Elizabeth M., and William L. Partridge, eds. 1978b. *Applied Anthropology in America.* New York: Columbia University Press.

———. 1986. *Applied Anthropology in America.* 2d ed. New York: Columbia University Press.

Eiselein, E. B., and Wes Marshall. 1976. "Mexican-American Television: Applied Anthropology and Public Television." *Human Organization* 35(2):147-156.

Elmendorf, Mary, and Patricia K. Buckles. 1978. *Socio-cultural Aspects of Water Supply and Excreta Disposal.* World Bank, Energy, Water and Telecommunications Department, Public Utilities notes (P.U. Report No. RES 15). Washington, D.C.: World Bank.

Elmendorf, Mary L., and Raymond B. Isely. 1981. *The Role of Women as Participants and Beneficiaries in Water Supply and Sanitation Programs.* Water and Sanitation for Health Project (WASH) Technical Report No. 11. Prepared for Office of Health, Bureau for Science and Technology. Washington, D.C.: U.S. Agency for International Development.

Elwin, Verrier. 1977. "Growth of a 'Philosophy.'" In *Anthropology in the Development Process*, Hari Mohan Mathur, ed. New Delhi: Vikas Publishing House.

Embree, John F. 1943a. "Resistance to Freedom—An Administrative Problem." *Applied Anthropology* 2(4):10-14.

———. 1943b. "Dealing with Japanese-Americans." *Applied Anthropology* 2(2):37-43.

———. 1944. "Community Analysis—An Example of Anthropology in Government." *American Anthropologist* 46(3):277-291.

———. 1946. "Military Government in Saipan and Tinian: A Report on the Organization of Susupe and Chuco, Together with Notes on the Attitudes of the People Involved." *Applied Anthropology* 5(1):1-39.

———. 1949. "American Military Government." In *Social Structure: Studies Presented to A. R. Radcliffe-Brown*, M. Fortes, ed. London: Oxford University Press.

Erasmus, Charles J. 1961. *Man Takes Control: Cultural Development and American Aid.* Minneapolis: University of Minnesota Press.

———. 1968. "Community Development and the Encogido Syndrome." *Human Organization* 27(1):65-74.

Ervin, Alexander M., Antonet T. Kaye, Giselle M. Marcotte, and Randy D. Belon. 1991. *Community Needs, Saskatoon—The 1990's: The Saskatoon Needs Assessment Project.* Saskatoon: University of Saskatchewan, Department of Anthropology.

Esber, George S., Jr. 1987. "Designing Apache Homes With Apaches." In *Anthropological Praxis: Translating Knowledge into Action*, R. Wulff and S. Fiske, eds. Boulder, Colo.: Westview Press.

Everhart, Robert B. 1975. "Problems in Doing Fieldwork in Educational Evaluation." *Human Organization* 34(2):205-215.

Fabrega, Horatio, Jr. 1972. "Medical Anthropology." In *Biennial Review of Anthropology*, B. J. Siegel, ed. Stanford: Stanford University Press.

Fallers, Lloyd A., 1955. "The Predicament of the Modern African Chief." *American Anthropologist* 57:290-305.

———. 1960. "The Role of Factionalism in Fox Acculturation." In *Documentary History of the Fox Project*, Frederick O. Gearing et al., eds., Chicago: University of Chicago, Department of Anthropology.

Fenton, William N., and Elizabeth L. Moore. 1974. *Introduction to Customs of the American Indians Compared with the Customs of Primitive Times.* Toronto: Champlain Society.

Fetterman, David M. 1987. "A National Ethnographic Evaluation of the Career Intern Program." In *Anthropological Praxis: Translating Knowledge into Action*, R. Wulff and S. Fiske, eds. Boulder, Colo.: Westview Press.

Fetterman, David M. 1988. *Qualitative Approaches to Evaluation in Education: The Silent Revolution.* New York: Praeger.

———. 1989. *Ethnography: Step by Step.* Newbury Park, Calif.: Sage Publications.

Fetterman, David M., and M. Pitman, eds. 1986. *Educational Evaluation: Ethnography in Theory, Practice, and Politics.* Beverly Hills, Calif.: Sage Publications.

Fine, S. H. 1981. *The Marketing of Ideas and Social Issues.* New York: Praeger.

Fiske, Shirley. 1991. Report to Governing Council of the National Association for the Practice of Anthropology.

Fitzsimmons, Stephen J. 1975. "The Anthropologist in a Strange Land." *Human Organization* 34(3):183-196.

Fleuret, Patrick, and Anne Fleuret. 1983. "Socio-economic Determinants of Child Nutrition in Taita, Kenya: A Call for Discussion." *Culture and Agriculture* 19: 8, 16-20.

Folch-Lyon, Evelyn, Luis de la Macorra, and S. Bruce Schearer. 1981. "Focus Groups and Survey Research on Family Planning in Mexico." *Studies in Family Planning* 12(12):409-412.

Forde, E. Daryll. 1953. "Applied Anthropology in Government: British Africa." In *Anthropology Today*, A. L. Kroeber, ed. Chicago: University of Chicago Press.

Fortes, Meyer, 1953. *Social Anthropology at Cambridge Since 1900*. Cambridge: Cambridge University Press.

Foster, George M. 1953. "Use of Anthropological Methods and Data in Planning and Operation." *Public Health Reports* 68(9):841-857.

————. 1962. *Traditional Cultures and the Impact of Technological Change*. New York: Harper and Row.

————. 1969. *Applied Anthropology*. Boston: Little, Brown.

Fuchs, Estelle, and Robert J. Havighurst. 1970. *To Live on this Earth: American Indian Education*. New York: Doubleday.

Gearing, Frederick O. 1960a. "The Strategy of the Fox Project." In *Documentary History of the Fox Project*, F. Gearing et al., eds. Chicago: University of Chicago, Department of Anthropology.

————. 1960b. "Program on Behalf of the Mesquakies and Nearby Whites of Iowa." In *Documentary History of the Fox Project*. F. Gearing et al. eds., Chicago: University of Chicago, Department of Anthropology.

————. 1960c. "Culture Contact, Free Choice and Progress." In *Documentary History of the Fox Project*, F. Gearing et al., eds. Chicago: University of Chicago, Department of Anthropology.

————. 1960d. "Coop Farming—A General Summary." In *Documentary History of the Fox Project*, F. Gearing et al., eds., Chicago: University of Chicago, Department of Anthropology.

————. 1970. *The Face of the Fox*. Chicago: Aldine Publishing.

————. 1988. *The Face of the Fox*. Reprint. Sheffield, Wisc.: Sheffield Publishing of Waveland Press.

Gearing, Frederick O., Robert McC. Netting, and Lisa R. Peattie, eds. 1960. *Documentary History of the Fox Project*. Chicago: University of Chicago, Department of Anthropology.

Geertz, Clifford. 1959. "The Japanese Kijaji: The Changing Role of a Culture Broker." *Comparative Studies in Society and History* 2:228-247.

Gilbert, E. H., David W. Norman, and F. E. Finch. 1980. *Farming Systems Research: A Critical Appraisal*. Michigan State University Development Paper no. 8. East Lansing.: Michigan State University.

Giovannini, Maureen J., and Lynne M. H. Rosansky. 1990. *Anthropology and Management Consulting: Forging a New Alliance*. NAPA Bulletin no. 9. Washington, D.C.: American Anthropological Association.

Gladwin, Thomas. 1950. "Civil Administration on Truk: A Rejoinder." *Human Organization* 9(4):15-23.

Glaser, B., and Anselm Straus. 1967. *The Discovery of Grounded Theory: Strategies for Qualitative Research*. Chicago: Aldine Publishing.

Glaser, Edward M., Harold H. Abelson, and Kathalee N. Garrison. 1983. *Putting Knowledge to Use: Facilitating the Diffusion of Knowledge and the Implementation of Planned Change*. San Francisco: Jossey-Bass.

Gluckman, Max. 1943. *Administrative Organization of the Barotse Native Authorities*. Communication 1. Northern Rhodesia: Rhodes-Livingstone Institute.

————. 1955. *The Judicial Process Among the Barotse of Northern Rhodesia*. Manchester: University of Manchester Press.

Goldschmidt, Walter C. 1947. *As You Sow: Three Studies in the Social Consequences of Agribusiness*. Glencoe, Ill.: The Free Press.

————. 1979. *The Uses of Anthropology*. Washington D.C.: American Anthropological Association.

Goldschmidt, Walter R., and Theodore H. Haas. 1946. "A Report to the Commissioner of Indian Affairs, Possessory Rights of the Natives of Southeastern Alaska." Mimeograph.

Goodenough, Ward H. 1963. *Cooperation in Change: An Anthropological Approach to Community Development*. New York: Russell Sage Foundation.

Gough, Kathleen. 1968. *Anthropology, Child of Imperialism*. London: London University, School of Oriental and African Studies, Third World Study Group.

Gouldner, Alvin W. 1957. Theoretical Requirements of the Applied Social Sciences. *American Sociological Review* 22:92-102.

Green, Edward C. 1982. *A Knowledge, Attitudes, and Practices Survey of Water and Sanitation in Swaziland*. Swaziland: Health Education Unit, Ministry of Health and Water Borne Disease Control Project.

Greenbaum, Thomas L. 1988. *The Practical Handbook and Guide to Focus Group Research*. Lexington, Mass.: D. C. Heath.

Grinstead, M. J. 1976. "Poverty, Race and Culture in a Rural Arkansas Community." *Human Organization* 35(1):33-34.

Hall, Edward T. 1949. "Military Government on Truk." *Human Organization* 9(2):25-30.

————. 1974. *Handbook for Proxemic Research*. Washington, D.C.: SAVICOM.

Halpern, Joel. 1972. *Some Reflections on the War in Laos, Anthropological or Otherwise*. Brussels: Centre d'Etude du Sud- Est Asiatique et de L'Extreme Orient.

Hammel, E. A. 1976. "Training Anthropologists for Effective Roles in Public Policy." In *Anthropology and the Public Interest*, Peggy Reeves Sanday, ed. New York: Academic Press.

Hansen, Asael T. 1946. "Community Analysis at Heart Mountain Relocation Center." *Applied Anthropology* 5(3):15-25.

Hanson, Karen J., John J. Conway, Jack Alexander, and H. Max Drake, eds. 1988. *Mainstreaming Anthropology: Experiences in Government Employment*. NAPA Bulletin no. 5. Washington, D.C.: American Anthropological Association.

Harza Engineering Company. 1980. *Environmental Design Considerations for Rural Development Projects*. Washington, D.C.: U.S. Agency for International Development.

Heider, Karl G. 1976. *Ethnographic Film*. Austin: University of Texas Press.

Held, Jan G. 1953. "Applied Anthropology in Government: The Netherlands." In *Anthropology Today*, A. L. Kroeber, ed. Chicago: University of Chicago Press.

Hess, G. Alfred, Jr. 1991. "Using Time-effective Ethnographic Evaluation to Reshape a Private-Public Partnership." In *Soundings: Rapid and Reliable Research Methods for Practicing Anthropologists*. NAPA Bulletin no. 10, John van Willigen and Timothy J. Finan, eds. Washington, D.C.: American Anthropological Association.

Hildebrand, Peter. 1976. *Generating Technology for Traditional Farmers: A Multidisciplinary Approach*. Guatemala: Instituto de Ciencia y Tecnologia Agricolas.

————. 1981. "Combining Disciplines in Rapid Appraisal: The Sondeo Approach." *Agricultural Administration* 8: 423-432.

Hill, Carole E., ed. 1984. *Training Manual in Medical Anthropology*. Washington, D.C.: American Anthropological Association.

Hinsley, Curtis M., Jr. 1976. "Amateurs and Professionals in Washington Anthropology, 1879 to 1903." In *American Anthropology, the Early Years*, John V. Murra, ed. 1974 Proceedings of the American Ethnological Society. New York: West Publishing.

————. 1979. "Anthropology as Science and Politics: The Dilemmas of the Bureau of American Ethnology, 1879 to 1904." In *The Uses of Anthropology*, Walter Goldschmidt, ed. Washington, D.C.: American Anthropological Association.

Hoben, S. J. 1980. *The Sociolinguistic Context of Literacy Programs: A Review of Nonformal Adult Literacy*. AID Contract 147-PE–70. Washington, D.C.: U.S. Agency for International Development.

Holmberg, Allan R. 1958. "The Research and Development Approach to the Study of Change." *Human Organization* 17:12-16.

————. 1971. "The Role of Power in Changing Values and Institutions of Vicos." In *Peasants, Power and Applied Social Change: Vicos as a Model*, Henry F. Dobyns, Paul L. Doughty, and Harold D. Lasswell, eds. Beverly Hills, Calif.: Sage Publications.

Holtz, Herman. 1983. *How to Succeed as an Independent Consultant*. New York: John Wiley and Sons.

Honadle, George. 1982. "Rapid Reconnaissance for Development Administration: Mapping and Moulding Organizational Landscapes." *World Development* 10 (8): 633-649.

Honigmann, John J. 1953. *Information for Pakistan: Report of Research on Intercultural Communication through Films*. Chapel Hill: Institute for Research in Social Science, University of North Carolina.

————. 1976. *The Development of Anthropological Ideas*. Homewood, Ill.: Dorsey Press.

Horowitz, Irving, ed. 1967. *The Rise and Fall of Project Camelot: Studies in the Relationship between Social Sciences and Practical Politics*. Cambridge, Mass.: M.I.T. Press.

Hostetler, John A. 1972. "Amish Schooling: A Study in Alternatives." *Council on Anthropology and Education* 3(2):1-4.

Huizer, Gerrit. 1975. "A Social Role of Social Scientists in Underdeveloped Countries: Some Ethical Considerations." In *Current Anthropology in the Netherlands*, Peter Kloos and Henri J. M. Claessen, eds. Rotterdam: Anthropological Branch of the Netherlands Sociology and Anthropology Society.

Hyland, Stanley, Linda A. Bennett, Thomas W. Collins, and Ruthbeth Finerman. 1988. "Developing Purposeful Internship Programs." In *Anthropology for Tomorrow: Creating Practitioner-Oriented Applied Anthropology Programs*, R. Trotter, ed. Washington, D.C.: American Anthropological Association.

Hyland, Stanley, and Sean Kirkpatrick. 1989. *Guide to Training Programs in the Applications of Anthropology*. 3d ed. Memphis, Tenn.: Society for Applied Anthropology.

Hymes, Dell, ed. 1974. *Reinventing Anthropology*. New York: Random House.

Ingersoll, Jasper. 1968. "Mekong River Basin Development: Anthropology in a New Setting." *Anthropological Quarterly* 41:147- 167.

————. 1969. *The Social Feasibility of PaMong Irrigation: A Report to the U.S. Bureau of Reclamation and the U.S. Agency for International Development*. Washington, D.C.: U.S. Agency for International Development.

Ingersoll, Jasper, Mark Sullivan, and Barbara Lenkerd. 1981. *Social Analysis of A.I.D. Projects: A Review of the Experience*. Washington, D.C.: U.S. Agency for International Development.

International Cooperation Administration. 1955. *Community Development Review*, no. 3. Washington, D.C.: International Cooperation Administration.

International Maize and Wheat Improvement Center. 1980. *Planning Technologies Appropriate to Farmers: Concepts and Procedures*. Mexico: CIMMYT.

Jacobs, Sue-Ellen. 1977. *Social Impact Assessment: Experiences in Evaluation Research, Applied Anthropology and Human Ethics*. Mississippi State University Occasional Papers in Anthropology, John H. Peterson, ed. Mississippi State: Department of Anthropology, Mississippi State University.

————. 1978. "'Top-down Planning': Analysis of Obstacles to Community Development in an Economically Poor Region of the Southwestern United States." *Human Organization* 37(3):246-256.

Jacobs, Sue-Ellen, Barbara A. Schleicher, and Raymond A. Ontiveros. 1974. "Preliminary Social and Cultural Profiles of the Human Communities in the Springer-Sangamon Impact Zones, Social Impact Assessment and Identification of Resource-Oriented Attributes of the Human Environment in the Springer-Sangamon Impact Zones—Phase 1." In *Annual Report FY74 for the Springer-Sangamon Environmental Research Program*, Bell, D. T. and F. L. Johnson, eds. Department of Forestry and Illinois Agricultural Experiment Station University of Illinois, Urbana-Champaign, Ill.

Jacobsen, Claire. 1973. *The Organization of Work in a Pre-school Setting: Work Relations Between Professionals and Para-professionals in Four Head Start Centers*. New York: Bank Street College of Education.

Jenks, Albert E. 1921. "The Relation of Anthropology to Americanization." *Scientific Monthly* 12:240-245.

Johnson, Jeffery, and David Griffith. 1985. *Perceptions and Preferences for Marine Fish: A Study of Recreational Fishermen in the Southeast*. Raleigh, N.C.: UNC Sea Grant Program.

Jones, Delmos. 1971. "Social Responsibility and Belief in Basic Research: An Example from Thailand." *Current Anthropology* 12(3):347.

————. 1976. "Applied Anthropology and the Application of Anthropological Knowledge." *Human Organization* 35:221-9.

Jones, Jeffrey. 1982. *Diagnostico Socio-economico Sobre el Consumo y Produccion de Lena in Fincas Pequeñas de la Peninsula de Azuero, Panama*. Turrialba, Costa Rica: Centro Agronomico Tropical de Investigation y Ensenanza.

Jorgensen, Joseph G. 1971. "On Ethics and Anthropology." *Current Anthropology* 12(3):321-334.

Joseph, Alice, Rosamond B. Spicer, and Jane Chesky. 1949. *The Desert People: A Study of the Papago Indians*. Chicago: University of Chicago Press.

Keefe, Susan Emley, ed. 1989. *Negotiating Ethnicity: The Impact of Anthropological Theory and Practice*. NAPA Bulletin no. 8. Washington, D.C.: American Anthropological Association.

Keith, Arthur. 1917. "How Can the Institute Best Serve the Needs of Anthropology?" *Journal of the Royal Anthropological Society* 47:12-30.

Kendall, Carl. 1989. "The Use and Non-Use of Anthropology: The Diarrheal Disease Control Program in Honduras." In *Making Our Research Useful: Case Studies in the Utilization of Anthropological Knowledge*, John van Willigen, Barbara Rylko-Bauer, and Ann McElroy, eds. Boulder, Colo.: Westview Press.

Kennard, Edward A., and Gordon MacGregor. 1953. "Applied Anthropology in Government: United States." In *Anthropology Today*, A. L. Kroeber, ed. Chicago: University of Chicago Press.

Kennedy, Raymond. 1944. "Applied Anthropology in the Dutch East Indies." *Transactions of the New York Academy of Sciences*. 2d ser., vol. 6:157-62.

Kerri, James N. 1977. "A Social Analysis of the Human Element in Housing: A Canadian Case." *Human Organization* 36(2):173-185.

Kessing, Felix M. 1949. "Experiments in Training Overseas Administrators." *Human Organization* 8(4):20-22.

Kimball, Solon T. 1946. *Community Government in the War Relocation Centers*. Washington, D.C.: Government Printing Office.

———. 1952. "Some Methodological Problems of the Community Self-Survey." *Social Forces* 31:160-164.

Kimball, Solon T., and Marion Pearsall. 1954. *The Talladega Story: A Study in Community Process*. University: University of Alabama Press.

Kimball, Solon T., and John H. Provinse. 1942. "Navaho Social Organization in Land Use Planning." *Applied Anthropology* 1(4):18-25.

Kiste, Robert C. 1974. "The Bikinians: A Study in Forced Migration." Menlo Park, Calif.: Cummings Publishing Company.

Kluckhohn, Clyde, and Dorothea C. Leighton. 1946. *The Navaho*. Cambridge: Harvard University Press.

Kluger, Richard. 1976. *Simple Justice: The History of Brown vs. Board of Education and Black America's Struggle for Equality*. New York: Knopf.

Koons, Adam, Beatrice Hackett, and John P. Mason, eds. 1989. *Stalking Employment in the Nation's Capital: A Guide for Anthropologists*. Washington, D.C.: Washington Association of Professional Anthropologists.

Kotler, Philip. 1975. *Marketing for Nonprofit Organizations*. Englewood Cliffs, N.J.: Prentice-Hall.

Kotler, Philip, and Eduardo L. Roberto. 1989. *Social Marketing: Strategies for Changing Public Behavior*. New York: Free Press.

Kotler, Philip, and Gerald Zaltman. 1971. "Social Marketing: An Approach to Planned Social Change." *Journal of Marketing* 35(July): 3-12.

Krueger, Richard A. 1988. *Focus Groups: A Practical Guide for Applied Research*. Newbury Park, Calif.: Sage Publications.

Kumar, Krishna. 1987. *Conducting Group Interviews in Developing Countries*. AID. Program Design and Evaluation Methodology Report No. 8. Washington, D.C.: Agency for International Development.

Kushner, Gilbert. 1978. "Applied Anthropology Training Programs." *Practicing Anthropology* 1(2):23.

Lackner, Helen. 1973. "Social Anthropology and Indirect Rule. The Colonial Administration and Anthropology in Eastern Nigeria: 1920–1940." In *Anthropology and the Colonial Encounter*, T. Asad, ed. New York: Humanities Press.

Lafitau, Joseph F. 1724. *Customs of the American Indians Compared with the Customs of Primitive Times*. Reprint. Toronto: Champlain Society, 1974.

Lample, Linda L., and Thomas A. Herbert. 1988. *The Integration of Fish, Seafood, and Aquaculture Products into the Florida Farmers' Market System*. Tallahassee, Fla.: T. A. Herbert and Associates.

Landman, Ruth H., and Katherine Spencer Halpern, eds. 1989. *Applied Anthropologist and Public Servant: The Life and Work of Philleo Nash*. NAPA Bulletin no. 7. Washington, D.C.: American Anthropological Association.

Landy, David. 1961. "A Halfway House for Women: Preliminary Report of a Study." In *Mental Patients in Transaction*. Springfield, Ill.: Charles C. Thomas.

Langer, Elinor. 1966. "Human Experimentation: New York Verdict Affirms Patient's Rights." *Science* 151:663-666.

Lantis, Margaret L. 1945. "Anthropology As Public Service." *Applied Anthropology* 4:20-32.

Lantis, Margaret L., and Evelyn B. Hadaway. 1957. "How Three Seattle Tuberculosis Hospitals Have Met the Needs of Their Eskimo Patients." Paper presented to the National Tuberculosis Association, Kansas City, Missouri.

Lasswell, Harold D., and Allen R. Holmberg. 1966. "Toward a General Theory of Directed Value Accumulation and Institutional Development." In *Comparative Theories of Social Change*, H. W. Peter, ed. Ann Arbor, Mich.: Foundation for Research on Human Behavior.

Lathrop, Richard. 1976. *Who's Hiring Who*. Reston, Va.: Reston Publishing.

————. 1989. *Who's Hiring Who: How to Find That Job Fast*. 12th ed. Berkeley, Calif.: Ten Speed Press.

Leacock, Eleanor, Nancie L. Gonzales, and Gilbert Kushner, eds. 1974. *Training Programs for New Opportunities in Applied Anthropology: A Symposium Sponsored by the Society for Applied Anthropology*. Washington, D.C.: American Anthropological Association.

Lefebvre, R. Craig, and June A. Flora. 1988. "Social Marketing and Public Health Intervention." *Health Education Quarterly* 15(3):299-315.

Lefley, Harriet P. 1975. "Approaches to Community Mental Health: The Miami Model." *Psychiatric Annals* 5(8):315-319.

Lefley, Harriet P., and Evalina W. Bestman. 1984. "Community Mental Health and Minorities: A Multi-Ethnic Approach." In *The Pluralistic Society: A Community Mental Health Perspective*, Stanley Sue and Thom Moore, eds. New York: Human Sciences Press.

Leighton, Alexander. 1949. *Human Relations in a Changing World: Observations on the Use of the Social Sciences*. New York: Dutton.

Leighton, Alexander H., et al. 1943. "Assessing Public Opinion in a Dislocated Community." *Public Opinion Quarterly* 7(4):652-658.

Leighton, Alexander H., and Dorothea C. Leighton. 1944. *The Navaho Door*. Cambridge: Harvard University Press.

Leighton, Dorothea C., and John Adair. 1946. *People of the Middle Place: A Study of the Zuni Indians*. New Haven: Human Relations Area Files.

Leviton, Laura C., and E.F.X. Hughes. 1981. "Research on the Utilization of Evaluations: A Review and Synthesis." *Evaluation Review* 5:525-48.

Loumala, Katharine. 1946. "California Takes Back Its Japanese Evacuees: The Readjustment of California to the Return of the Japanese Evacuees.'' *Applied Anthropology* 5(3):25-39.

———. 1947. ''Community Analysis by the War Relocation Authority Outside the Relocation Centers.'' *Applied Anthropology* 6(1):25-31.

———. 1948. ''Research and the Records of the War Relocation Authority.'' *Applied Anthropology* 7(1):23-32.

Low, Setha M., and Elaine L. Simon. 1984. ''Working Landscapes: A Report on the Social Uses of Outside Space in Corporate Centers and Program Recommendations for Carnegie Center.'' Xeroxed typescript.

Lurie, Nancy Oestreich. 1955. ''Anthropology and Indian Claims Litigation: Problems, Opportunities, and Recommendations.'' *Ethnohistory* 2:357-375.

McCay, Bonnie J., and Carolyn F. Creed. 1990. ''Social Structure and Debates on Fisheries Management in the Atlantic Surf Clam Fishery.'' *Ocean and Shoreline Management* 13:199-229.

Maccoby, N., et al. 1977. ''Reducing the Risk of Cardiovascular Disease.'' *Journal of Community Health* 100-114.

McCorkle, Constance M. 1989. *The Social Sciences in International Agricultural Research: Lessons from the CRSPs*. Boulder, Colo.: Lynne Reinner Publishers.

MacGregor, Gordon. 1946. *Warriors Without Weapons*. Chicago: University of Chicago Press.

———. 1955. ''Anthropology in Government: United States.'' In *Yearbook of Anthropology—1955*. New York: Wenner-Gren.

McGuire, Thomas R., and Marshall A. Worden. 1984. *Social-cultural Impact Assessment of the San Xavier Planned Community, Papago Indian Reservation, Pima County, Arizona*. Tucson: Bureau of Applied Research in Anthropology, University of Arizona.

McKillip, Jack. 1987. *Need Analysis: Tools for the Human Services and Education*. Newbury Park, Calif.: Sage Publications.

McPherson, Laura, ed. 1978. *The Role of Anthropology in the Agency for International Development*. Binghamton, N.Y.: Institute for Development of Anthropology.

McRobie, George. 1981. *Small Is Possible*. New York: Harper and Row.

Maday, Bela C. 1975. *Anthropology and Society*. Washington, D.C.: Anthropological Society of Washington.

Mair, Lucy P. 1968. ''Applied Anthropology.'' In *International Encyclopedia of Social Sciences*. New York: Macmillan.

Maloney, Clarence, K.M.A. Aziz, and Profulla C. Sarker. 1980. *Beliefs and Fertility in Bangladesh*. Rajshahi, Bangladesh: Institute of Bangladesh Studies, Rajshahi University.

Manoff, Richard K. 1985. *Social Marketing: New Imperative for Public Health*. New York: Praeger.

———. 1988. Rationale for Application of Social Marketing and Use of Mass Media in Prevention. in Social Marketing: Accepting the Challenge in Public Health. Atlanta: Centers for Disease Control Renne Dunmere, ed.

Mark, Melvin M., and R. Lance Shotland. 1985. ''Stakeholder Based Evaluation and Value Judgements.'' *Evaluation Review* 9(5):605-625.

Marshall, Patricia. 1979. *Executive Summary Interim Report: Rural Alcohol Initiative*. Ashland, Ky.: Lansdowne Mental Health Center.

Maruyama, Magorah. 1973. ''Cultural, Social and Psychological Considerations in the

Planning of Public Works." *Technological Forecasting and Social Change* 5:135-143.

Mason, John. 1979. *Social Research of Resident Preference, Need and Ability to Pay: Towards a Framework for Physical Planning Standards in Botswana's Self-Help Housing in Site and Service Areas*. Washington, D.C.: FCH International.

Mason, Leonard E. 1947. *Economic and Human Resources—Marshall Islands*. Ponape: U.S. Commercial Company.

———. 1950. "The Bikinians: A Transplanted Population." *Human Organization* 9(1):5-15.

———. 1958. "Kili Community in Transition." *South Pacific Commission Quarterly Bulletin* 18:32-35.

Mathur, Hari Mohan. 1977. "Anthropology, Government, and Development Planning in India." In *Anthropology in the Development Process*, ed. Hari Mohan Mathur. New Delhi: Vikas Publishing House.

Matlon, P., R. Cantrell, D. King, and M. Benoit-Cattin. 1984. *Coming Full Circle: Farmer's Participation in the Development of Technology*. Ottawa: IDRC.

Mead, Margaret. 1977. "Applied Anthropology: The State of the Art." In *Perspectives on Anthropology, 1976*, A.F.C. Wallace, ed. Washington, D.C.: American Anthropological Association.

Mead, Margaret, ed. 1955. *Cultural Patterns and Technical Change*. New York: American Library.

Mead, Margaret, Eliot D. Chapple and G. Gordon Brown. 1949. Report of the Committee on Ethics. *Human Organization* 8(2):20-21.

Mekeel, H. Scudder. 1944. "An Appraisal of the Indian Reorganization Act." *American Anthropologist* 46(2):209-217.

Merton, Robert K., Marjorie Fiske, and Patricia L. Kendall. 1990. *The Focused Interview: A Manual of Problems and Procedures*. 2nd ed. New York: Free Press.

Merton, Robert K., and Patricia L. Kendall. 1946. "The Focused Interview." *American Journal of Sociology* 51:541-557.

Messing, Simon D. 1965. "Application of Health Questionnaires to Pre-Urban Communities in a Developing Country." *Human Organization* 24(3):365-372.

Messing, Simon D., et al. 1964. "Health Culture Research in a Developing Country." *American Behavioral Scientist* 7(8):29-30.

Metraux, Rhoda. 1943. "Qualitative Attitude Analysis, A Technique for the Study of Verbal Behavior." In *The Problem of Changing Food Habits*. Washington, D.C.: National Research Council.

Mezirow, Jack D. 1963. *Dynamics of Community Development*. New York: Scarecrow Press.

Miles, M. B., and A. M. Huberman. 1984. *Qualitative Data Analysis: A Sourcebook of New Methods*. Beverly Hills, Calif.: Sage Publications.

Miller, Barbara D. 1980. *Local Social Organizations and Local Project Capacity*. Syracuse, N.Y.: Local Revenue Administration Project, Maxwell School, Syracuse University.

Millsap, William. 1978. "New Tools for an Old Trade: Social Impact Assessment in Community and Regional Development." In *Social Science Education for Development*, William T. Vickers and Glenn R. Howze, eds. Tuskegee Institute, Alabama: Tuskegee Institute, Center for Rural Development.

Millsap, William, ed. 1984. *Applied Social Science for Environmental Planning*. Boulder, Colo.: Westview Press.

Montgomery, Edward, and John W. Bennett. 1979. ''Anthropological Studies of Food and Nutrition: The 1940's and the 1970's.'' In *The Uses of Anthropology*, Walter Goldschmidt, ed. Washington, D.C.: American Anthropological Association.

Mooney, James. 1896. *The Ghost Dance Religion and the Sioux Outbreak of 1890*. Fourteenth Annual Report. Washington, D.C.: Bureau of American Ethnology.

Moore, John. 1971. ''Perspective for a Partisan Anthropology.'' *Liberation*, November, pp. 34-43.

Morgan, David L. 1988. *Focus Groups as Qualitative Research*. Newbury Park, Calif.: Sage Publications.

Murdock, George P., et al. 1982. *Outline of Cultural Materials*. 5th rev. ed. New Haven: Human Relations Area Files.

Murray, Gerald F. 1987. ''The Domestication of Wood in Haiti: A Case Study in Applied Evolution.'' In *Anthropological Praxis: Translating Knowledge into Action*, R. Wulff and S. Fiske, eds. Boulder, Colo.: Westview Press.

Myres, J. L. 1928. ''The Science of Man in the Service of the State.'' *Journal of the Royal Anthropological Institute of Great Britain and Ireland* 59:19-52.

Nadel, S. F. 1947. *The Nuba: An Anthropological Study of the Hill Tribes of Kordofan*. London: Oxford University Press.

National Association for the Practice of Anthropology. 1991. *NAPA Directory of Practicing Anthropologists*. Washington, D.C.: American Anthropological Association.

Naylor, Larry L. 1976. *Native Hire on Trans-Alaska Pipeline*. Report prepared for Arctic Gas Pipeline Company. Fairbanks: Department of Anthropology, University of Alaska.

Nellemann, George. 1969. ''Hinrich Rink and Applied Anthropology in Greenland in the 1860s.'' *Human Organization* 28:166-174.

Neuber, Keith A. 1980. *Needs Assessment: A Model for Community Planning*. Beverly Hills, Calif.: Sage Publications.

Nicaise, Joseph. 1960. ''Applied Anthropology in the Congo and Ruanda-Urandi.'' *Human Organization* 19:112-117.

Norman, David W., and Emmy B. Summons. 1982. *Farming Systems in the Nigerian Savanna: Research Strategies for Development*. Boulder, Colo.: Westview Press.

Nugent, Jeffery B., William L. Partridge, Antoinette B. Brown, and John D. Rees. 1978. *An Interdisciplinary Evaluation of the Human Ecology and Health Impact of the Aleman Dam*. Mexico: Center for Human Ecology and Health, Pan American Health Organization.

Oberg, Kalervo, Allan G. Harper, and Andrew R. Cordova. 1943. *Man and Resources in the Middle Rio Grande Valley*. Albuquerque: University of New Mexico Press.

Oliver, Douglas L., ed. 1951. *Planning Micronesia's Future: A Summary of the United States Commercial Company's Economic Survey of Micronesia, 1946*. Cambridge: Harvard University Press.

Opler, Marvin K. 1945. ''A Sumo Tournament at Tule Lake Center.'' *American Anthropologist* 47:134-39.

Orbach, Michael. 1979. ''Qualifications for the Performance of Social Impact Assessment.'' Report submitted to the Executive Committee of the Society for Applied Anthropology, for the Social Impact Assessment Committee. Typescript.

O'Reilly, Kevin R., and Michael E. Dalmat. 1987. "Marketing Program Evaluation: Birth Attendant Training in Kenya." *Practicing Anthropology* 9(1):12-13.

Ortolano, Leonard, and William W. Hill. 1972. *An Analysis of Environmental Statements for the Corps of Engineers Water Projects.* Fort Belvoir, Va.: U.S. Army Engineer Institute.

Padfield, Harland, and Courtland L. Smith. 1968. "Water and Culture." *Rocky Mountain Social Science Journal* 5(2):23-32.

Papago Community Action Program Staff. 1966. *Component Project No. 7-2: Application to the Office of Economic Opportunity.* Sells, Ariz.: Papago Tribe of Arizona.

Parker, Patricia L., and Thomas F. King. 1987. "Intercultural Mediation at Truk International Airport." In *Anthropological Praxis: Translating Knowledge into Action,* R. Wulff and S. Fiske, eds. Boulder, Colo.: Westview Press.

Partridge, William L. 1984. *Training Manual in Development Anthropology.* Washington, D.C.: American Anthropological Association.

Partridge, William L., and Elizabeth M. Eddy. 1978. "The Development of Applied Anthropology in America." In *Applied Anthropology in America,* Elizabeth M. Eddy and William L. Partridge, eds. New York: Columbia University Press.

Patton, Michael Quinn. 1986. *Utilization-Focused Evaluation.* 2d ed. Beverly Hills, Calif.: Sage Publications.

Paul, Benjamin D., ed. 1955. *Health, Culture, and Community: Case Studies of Public Reactions to Health Problems.* New York: Russell Sage Foundation.

Pearsall, Marion, and M. Sue Kern. 1967. "Behavioral Science, Nursing Services, and the Collaborative Process: A Case Study." *Journal of Applied Behavioral Science* 3(2):253-270.

Peattie, Lisa R. 1960a. "Being a Mesquakie Indian." In *Documentary History of the Fox Project,* F. Gearing et al., eds. Chicago: University of Chicago, Department of Anthropology.

———. 1960b. "The Failure of the Means-Ends Scheme in Action Anthropology." In *Documentary History of the Fox Project,* F. Gearing et al., eds. Chicago: University of Chicago, Department of Anthropology.

———. 1968. "Reflections on Advocacy Planning." *American Institute of Planners* 34:80-87.

———. 1969a. "Conflicting Views of the Project: Caracas Versus the Site." In *Regional Planning for Development: The Experience of the Guayani Program of Venezuela,* Lloyd Rodwin, ed. Cambridge, Mass.: M.I.T. Press.

———. 1969b. "Social Mobility and Economic Development." In *Regional Planning for Development: The Experience of the Guayani Program of Venezuela,* Lloyd Rodwin, ed. Cambridge, Mass.: M.I.T. Press.

———. 1971a. "Public Housing: Urban Slums under Public Management." In *Race, Change and Urban Society, Urban Affairs Annual Review,* P. Orleans and W. Ellis, eds. Beverly Hills, Calif.: Sage Publications.

———. 1971b. *Conventional Public Housing.* Working Paper no. 3. Joint Center for Urban Studies.

Pelto, Pertti J., and Gretel H. Pelto. 1975. "Intra-cultural Diversity: Some Theoretical Issues." *American Ethnologist* 2(1):1-18.

———. 1978. *Anthropological Research: The Structure of Inquiry.* New York: Cambridge University Press.

Pelzer, Karl, and Edward T. Hall. 1947. *Economic and Human Resources—Truk Islands, Central Carolines*. Ponape: U.S. Commercial Company.

Peterson, John H., Jr. 1970. *Socio-Economic Characteristics of the Mississippi Choctaw Indians*. Social Science Research Center Report no. 34. Mississippi State: Mississippi State University.

————. 1972. "Assimilation, Separation and Out-Migration in an American Indian Community." *American Anthropologist* 74:1286-1295.

————. 1978. "The Changing Role of an Applied Anthropologist." In *Applied Anthropology in America*. Elizabeth M. Eddy and William L. Partridge, eds. New York: Columbia University Press.

Peterson, John H., Jr., and Sue-Ellen Jacobs. 1977. "Anthropologists in Social Impact Assessment." Paper presented at Society for Applied Anthropology Meetings, Philadelphia.

Pillsbury, Barbara. 1986. *Executive Summaries of Evaluations and Special Studies Conducted for AID. in Asia in Fiscal Year 1985*. Washington, D.C.: Agency for International Development.

Pollard, Richard. 1987. *Social Marketing of Vitamin A: Final Creative and Promotional Strategy*. West Sumatra Vitamin A Project Report. Washington, D.C.: The Manoff Group.

Powdermaker, Hortense. 1943. "Summary of Methods of a Field Work Class Cooperating with the Committee on Food Habits." In *The Problem of Changing Food Habits*. Washington, D.C.: National Research Council.

Powell, John Wesley. 1881. *First Annual Report of the Bureau of American Ethnology*. Washington, D.C.: Government Printing Office.

Practical Concepts, Inc. 1980. *Planning Rural Energy Projects: A Rural Energy Survey and Planning Methodology for Bolivia*. Washington, D.C.: Practical Concepts, Inc.

Preister, Kevin. 1987. "Issue-Centered Social Impact Assessment." In *Anthropological Praxis: Translating Knowledge into Action, R. Wulff and S. Fiske, eds. Boulder, Colo.: Westview Press*.

Price, Derek J. de Solla. 1964. "Ethics of Scientific Publication." *Science* 144:655-657.

Price, John A. 1987. *Applied Anthropology: Canadian Perspectives*. Downsview, Ontario: SAAC/York University.

Provinse, John H. 1942. "Cultural Factors in Land Use Planning." In *The Changing Indian*, Oliver La Farge, ed. Norman: University of Oklahoma Press.

Provinse, John H., and Solon T. Kimball. 1946. "Building New Communities During Wartime." *American Sociological Review* 11:396-410.

Quandt, Sara A., and Cheryl Ritenbaugh, eds. 1986. *Training Manual in Nutritional Anthropology*. Washington, D.C.: American Anthropological Association.

Ralston, Lenore, James Anderson, and Elizabeth Colson. 1981. *Voluntary Efforts in Decentralized Management: Final Report, Project on Managing Decentralization*. Berkeley: Institute of International Studies, University of California.

Read, C. H. 1906. Anthropology at the Universities. *Man* 38:56-59.

Reeves, Edward B., and Timothy Frankenberger. 1981. *Socio-economic Constraints to the Production, Distribution, and Consumption of Millet, Sorghum, and Cash Crops in North Kordofan, Sudan*. Report no. 1. Lexington: University of Kentucky, College of Agriculture, Department of Sociology.

————. 1982. *Farming Systems Research in North Kordofan, Sudan*. Report no. 2.

Lexington: University of Kentucky, College of Agriculture, Department of Sociology.

Reining, Conrad C. 1962. "A Lost Period of Applied Anthropology." *American Anthropologist* 64:593-600.

Rhoades, Robert E. 1982. *The Art of the Informal Agricultural Survey.* Training Document 1982-2. Lima: Social Science Department, International Potato Center.

———. 1984. *Breaking New Ground: Agricultural Anthropology.* Lima, Peru: International Potato Center.

Rhoades, Robert E., and R. Booth. 1982. *Farmer-Back-to-Farmer: A Model for Generating Acceptable Technology.* International Potato Center, Social Sciences Department Working Paper, 1982-1. Lima: International Potato Center.

Rhoades, R., R. Booth, R. Shaw, and R. Werge. 1982. "The Involvement and Interaction of Anthropological and Biological in the Development and Transfer of Post-Harvest Technology at CIP." In *The Role of Anthropologists and other Social Scientists in Interdisciplinary Teams Developing Improved Food Production Technology.* Los Banos, Philippines: International Rice Research Institute.

Rich, R. F. 1975. "Selective Utilization of Social Science Related Information by Federal Policy Makers." *Inquiry* 12:239-45.

Riecken, Henry W. 1972. "Memorandum on Program Evaluation, Ford Foundation." In *Evaluating Action Programs: Readings in Social Action and Education,* Carol A. Weiss, ed. Boston: Allyn and Bacon.

Roberts, A. 1978. Mid-term Evaluation: Social Impact, Tangaye Solar Energy Demonstration. Ann Arbor, Mich.: University of Michigan.

———. 1981. *The Social Impact of the Tangaye (Upper Volta) Solar Energy Demonstration: A Summary Report.* Ann Arbor: University of Michigan, Center for Afro-American and African Studies.

Rodnick, David. 1936. *Report on the Indians of Kansas.* Applied Anthropology Unit Report Series. Washington, D.C.: Office of Indian Affairs, Department of the Interior.

———. 1948. *Postwar Germans: An Anthropologist's Account.* New Haven: Yale University Press.

Rothman, Jack. 1980. *Using Research in Organizations.* Beverly Hills, Calif.: Sage Publications.

Ruthenberg, Hans, with J. D. MacArthur, H. D. Zandstra, and M. P. Collinson. 1980. *Farming Systems in the Tropics.* 3rd ed. Oxford: Clarendon Press.

Ruttan, V. W. 1977. "The Green Revolution: Seven Generalisations." *International Development Review* 4:15-23.

Rylko-Bauer, Barbara, and John van Willigen. 1993. A Framework for Conducting Utilization-Focused Policy Research in Anthropology. In *Speaking the Language of Power: Communication, Collaboration and Advocacy.* David Fetterman, ed. London, Eng.: Falmer.

Rynkiewich, Michael A., and James P. Spradley. 1976. *Ethics and Anthropology: Dilemmas in Fieldwork.* New York: John Wiley and Sons.

Sachchidananda. 1972. "Planning, Development and Applied Anthropology." *Journal of the Indian Anthropological Society* 7:11-28.

Sackman, Harold. 1975. *Delphi Critique: Expert Opinion, Forecasting and Group Process.* Lexington, Mass.: Lexington Books.

Sanday, Peggy Reeves, ed. 1976. *Anthropology and the Public Interest: Fieldwork and Theory*. New York: Academic Press.

Sanders, Irwin T. 1958. "Theories of Community Development." *Rural Sociology* 23(1):1-32.

————. 1970. "The Concept of Community Development." In *Community Development as a Process*, Lee J. Cary, ed. Columbia: University of Missouri Press.

Sandoval, Mercedes C., and Leon Tozo. 1975. "An Emergent Cuban Community." *Psychiatric Annals* 5(8):324-332.

Sands, Deborah Merrill. 1985. *A Review of Farming Systems Research*. Prepared for Technical Advisory Committee/CGIAR. Rome: CGIAR.

Sasaki, Tom T. 1960. *Fruitland, New Mexico: A Navaho Community in Transition*. Ithaca, N.Y.: Cornell University Press.

Sasaki, Tom T., and John Adair. 1952. "New Land to Farm: Agricultural Practices Among the Navaho Indians of New Mexico." In *Human Problems in Technological Change*, Edward H. Spicer, ed. New York: Russell Sage Foundation.

Scaglion, Richard. 1981. "Samukundi Abelam Conflict Management: Implications for Legal Planning in Papua New Guinea." *Oceania* 52:28-38.

Schapera, Isaac. 1947. *Migrant Labour and Tribal Life*. London: Oxford University Press.

Schearer, S. Bruce. 1981. "The Value of Focus Group Research for Social Action Programs." *Studies in Family Planning* 12(12):407-408.

Schein, Edgar. 1969. *Process Consultation: Its Role in Organizational Development*. Reading, Mass.: Addison Wesley.

Schellstede, W. P., and R. L. Ciszewski. 1984. "Social Marketing of Contraceptives in Bangladesh." *Studies in Family Planning* 15(1)

Schensul, Jean J. 1987. "Knowledge Utilization: An Anthropological Perspective." *Practicing Anthropology* 9(1):6-8.

Schensul, Stephen L. 1973. "Action Research: The Applied Anthropologist in a Community Mental Health Program." In *Anthropology Beyond the University*, A. Redfield, ed. Southern Anthropological Society Proceedings no. 7. Athens: University of Georgia Press.

————. 1974. "Skills Needed in Action Anthropology: Lessons from El Centro de La Causa." *Human Organization* 33(2):203-208.

Schensul, Stephen L. and Jean J. Schensul. 1978. "Advocacy and Applied Anthropology." In *Social Scientists as Advocates*, George H. Weber and George J. McCall, eds. Beverly Hills, Calif.: Sage Publications.

Schlesier, Karl H. 1974. "Action Anthropology and the Southern Cheyenne." *Current Anthropology* 15(3):277-283.

Schoolcraft, Henry R. 1852-1857. *Information Respecting the History, Condition and Prospects of the Indian Tribes of the United States*. Philadelphia: Lippincott.

Schultz, T. W. 1964. *Transforming Traditional Agriculture*. New Haven: Yale University Press.

Schumacher, E. F. 1973. *Small Is Beautiful*. London: Blond and Briggs.

Scott, Eugenie C., Billie R. DeWalt, Elizabeth Adelski, Sara Alexander, and Mary Beebe. 1982. *Landowners, Recreationists, and Government: Cooperation and Conflict in Red River Gorge*. Lexington: University of Kentucky, Water Resources Research Institute.

Scrimshaw, Susan C. M., and Elena Hurtado. 1987. *Rapid Assessment Procedures for*

Nutrition and Primary Health Care: Anthropological Approaches to Improving Program Effectiveness (RAP). Los Angeles: UCLA Latin American Center Publications.

Scriven, Michael. 1973. "The Methodology of Evaluation." In *Educational Evaluation: Theory and Practice*, Blaine R. Worthen and James R. Sanders, eds. Belmont, Calif.: Wadsworth Publishing.

Scriven, Michael, and J. Roth. 1978. "Needs Assessment: Concept and Practice." *New Directions for Program Evaluation* 1:1-11.

Scudder, Thayer. 1962. *The Ecology of the Gwembe Tonga*. Rhodes-Livingstone Institute, Kariba Studies, vol. 2. Manchester: Manchester University Press.

———. 1966. "Man-made Lakes and Social Change." *Engineering and Science* 24:19-22.

———. 1968. "Social Anthropology, Man-Made Lakes and Population Relocation in Africa." *Anthropological Quarterly* 41:168-76.

Scurlock, Reagan. 1975. *Government Contracts and Grants for Research: A Guide for Colleges and Universities*. Washington, D.C.: Committee on Governmental Relations, National Association of College and University Business Officers.

Seidel, J., et al. 1988. The Ethnograph. Version 3.0. Littleton, Colo.: Qualis Associates.

Seligman, C. G. 1932. *Pagan Tribes of the Nilotic Sudan*. London: G. Routledge.

Service, Elman R. 1960. *Primitive Social Organization*. New York: Random House.

Shaner, W. W., P. F. Philipp, and W. R. Schmehl. 1982. *Farming Systems Research and Development: A Guideline for Developing Countries*. Boulder, Colo.: Westview Press.

Siegel, Karolynn, and Peter Tuckel. 1985. "The Utilization of Evaluation Research. A Case Analysis." *Evaluation Review* 9(3):307-28.

Simmonds, N. W. 1984. "The State of the Art of Farming Systems Research." Paper prepared for the Agriculture and Rural Development Department of the World Bank, Washington, D.C.

Simon, Elaine, and Karen Curtis. 1983. "Evaluation of the Job Shop/Job Club Program of the Community Education Center." Typescript.

Sinha, Surajit. 1986. *Nirmal Kumar Bose, Scholar–Wanderer*. New Delhi: National Book Trust.

Sjoberg, Gideon, ed. 1967. *Ethics, Politics and Social Research*. Cambridge, Mass.: Schenkman Publishing.

Smucker, Glenn R. 1981. *Trees and Charcoal in Haitian Peasant Economy, a Feasibility Study of Reforestation*. Port-au-Prince: U.S. Agency for International Development Mission.

Society for Applied Anthropology. 1978. *Practicing Anthropology: A Career-Oriented Publication of the Society for Applied Anthropology*. College Park, Md.: Society for Applied Anthropology.

Society for Applied Anthropology. 1989. *Guide to Training Programs in the Applications of Anthropology*. Oklahoma City, Okla.: Society for Applied Anthropology.

Softestad, Lars T. 1990. "On Evacuation of People in the Kotmale Hydro Power Project: Experience from a Socio Economic Impact Study." *Bistandsantropogen [Development Anthropologist]* 15:22-32.

Sorenson, John L., and Larry L. Berg. 1967. *Evaluation of Indian Community Action Programs at Arizona State University, University of South Dakota and University of Utah (CR–82-1)*. Santa Barbara, Calif.: General Research Corporation.

Southern Regional Council. 1961. *The Negro and Employment Opportunities in the South.* Atlanta, Ga.: Southern Regional Council.

Spicer, Edward H. 1946a. "The Use of Social Scientists by the War Relocation Authority." *Applied Anthropology* 5(2):16-36.

―――. 1946b. *Impounded People: Japanese-Americans in the Relocation Centers.* Washington, D.C.: Department of the Interior, War Relocation Authority.

―――. 1952. *Human Problems in Technological Change.* New York: Russell Sage Foundation.

―――. 1976. "Beyond Analysis and Explanation? The Life and Times of the Society for Applied Anthropology." *Human Organization,* 35(4):335-343.

―――. 1977. "Early Applications of Anthropology, 1976." In *Perspectives on Anthropology 1976,* A.F.C. Wallace et al. eds. Washington, D.C.: American Anthropological Association.

―――. 1979. "Anthropologists and the War Relocation Authority." In *The Uses of Anthropology,* Walter Goldschmidt, ed. Washington, D.C.: American Anthropological Association.

―――. 1952a. "Reluctant Cotton-Pickers: Incentive to Work in a Japanese Relocation Center." In *Human Problems in Technological Change,* Edward H. Spicer, ed. New York: Russell Sage Foundation.

―――. 1952b. "Resistance to Freedom: Resettlement from the Japanese Relocation Centers During World War II." In *Human Problems in Technological Change,* Edward H. Spicer, ed. New York: Russell Sage Foundation.

Spicer, Edward H., and Theodore E. Downing. 1974. "Training for Non-Academic Employment: Major Issues." In *Training Programs for New Opportunities in Applied Anthropology,* E. Leacock, N. Gonzalez, and G. Kushner, eds. Washington, D.C.: American Anthropological Association.

Spillius, James. 1957. "Natural Disaster and Political Crisis in a Polynesian Society: An Exploration of Operational Research II." *Human Relations* 10(2):113-125.

Stern, Gwen. 1985. "Research, Action, and Social Betterment." *American Behavioral Scientist* 29(2):229-48.

Stewart, Frances. 1977. *Technology and Underdevelopment.* Boulder, Colo.: Westview Press.

Stewart, Omer C. 1961. *Kroeber and the Indian Claims Commission Cases.* Kroeber Anthropology Society Paper no. 25. Berkeley, Calif.: Kroeber Anthropology Society.

Stoffle, Richard W. 1986. *Caribbean Fisherman Farmers: A Social Assessment of Smithsonian King Crab Mariculture.* Ann Arbor: Institute for Social Research, University of Michigan.

Stoffle, Richard W., Michael J. Evans, and Florence V. Jensen. 1987. *Native American Concerns and State of California Low-Level Waste Disposal Facility: Mohave, Navajo, Chemehuevi, and Nevada Paiute Responses.* Menlo Park, Calif.: Cultural Systems Research.

Stoffle, Richard W., Florence V. Jensen, and Danny L. Rasch. 1981. *Coho Stocking and Salmon Stamps: Lake Michigan Anglers Assess Wisconsin's DNR Policies.* Kenosha: University of Wisconsin-Parkside.

Stoffle, Richard W., Michael W. Traugott, Florence V. Jensen, and Robert Copeland. 1987. *Social Assessment of High Technology: The Superconducting Super Collider*

in Southeast Michigan. Ann Arbor: Institute for Social Research, University of
Michigan.

Straus, Robert. 1957. "The Nature and Status of Medical Sociology." *American Sociological Review* 22:200-204.

Stufflebeam, Daniel L. 1973. "Excerpts from 'Evaluation as Enlightenment for Decision-
Making.' " In *Educational Evaluation: Theory and Practice.* Belmont, Calif.:
Wadsworth Publishing.

Stull, Donald D. 1979. "Action Anthropology among the Kansas Kickapoo." Paper
presented at meetings of the Society for Applied Anthropology, Philadelphia.

Stull, Donald D., and Jean J. Schensul, eds. 1987. *Collaborative Research and Social
Change: Applied Anthropology in Action.* Boulder, Colo.: Westview Press.

Sussex, James N., and Hazel H. Weidman. 1975. "Toward Responsiveness in Mental
Health Care." *Psychiatric Annals* 5(8):306-311.

Tax, Sol. 1945. "Anthropology and Administration." *American Indigena* 5(1):21-33.

———. 1958. "The Fox Project." *Human Organization* 17:17-19.

———. 1960a. "Extracts from 'Introduction' to A Reader in Action Anthropology." In
Documentary History of the Fox Project, F. Gearing et al., eds. Chicago: University of Chicago, Department of Anthropology.

———. 1960b. "Action Anthropology." In *Documentary History of the Fox Project*,
F. Gearing et al., eds. Chicago: University of Chicago, Department of
Anthropology.

Textor, Robert B., ed. 1966. *Cultural Frontiers of the Peace Corps.* Cambridge, Mass.:
M.I.T. Press.

Thompson, Laura. 1950. "Action Research Among American Indians." *Scientific
Monthly.* 70:34-40.

———. 1956. "U.S. Indian Reorganization Viewed as an Experiment in Social Action
Research." In *Estudios Antropologicos Publicado en Homenaje a Doctor Manuel
Gamio.* Mexico: Direccion General de Publicaciones.

Thompson, Laura, and Alice Joseph. 1944. *The Hopi Way.* New York: Russell Sage
Foundation.

Trend, M. G. 1976. "The Anthropologist as Go-fer." Paper presented at meetings of
the Society for Applied Anthropology, St. Louis.

———. 1977. "Anthropological Research Services: Some Observations." *Human Organization* 36(2):211-212.

———. 1978a. "On the Reconciliation of Qualitative and Quantitative Analyses: A Case
Study." *Human Organization* 37:345-354.

———. 1978b. "Research in Progress: The Minnesota Work Equity Project Evaluation."
Human Organization 37(4):398-399.

Tripp, Robert. 1982. *Including Dietary Concerns in On-farm Research: An Example
from Imbabura, Ecuador.* Mexico: Centro International de Mejoramiento de Maiz
y Trigo.

———. 1985. "Anthropology and On-Farm Research." *Human Organization* 44(2):114-
124.

Trotter, Robert T., II. 1987. "A Case of Lead Poisoning from Folk Remedies in Mexican
American Communities." In *Anthropological Praxis.* R. Wulff and S. Fiske, eds.
Boulder, Colo.: Westview Press.

Trotter, Robert T., II. 1988. *Anthropology for Tomorrow: Creating Practitioner-Oriented*

Applied Anthropology Programs. Washington, D.C.: American Anthropological Association.

Turner, Allen C. 1974. *Southern Paiute Research and Development Program: A Pre-Proposal*. Cedar City, Utah: Southern Utah State College.

Uhlman, Julie M. 1977a. "Anthropologists in a Multidisciplinary Training Program." Paper presented at meetings of the American Anthropological Association, Houston, Tex.

———. 1977b. "The Delivery of Human Services in Wyoming Boomtowns." In *Socio-Economic Impact of Western Energy Development*, Berry Crawford and Edward H. Allen, eds. Ann Arbor, Mich.: Science Publishers.

University of Chicago, Department of Anthropology. 1960. "The 'Tama Indian Crafts' Project." In *Documentary History of the Fox Project*, F. Gearing et al., eds. Chicago: University of Chicago, Department of Anthropology.

U.S. Agency for International Development. 1975. *Handbook 3: Project Assistance*. Washington, D.C.: U.S. Agency for International Development.

U.S. Congress. 1971. "National Environmental Policy Act of 1969, (PL 91-190)." *United States Statutes at Large* 83: 852-856.

———. 1972. "River and Harbor and Flood Control Acts of 1970, (PL 91- 6ll)." *United States Statutes at Large* 84:1818-1835.

U.S. Department of the Treasury, Internal Revenue Service. 1988. *Tax Exempt Status for Your Organization*. Publication 557. Washington, D.C.: Government Printing Office.

U.S. Public Health Service. 1991. *Healthy People 2000: National Health Promotion and Disease Prevention Objectives*. Publication (PHS)91-50212. Washington, D.C.: U.S. Public Health Service.

Useem, John. 1947. *Economic and Human Resources—Yap and Palau, Western Carolines*. Ponape: U.S. Commercial Company.

Van Tassell, Jon, and Karen L. Michaelson. 1977. *Social Impact Assessment: Methods and Practice (Interstate 88 in New York)*. Final Report: National Science Foundation, Student-Originated-Study Grant, Summer, 1976. Binghamton, N.Y.: Department of Anthropology, SUNY Binghamton.

van Willigen, John. 1971. "The Papago Community Development Worker." *Community Development Journal* 6(2):85-91.

———. 1973. "Abstract Goals and Concrete Means: Papago Experiences in the Application of Development Resources." *Human Organization* 32(1):1-8.

———. 1976. "Applied Anthropology and Community Development Administration: A Critical Assessment." In *Do Applied Anthropologists Apply Anthropology?*, M. Angrosino, ed. Athens: University of Georgia Press.

———. 1977. "Administrative Problems in an Arizona Community Development Programme." *Community Development Journal* 12(1):30-35.

———. 1979. "Recommendations for Training and Education for Careers in Applied Anthropology: A Literature Review." *Human Organization* 38(4):411-416.

———. 1981a. *Anthropology in Use: A Bibliographic Chronology of the Development of Applied Anthropology*. Pleasantville, N.Y.: Redgrave Publishers.

———. 1981b. "Applied Anthropology and Cultural Persistence." In *Persistent Peoples: Cultural Enclaves in Perspective*. George Pierre Castile and Gilbert Kushner, eds. Tucson: University of Arizona Press.

———. 1982. "The Great Transformation? Applied Training and Disciplinary Change." *Practicing Anthropology* 4(3-4):16-17.

———. 1985. *Guide to Training Programs in the Applications of Anthropology.* Washington, D.C.: Society for Applied Anthropology.

———. 1987. *Becoming a Practicing Anthropologist: A Guide to Careers and Training Programs in Applied Anthropology.* NAPA Bulletin no. 3. Washington, D.C.: American Anthropological Association.

———. 1988. "Types of Programs." In *Anthropology for Tomorrow: Creating Practitioner-Oriented Applied Anthropology Programs*, R. Trotter, ed. Washington, D.C.: American Anthropological Association.

———. 1991. *Anthropology in Use: A Source Book on Anthropological Practice.* Boulder, Colo.: Westview Press.

van Willigen, John, and Billie R. DeWalt. 1985. *Training Manual in Policy Ethnography.* Washington, D.C.: American Anthropological Association.

van Willigen, John, Billie R. DeWalt, Timothy Frankenberger, and John Lichte. 1985. "Rapid Rural Reconnaissance." In *Training Manual for Policy Ethnography.* Washington, D.C.: American Anthropological Association.

van Willigen, John, and Timothy L. Finan, eds. 1991. *Soundings: Rapid and Reliable Research Methods for Practicing Anthropologists.* NAPA Bulletin no. 10. Washington, D.C.: American Anthropological Association.

van Willigen, John, Barbara Rylko-Bauer, and Ann McElroy, eds. 1989. *Making Our Research Useful: Case Studies in the Utilization of Anthropological Knowledge.* Boulder, Colo.: Westview Press.

Villa-Rojas, Alfonso. 1955. *Los Mazatecas y el Problema Indigena de la Cuenca del Papaloapan.* Mexico: I.N.I.

Vlachos, Evan, ed. 1975. *Social Impact Assessment: An Overview.* Fort Belvoir, Va.: Army Corps of Engineers, Institute of Water Resources.

Vlachos, Evan, Walter Buckley, William F. Filstead, Sue-Ellen Jacobs, Magoroh Maruyama, John H. Peterson, Jr., and Gene Willeke. 1975. *Procedural Guidelines for Social Impact Assessment.* Arlington, Va.: U.S. Army Corps of Engineers Institute for Water Resources.

Voget, Fred W. 1975. *A History of Ethnology.* New York: Holt, Rinehart and Winston.

Wallace, Anthony F. C. 1976. "Some Reflections on the Contributions of Anthropologists to Public Policy." In *Anthropology and the Public Interest, Fieldwork and Theory*, Peggy Reeves Sanday, ed. New York: Academic Press.

Ward, G. W. 1984. "The National High Blood Pressure Education Program: An Example of Social Marketing." In *Marketing Health Behavior: Principles, Techniques and Applications*, L. Frederickson, L. J. Solomon, and K. A. Brehony, eds. New York: Plenum.

Warren, Roland L. 1970. "The Context of Community Development." In *Community Development as a Process*, Lee J. Cary, ed. Columbia: University of Missouri Press.

Wax, Murray L., and Robert G. Breunig. 1973. *Study of the Community Impact of the Hopi Follow Through Program.* Final Report, Project O. 2-0647, Grant No. OEG–0-72-3946. Washington, D.C.: U.S. Department of Health, Education and Welfare, Office of Education, National Institute of Education.

Wax, Rosemary H. 1971. *Doing Fieldwork: Warnings and Advice.* Chicago: University of Chicago Press.

Weaver, Thomas. 1973. *To See Ourselves: Anthropology and Modern Social Issues.* New York: Scott, Foresman.

Weaver, Thomas, et al. 1971. *Political Organization and Business Management in the Gila River Indian Community.* Tucson: Bureau of Ethnic Research, University of Arizona.

Weaver, Thomas, and Theodore Downing, eds. 1975. *The Douglas Report: The Community Context of Housing and Social Problems.* Tucson: Bureau of Ethnic Research, University of Arizona.

Weber, George H., and George J. McCall, eds. 1978. *Social Scientists as Advocates: Views from the Applied Disciplines.* Beverly Hills, Calif.: Sage Publications.

Weidman, Hazel H. 1973. "Implications of the Culture-broker Concept for the Delivery of Health Care." Paper presented at meetings of the Southern Anthropological Society, Wrightsville Beach, North Carolina.

———. 1974. "Toward the Goal of Responsiveness in Mental Health Care." Paper presented at the Department of Psychiatry, University of Miami.

———. 1975. *Concepts as Strategies for Change.* A Psychiatric Annals Reprint. New York: Insight Communications, Inc.

———. 1976. "In Praise of the Double-Bind Inherent in Anthropological Application." In *Do Applied Anthropologists Apply Anthropology?*, M. V. Angrosino, ed. Proceedings of the Southern Anthropological Society no. 10. Athens: University of Georgia Press.

———. 1979. "The Transcultural View: Prerequisite to Interethnic (Intercultural) Communication in Medicine." *Social Science and Medicine* 13B:85-87.

———. 1982. "Research Strategies, Structural Alterations and Clinically Applied Anthropology." In *Clinically Applied Anthropology*, N. J. Chrisman and T. W. Maretzki, eds. Dordrecht: D. Reidel Publishing.

———. 1985 Personal correspondence.

Weiss, Carol H. 1972. *Evaluating Action Programs: Readings in Social Action and Education.* Boston: Allyn and Bacon.

———. 1977. "Introduction." In *Using Social Research in Public Policy Making*, Carol H. Weiss, ed. Lexington, Mass.: D. C. Heath.

———. 1981. "Measuring the Use of Evaluations." In *Utilizing Evaluation.* James A. Ciarlo, ed. Beverly Hills, Calif.: Sage Publications.

Weiss, Carol H., and Michael Bucuvalas. 1980. "Truth Test and Utility Test: Decision Makers' Frame of Reference for Social Science Research." *American Sociological Review* 45:302-313.

Wellhausen, Edwin J. 1976. "The Agriculture of Mexico." *Scientific American* 235:128-50.

Weppner, Robert S. 1973. "An Anthropological View of the Street Addict's World." *Human Organization* 32(2):111-112.

Werge, Robert W. 1977. *Anthropology and Agricultural Research: The Case of Potato Anthropology.* Lima: International Potato Center.

Whiteford, Linda M. 1987. "Staying Out of the Bottom Drawer." *Practicing Anthropology* 9(1):9-11.

Willard, William. 1977. "The Agency Camp Project." *Human Organization* 36(4):352-362.

Williams, Bruce T. 1980. *Integrated Basic Services Project: A Baseline Survey.* UNICEF/Malawi: Centre for Social Research, University of Malawi.

————. 1981. *UNICEF-Assisted Women's Programs in Malawi, An Evaluation and Summary of Findings on the Homecraft Workers' Program and the Female Community Development Assistant's Program*. UNICEF/Malawi: Centre for Social Research, University of Malawi.

Wilson, Stephen. 1977. "The Use of Ethnographic Methods in Educational Evaluation." *Human Organization* 36(2):200-203.

Wolf, Eric R. 1956. "Aspects of Group Relations in a Complex Society: Mexico." American Anthropologist 58:1065-1078.

Wolfe, Alvin W., Erve Chambers, and J. Jerome Smith. 1981. *Internship Training in Applied Anthropology: A Five Year Review*. Tampa: Human Resources Institute, University of South Florida.

Wolfe, Alvin W., with Linda Whiteford Dean. 1974. *Social Network Effects on Employment*. Report submitted to the Manpower Administration, U.S. Department of Labor. Milwaukee, Wis.: Manpower Administration, U.S. Department of Labor.

Worthen, Blaine R., and James R. Sanders. 1973. *Educational Evaluation: Theory and Practice*. Belmont, Calif.: Wadsworth Publishing.

Wulff, Robert N. 1972. *Housing the Papago: An Analytical Critique of a Housing Delivery System*. Los Angeles: International Housing Productivity Project, University of California, Los Angeles.

————. 1976a. "Anthropology in the Urban Planning Process: A Review and an Agenda." In *Do Applied Anthropologists Apply Anthropology?*, M. Angrosino, ed. Athens: University of Georgia Press.

————. 1976b. *Tampa's Community Centers: An Analysis of Recreation Programming and Policy*. Tampa: Human Resources Institute and Center of Applied Anthropology, University of South Florida.

————. 1977. *Vicos in Watts: Testing Anthropological Change Strategies in Urban America*. ERIC Microfiche. Princeton, N.J.: Educational Testing Service.

Zilverberg, Grace M., and Anita Courtney. 1984. *The Status and Potential of the Fruit and Vegetable Market in the Kentucky Bluegrass Region*. Frankfort: Kentucky Department of Agriculture.

Index

About the Author

JOHN VAN WILLIGEN is Professor of Anthropology at the University of Kentucky and Director of the Applied Anthropology Documentation Project which he founded in 1978. He is foremost in his field and has written many books including *Making Our Research Useful* (1989) and *Anthropology in Use: A Source Book on Anthropological Practice* (1991).